Customer Service For Dummies

P9-CJG-055

Sheet

1. Attitude

The bottom line — it's all a matter of attitude.

1. Learn to view your customer as the job, rather than an interruption of it.

2. Understand that your co-workers are internal customers and treat them with the same respect you do your customers.

3. Service excellence starts at the top. As a manager, what you say about service is not nearly as important as what you do.

4. A customer focused company is created when the person at the top believes that service is so critical to the success of the business that he or she invests time, resources, and effort to make it happen.

2. Six Basic Customer Needs

Customers ask for what they want; what they need is a whole lot more.

1. Friendliness

2. Understanding and empathy

3. Fairness

4. Control

5. Options and alternatives

6. Information

4. Service Improvement Strategy

Create a plan of action for your company.

1. Put together a team whose job it is to create and implement the overall service improvement strategy.

2. If you don't already have one, write a mission statement for your company that stresses the importance of customer service.

3. Do staff/customer surveys for feedback on how your company provides service.

4. Train your staff and managers in the skills they need for the best service possible.

5. Improve your processes and procedures through quality groups.

6. Create and implement specific service standards.

7. Reward and recognize your staff for service excellence.

3. A Winning Telephone Style

One of the most valuable business skills you can acquire.

1. Eighty-six percent of the message the customer gets over the phone is from your tone of voice. By using inflection, pacing, and volume, you can achieve a great telephone voice.

2. Telephone etiquette can make or break your service on the phone. Knowing proper telephone etiquette for how to answer the phone, put callers on hold, and transfer calls puts you ahead of the game.

3. A good technique for improving your phone tone is to record yourself on a tape recorder during a phone conversation and then play the tape back.

. . .For Dummies: The Best-Selling Book Series for Beginners

BUSINESS AND
GENERAL
REFERENCE
BOOK SERIES
FROM IDG

Customer Service For Dummies®

Cheat Sheet

5. Six Steps for Handling Difficult Customers

1. Let the customers vent their feelings. Don't tell them to *calm down* — this will make things worse. Learn to zip your lip and not take what they are saying personally.

2. Don't get trapped in your negative filter about the customer. Instead, focus on asking yourself the question, "What does this person need and how can I provide it?"

3. Express empathy for the customer's situation by using empathic phrases and apologizing.

4. Work to actively solve the problem. Gather the information you need by using the questioning technique and the bridging technique.

5. Double-check all the facts with the mirroring technique.

6. Come to a mutual agreement on the solution with the customer. Remember to *under* promise and *over* deliver.

6. Reward and Recognition

You can reward staff in many ways for going above and beyond with their customers.

Send a thank you note.

Have a pizza party.

Give a gift certificate.

Send flowers.

Hand out a plaque.

Send a letter of praise.

Give them a day off.

Treat them to dinner for two.

7. Working Styles

There are four basic working styles that you need to know to get in step with.

1. The *Driver* Working Style: Focuses on bottom line results, wants things how they want them, when they want them, with as few problems as possible.

2. The *Analytical* Working Style: Wants to know the facts, is less interested in the feelings. Looks at the world through logic and details.

3. The *Expressive* Working Style: Enthusiastic and fun loving, likes to be around people. Puts into motion the ideas they like now and worries about details later.

4. The *Amiable* Working Style: Feelings are more important than tasks. Takes time to decide and does not like to be pressured. On the quiet side.

IDG
BOOKS
WORLDWIDE

Copyright © 1995 IDG Books Worldwide, Inc.
All rights reserved.

Cheat Sheet $2.95 value. Item 391-7.

For more information about IDG Books,
call 1-800-762-2974.

...For Dummies: The Best-Selling Book Series for Beginners

Praise for Karen and Keith

"Karen and Keith consistently rate among our top speakers at conferences. The overwhelming positive feedback we receive from attendees about them is that they are practical, fun, and have valuable information to contribute to any growing company. There are few speakers out there who know this audience as well as they do!"

— Craig Lis, Conference Producer, *Inc. Magazine*

"Our president, managers, and staff who participated in your program shared their overwhelmingly positive feedback with me. They not only enjoyed the content of the training but were delighted with the presentation. I applaud your ability to consistently connect the content of your programs with our corporate culture."

— Magali Akle, Director, Quality Service, **Avis Rent A Car**

"I must confess that your seminar on *Service Management* was the biggest eye opener I have had in years. It was also one of the best presentations I have had the opportunity to attend."

— Howard Cowell, Managing Director, **SC Johnson Wax**

"A unique advantage that you (SCG) bring to an organization is your exceptional ability to make the presentations very practical and real. This has been a key factor in the success of the project at Marriott."

— Gary Dzurec, HR Manager, **Courtyard By Marriott**

"Thank you for the fantastic program that you presented. Helping our staff and ourselves to deal with stress on the job is vital to our business needs today. Your presentation gave us much to consider."

— Vickie Pilotti, Program Chair, **Society of Consumer Affairs**

"Your work has a keen sensibility not usually found in comparable training programs. I continue to be impressed with its quality and your results."

— Earl W. Hinton, Director, Professional Development, **Fidelity Investments**

"Thank you so much for the terrific job you did in meeting the objectives I had for the customer service training. Your session was fast paced, fun, and interactive. We have received great feedback from the 250 participants, and, as you know, we have a tough group to please."

> — Andrew Campbell, Director of Training, **Kinko's Copy Centers**

"I've sat back, looking for the right words, and the ones that keep coming up are *Thank you!* Your presentation at the conference was fantastic."

> — Kathleen Geier, Senior Account Executive, **AT&T**

"You listened to our problems and gave us the tools to solve them ourselves. Your enthusiasm and commitment were apparent throughout the whole project. Our staff left the workshops both educated and motivated."

> — Mary Jane Palmieri, Customer Service Manager, **Perkin Elmer**

"Every one of my staff has come back from the program excited and enthusiastic about what they learned from Karen and Keith. Their blend of energy and practical advice makes an unbelievable combination! I have staff asking me when they get to attend the seminar."

> — Steve Shaper, Executive Vice President, Marketing, **Telecheck**

"Keith and Karen deliver! I've used hundreds of presenters for our magazine's conferences and for seminars at the American Management Association. Keith and Karen were rated oustanding by a challenging audience of presidents and CEOs of fast-growing companies. Their material and message were right on target."

> — Marlene Sholod, Director, Events Marketing, ***Sales & Marketing Management Magazine***

TM

BUSINESS AND GENERAL REFERENCE BOOK SERIES FROM IDG

References for the Rest of Us!™

Do you find that traditional reference books are overloaded with technical details and advice you'll never use? Do you postpone important life decisions because you just don't want to deal with them? Then our *...For Dummies*™ business and general reference book series is for you.

...For Dummies business and general reference books are written for those frustrated and hard-working souls who know they aren't dumb, but find that the myriad of personal and business issues and the accompanying horror stories make them feel helpless. *...For Dummies* books use a lighthearted approach, a down-to-earth style, and even cartoons and humorous icons to diffuse fears and build confidence. Lighthearted but not lightweight, these books are perfect survival guides to solve your everyday personal and business problems.

> *"More than a publishing phenomenon, 'Dummies' is a sign of the times."*
> — The New York Times

> *"A world of detailed and authoritative information is packed into them..."*
> — U.S. News and World Report

> *"... you won't go wrong buying them."*
> — Walter Mossberg, Wall Street Journal, on IDG's ...For Dummies™ books

Already, hundreds of thousands of satisfied readers agree. They have made *...For Dummies* the #1 introductory level computer book series and a best-selling business book series. They have written asking for more. So, if you're looking for the best and easiest way to learn about business and other general reference topics, look to *...For Dummies* to give you a helping hand.

IDG BOOKS WORLDWIDE™

7/96r

CUSTOMER SERVICE

FOR DUMMIES™

CUSTOMER SERVICE FOR DUMMIES™

by Keith Bailey
and Karen Leland

IDG BOOKS WORLDWIDE

IDG Books Worldwide, Inc.
An International Data Group Company

Foster City, CA ♦ Chicago, IL ♦ Indianapolis, IN ♦ Southlake, TX

Customer Service For Dummies™

Published by
IDG Books Worldwide, Inc.
An International Data Group Company
919 E. Hillsdale Blvd.
Suite 400
Foster City, CA 94404
http://www.dummies.com (IDG Books Worldwide Web Site)
http://www.idgbooks.com (Dummies Press Web Site)

Library of Congress Catalog Card No.: 95-81423

ISBN: 1-56884-391-7

Printed in the United States of America

10 9 8 7 6

1E/RU/QU/ZX/IN

Distributed in the United States by IDG Books Worldwide, Inc.

Distributed by Macmillan Canada for Canada; by Transworld Publishers Limited in the United Kingdom and Europe; by WoodsLane Pty. Ltd. for Australia; by WoodsLane Enterprises Ltd. for New Zealand; by Longman Singapore Publishers Ltd. for Singapore, Malaysia, Thailand, and Indonesia; by Simron Pty. Ltd. for South Africa; by Toppan Company Ltd. for Japan; by Distribuidora Cuspide for Argentina; by Livraria Cultura for Brazil; by Ediciencia S.A. for Ecuador; by Addison-Wesley Publishing Company for Korea; by Ediciones ZETA S.C.R. Ltda. for Peru; by WS Computer Publishing Company, Inc., for the Philippines; by Unalis Corporation for Taiwan; by Contemporanea de Ediciones for Venezuela. Authorized Sales Agent: Anthony Rudkin Associates for the Middle East and North Africa.

For general information on IDG Books Worldwide's books in the U.S., please call our Consumer Customer Service department at 800-762-2974. For reseller information, including discounts and premium sales, please call our Reseller Customer Service department at 800-434-3422.

For information on where to purchase IDG Books Worldwide's books outside the U.S., please contact our International Sales department at 415-655-3023 or fax 415-655-3299.

For information on foreign language translations, please contact our Foreign & Subsidiary Rights department at 415-655-3021 or fax 415-655-3281.

For sales inquiries and special prices for bulk quantities, please contact our Sales department at 415-655-3200 or write to the address above.

For information on using IDG Books Worldwide's books in the classroom or for ordering examination copies, please contact our Educational Sales department at 800-434-2086 or fax 817-251-8174.

For press review copies, author interviews, or other publicity information, please contact our Public Relations department at 415-655-3000 or fax 415-655-3299.

For authorization to photocopy items for corporate, personal, or educational use, please contact Copyright Clearance Center, 222 Rosewood Drive, Danvers, MA 01923, or fax 508-750-4470.

is a trademark under exclusive license to IDG Books Worldwide, Inc., from International Data Group, Inc.

About the Authors

Karen Leland and Keith Bailey are co-founders of Sterling Consulting Group, Inc., an international management consulting firm specializing in quality service and managing rapid growth. They have a combined 25 years of experience in this field and have worked with over 100,000 executives, managers, and front-line staff from a wide variety of industries including retail, transportation, hospitality, banking, and consumer goods.

Their consulting work in corporations and public speaking engagements has taken them throughout North America, Southeast Asia, and Europe. Their clients have included such companies as AT&T, American Express, Ameritech, Apple Computer, Avis Rent A Car, Bank of America, Bristol Myers-Squibb, The British Government, Dupont, S.C. Johnson Wax, Lufthansa German Airlines, Pacific Bell, Telecheck, and Xerox, to name a few.

In addition to their consulting work, Karen and Keith are sought after by the media as experts on quality service. They have been interviewed by dozens of newspapers, magazines, and television and radio stations including The Associated Press International, The British Broadcasting Company, CBS, CNN, *Executive Excellence*, *Fortune*, *Management Today*, *Newsweek*, *The New York Times*, *Sales and Marketing*, *Time Magazine*, and *The Oprah Winfrey Show*.

Their most recent venture is the formation of the *International Association of Quality Service*, which has more than 5,000 charter members. The purpose of the *Association* is to promote the principles and ideas of quality service throughout businesses worldwide. To receive a copy of the *Association's* newsletter "Excellence," please contact Sterling Consulting Group.

ABOUT IDG BOOKS WORLDWIDE

Welcome to the world of IDG Books Worldwide.

IDG Books Worldwide, Inc., is a subsidiary of International Data Group, the world's largest publisher of computer-related information and the leading global provider of information services on information technology. IDG was founded more than 25 years ago and now employs more than 8,500 people worldwide. IDG publishes more than 275 computer publications in over 75 countries (see listing below). More than 60 million people read one or more IDG publications each month.

Launched in 1990, IDG Books Worldwide is today the #1 publisher of best-selling computer books in the United States. We are proud to have received eight awards from the Computer Press Association in recognition of editorial excellence and three from *Computer Currents'* First Annual Readers' Choice Awards. Our best-selling *...For Dummies®* series has more than 30 million copies in print with translations in 30 languages. IDG Books Worldwide, through a joint venture with IDG's Hi-Tech Beijing, became the first U.S. publisher to publish a computer book in the People's Republic of China. In record time, IDG Books Worldwide has become the first choice for millions of readers around the world who want to learn how to better manage their businesses.

Our mission is simple: Every one of our books is designed to bring extra value and skill-building instructions to the reader. Our books are written by experts who understand and care about our readers. The knowledge base of our editorial staff comes from years of experience in publishing, education, and journalism — experience we use to produce books for the '90s. In short, we care about books, so we attract the best people. We devote special attention to details such as audience, interior design, use of icons, and illustrations. And because we use an efficient process of authoring, editing, and desktop publishing our books electronically, we can spend more time ensuring superior content and spend less time on the technicalities of making books.

You can count on our commitment to deliver high-quality books at competitive prices on topics you want to read about. At IDG Books Worldwide, we continue in the IDG tradition of delivering quality for more than 25 years. You'll find no better book on a subject than one from IDG Books Worldwide.

John J. Kilcullen

John Kilcullen
CEO
IDG Books Worldwide, Inc.

Eighth Annual Computer Press Awards ≥1992

Ninth Annual Computer Press Awards ≥1993

Tenth Annual Computer Press Awards ≥1994

Eleventh Annual Computer Press Awards ≥1995

IDG Books Worldwide, Inc., is a subsidiary of International Data Group, the world's largest publisher of computer-related information and the leading global provider of information services on information technology. International Data Group publishes over 275 computer publications in over 75 countries. Sixty million people read one or more International Data Group publications each month. International Data Group's publications include: **ARGENTINA:** Buyer's Guide, Computerworld Argentina, PC World Argentina; **AUSTRALIA:** Australian Macworld, Australian PC World, Australian Reseller News, Computerworld, IT Casebook, Network World, Publish, Webmaster; **AUSTRIA:** Computerwelt Österreich, Networks Austria, PC Tip Austria; **BANGLADESH:** PC World Bangladesh; **BELARUS:** PC World Belarus; **BELGIUM:** Data News; **BRAZIL:** Annuário de Informática, Computerworld, Connections, Macworld, PC Player, PC World, Publish, Reseller News, Supergamepower; **BULGARIA:** Computerworld Bulgaria, Network World Bulgaria, PC & MacWorld Bulgaria; **CANADA:** CIO Canada, Client/Server World, ComputerWorld Canada, InfoWorld Canada, NetworkWorld Canada, WebWorld; **CHILE:** Computerworld Chile, PC World Chile; **COLOMBIA:** Computerworld Colombia, PC World Colombia; **COSTA RICA:** PC World Centro America; **THE CZECH AND SLOVAK REPUBLICS:** Computerworld Czechoslovakia, Macworld Czech Republic, PC World Czechoslovakia; **DENMARK:** Communications World Danmark, Computerworld Danmark, Macworld Danmark, PC World Danmark, Techworld Denmark; **DOMINICAN REPUBLIC:** PC World Republica Dominicana; **ECUADOR:** PC World Ecuador; **EGYPT:** Computerworld Middle East, PC World Middle East; **EL SALVADOR:** PC World Centro America; **FINLAND:** MikroPC, Tietoverkko, Tietoviikko; **FRANCE:** Distributique, Hebdo, Info PC, Le Monde Informatique, Macworld, Reseaux & Telecoms, WebMaster France; **GERMANY:** Computer Partner, Computerwoche, Computerwoche Extra, Computerwoche FOCUS, Global Online, Macwelt, PC Welt; **GREECE:** Amiga Computing, GamePro Greece, Multimedia World; **GUATEMALA:** PC World Centro America; **HONDURAS:** PC World Centro America; **HONG KONG:** Computerworld Hong Kong, PC World Hong Kong, Publish in Asia; **HUNGARY:** ABCD CD-ROM, Computerworld Szamitastechnika, Internetto online Magazine, PC World Hungary, PC-X Magazin Hungary; **ICELAND:** Tolvuheimur PC World Island; **INDIA:** Information Communications World, Information Systems Computerworld, PC World India, Publish in Asia; **INDONESIA:** InfoKomputer PC World, Komputek Computerworld, Publish in Asia; **IRELAND:** ComputerScope, PC Live!; **ISRAEL:** Macworld Israel, People & Computers/Computerworld; **ITALY:** Computerworld Italia, Macworld Italia, Networking Italia, PC World Italia; **JAPAN:** DTP World, Macworld Japan, Nikkei Personal Computing, OS/2 World Japan, SunWorld Japan, Windows NT World, Windows World Japan; **KENYA:** PC World East African; **KOREA:** Hi-Tech Information, Macworld Korea, PC World Korea; **MACEDONIA:** PC World Macedonia; **MALAYSIA:** Computerworld Malaysia, PC World Malaysia, Publish in Asia; **MALTA:** PC World Malta; **MEXICO:** Computerworld Mexico, PC World Mexico; **MYANMAR:** PC World Myanmar; **NETHERLANDS:** Computer! Totaal, LAN Internetworking Magazine, LAN World Buyers Guide, Macworld Netherlands, Net, WebWereld; **NEW ZEALAND:** Absolute Beginners Guide and Plain & Simple Series, Computer Buyer, Computer Industry Directory, Computerworld New Zealand, MTB, Network World, PC World New Zealand; **NICARAGUA:** PC World Centro America; **NORWAY:** Computerworld Norge, CW Rapport, Datamagasinet, Financial Rapport, Kursguide Norge, Macworld Norge, Multimediaworld Norge, PC World Ekspress Norge, PC World Nettverk, PC World Norge, PC World ProduktGuide Norge; **PAKISTAN:** Computerworld Pakistan; **PANAMA:** PC World Panama; **PEOPLE'S REPUBLIC OF CHINA:** China Computer Users, China Computerworld, China InfoWorld, China Telecom World Weekly, Computer & Communication, Electronic Design China, Electronics Today, Electronics Weekly, Game Software, PC World China, Popular Computer Week, Software Weekly, Software World, Telecom World; **PERU:** Computerworld Peru, PC World Profesional Peru, PC World SoHo Peru; **PHILIPPINES:** Click!, Computerworld Philippines, PC World Philippines, Publish in Asia; **POLAND:** Computerworld Poland, Computerworld Special Report Poland, Cyber, Macworld Poland, Networld Poland, PC World Komputer; **PORTUGAL:** Cerebro/PC World, Computerworld/Correio Informático, Dealer World Portugal, Mac*In/PC*In Portugal, Multimedia World; **PUERTO RICO:** PC World Puerto Rico; **ROMANIA:** Computerworld Romania, PC World Romania, Telecom Romania; **RUSSIA:** Computerworld Russia, Mir PK, Publish, Seti; **SINGAPORE:** Computerworld Singapore, PC World Singapore, Publish in Asia; **SLOVENIA:** Monitor; **SOUTH AFRICA:** Computing SA, Network World SA, Software World SA; **SPAIN:** Communicaciones World España, Computerworld España, Dealer World España, Macworld España, PC World España; **SRI LANKA:** Infolink PC World; **SWEDEN:** CAP&Design, Computer Sweden, Corporate Computing Sweden, Internetworld Sweden, it.branschen, Macworld Sweden, MaxiData Sweden, MikroDatorn, Nätverk & Kommunikation, PC World Sweden, PCAktiv, Windows World Sweden; **SWITZERLAND:** Computerworld Schweiz, Macworld Schweiz, PCtip; **TAIWAN:** Computerworld Taiwan, Macworld Taiwan, NEW ViSiON/Publish, PC World Taiwan, Windows World Taiwan; **THAILAND:** Publish in Asia, Thai Computerworld; **TURKEY:** Computerworld Turkiye, Macworld Turkiye, Network World Turkiye, PC World Turkiye; **UKRAINE:** Computerworld Kiev, Multimedia World Ukraine, PC World Ukraine; **UNITED KINGDOM:** Acorn User UK, Amiga Action UK, Amiga Computing UK, Apple Talk UK, Computing, Macworld, Parents and Computers UK, PC Advisor, PC Home, PSX Pro, The WEB; **UNITED STATES:** Cable in the Classroom, CIO Magazine, Computerworld, DOS World, Federal Computer Week, GamePro Magazine, InfoWorld, I-Way, Macworld, Network World, PC Games, PC World, Publish, Video Event, THE WEB Magazine, and WebMaster; online webzines: JavaWorld, NetscapeWorld, and SunWorld Online; **URUGUAY:** InfoWorld Uruguay; **VENEZUELA:** Computerworld Venezuela, PC World Venezuela; and **VIETNAM:** PC World Vietnam. 2/14/97

Speeches, Seminars, and Consulting

Karen and Keith are among the highest-rated presenters on the speaking circuit and offer keynote presentations that are

- ✔ customized to reflect your specific needs, concerns, and industry
- ✔ highly interactive, creating presentations that are fun and lively
- ✔ based on practical, real-world information that attendees can use immediately
- ✔ conducted in a unique and effective co-presentation style

Karen and Keith would be delighted to speak at your next business meeting, conference, or convention. For more information on keynote presentations, training, or consulting, contact Karen Leland/ Keith Bailey at:

Sterling Consulting Group, Inc.
180 Harbor Drive #212
Sausalito, CA 94965
Phone: (415) 331-5200
Fax: (415) 331-5272
E-mail: sterconinc@aol.com

Dedication

To my parents for always giving me the freedom to make my own choices, and to Deborah, my wife, for her open heart and limitless love.

– Keith Bailey

To my husband, Jon, I am deeply grateful for your love, support, and enthusiasm for life.

To my mother, Barbara Tiber, the most well-read person I know. Thanks for giving me my love of books and for always being there when I needed you.

To my father, Norman Tiber, who told me to get a degree in Astronomy because "you will always be able to find a job." I'm glad I didn't listen to you, but thanks for your support and passing on your great sense of humor.

– Karen Frances Leland

Publisher's Acknowledgments

We're proud of this book; please send us your comments about it by using the Reader Response Card at the back of the book or by e-mailing us at `feedback/dummies@idgbooks.com`. Some of the people who helped bring this book to market include the following:

Acquisitions, Development, & Editorial

Project Editor: Bill Helling

Product Development Manager: Mary Bednarek

Permissions Editor: Joyce Pepple

Copy Editor: Tamara S. Castleman

Technical Reviewer: Suzanne Saxe

Editorial Assistants: Chris Collins, Ann Miller

Production

Project Coordinator: J. Tyler Connor

Layout and Graphics: Shawn Aylsworth, Cameron Booker, Linda M. Boyer, Todd Klemme, Jane Martin, Tom Missler, Mark C. Owens, Laura Puranen, Anna Rohrer, Kate Snell, Michael Sullivan, Angela F. Hunckler, Carla C. Radzikinas, Gina Scott

Proofreaders: Mary C. Oby, Christine Meloy Beck, Gwenette Gaddis, Dwight Ramsey, Robert Springer

Indexer: David Heiret

General and Administrative

IDG Books Worldwide, Inc.: John Kilcullen, CEO; Steven Berkowitz, President and Publisher

IDG Books Technology Publishing: Brenda McLaughlin, Senior Vice President and Group Publisher

Dummies Technology Press and Dummies Editorial: Diane Graves Steele, Vice President and Associate Publisher; Judith A. Taylor, Brand Manager; Kristin A. Cocks, Editorial Director

Dummies Trade Press: Kathleen A. Welton, Vice President and Publisher; Stacy S. Collins, Brand Manager

IDG Books Production for Dummies Press: Beth Jenkins, Production Director; Cindy L. Phipps, Supervisor of Project Coordination, Production Proofreading, and Indexing; Kathie S. Schutte, Supervisor of Page Layout; Shelley Lea, Supervisor of Graphics and Design; Debbie J. Gates, Production Systems Specialist; Tony Augsburger, Supervisor of Reprints and Bluelines; Leslie Popplewell, Media Archive Coordinator

Dummies Packaging and Book Design: Patti Sandez, Packaging Specialist; Lance Kayser, Packaging Assistant; Kavish+Kavish, Cover Design

♦

The publisher would like to give special thanks to Patrick J. McGovern, without whom this book would not have been possible.

♦

Acknowledgments

First we would like to thank our clients who, over the years, have taught us more about customer service than we could ever write in one book. Thank you for helping us to turn good ideas into practical applications.

We are very grateful to Kathy Welton, at IDG Books, for contacting us about writing *Customer Service For Dummies,* reigniting our desire to write a book, and then being our champion in getting it published.

Another thank you goes to our book representative Marc Jaffe at ELO. Thanks for guiding us through the turns and twists of the publishing world with such calm certainty.

Thank you to Milton Woolley, MS, whose insights into human behavior and emotions helped us in writing the book and have benefited us personally over the years.

A special thanks to Suzanne Saxe, Ph.D., for being our good friend and technical advisor on the book.

To the folks at *Inc. Magazine*: Linda, Ellen, Nancy, Craig, George, Bob, Caty, and Jim. We have enjoyed working with you over the years and look forward to many more conferences together.

To the various people in our community who contributed in one way or another to this book including: Westamerica Bank, Irving Bernstein-CPA, Melba Beales, Tom Schofield, Charlene and Judy at Travel Associates, Jose, our mailman, and Bert, our neighbor.

Special thanks go to the wonderful staff at IDG Books who have helped us through this process: Stephanie Britt, whose insight got us off on the right foot; Bill Helling and Tammy Castleman, our editors, who kept us on track with a sense of humor and a very active e-mail account; and Stacy Collins, for being our cheerleader and believing in the value of this book.

Contents at a Glance

· ·

Cartoons at a Glance

By Rich Tennant • Fax: 508-546-7747 • E-mail: the5wave@tiac.net

"And that's why you're in the back of the store instead of in the front!"

page 45

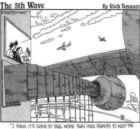

"I THINK IT'S GOING TO TAKE MORE THAN FREE PEANUTS TO KEEP THE PASSENGERS HAPPY AFTER THIS ONE, SIR."

page 3

page 237

"JERRY! OVER THERE, NEAR THE ESCALATOR...I THINK IT'S A SALES CLERK...QUICK! LIGHT ANOTHER TIE ON FIRE!"

page 326

page 288

page 117

"As a bonus to our customers, we're throwing in a wrist-lock, a neck breaker and a stomp-to-the-groin, free of charge."

page 188

page 305

"WHOA, WHOA, FELLOWS, TONE IT DOWN! WHAT ARE YOU TRYIN' TO DO, IMPRESS SOMEONE.?"

page 68

page 18

Table of Contents

Part III: Six Steps to Service Success:
Company Strategies *117*

Chapter 9: Taking Your Company's Pulse: How to
Survey Your Customers 119

Chapter 16: Wrinkled Foreheads and Clenched Fists:
Stress Management **249**

Chapter 17: It Takes Two to Tango: Getting in
Step with Your Customer **265**

Introduction

• •

*W*elcome to *Customer Service For Dummies*. Have you ever noticed how easy it is to get annoyed (or even ready to kill in some cases) when you get bad service? But when the shoe is on the other foot, you know how frustrating it can be trying to help your customers and feeling like you're not getting anywhere!

The bottom line is that quality service touches our lives in two important ways: the service we give and the service we receive. *Customer Service For Dummies* will help you to not only be a better business-person but also a better customer.

Customer Service For Dummies is a down-to-earth, step-by-step guide that takes the mystery out of providing the best possible service to your customers. This book is filled with hot tips, techniques, and lots of suggestions for giving your customers the kind of service that you yourself would like to receive.

- ✔ *Customer Service For Dummies* contains lots of practical advice for getting through the everyday challenges at work. It teaches you how to keep your sanity when an angry customer is calling you (and your mother) unflattering names over the phone; how to manage and develop your staff so they can become service heroes to their customers; and it provides you with tried and true techniques for achieving gold level service at bronze level cost.

- ✔ And for you empire builders out there (business owners and entrepreneurs), we provide a blueprint that will help you take over the world, or at least improve your market share. In fact, we've made it as easy as 1-2-3 with a specific and detailed six-step process that makes any company, large or small, more customer oriented.

- ✔ Everyone in the world is a customer. Chapter 2 tells you about becoming a better customer and getting better service by getting the service provider on your side and expressing yourself in style.

Oh, by the way, the dictionary definition of the word *customer* includes *a person with whom one has dealings.* So please feel free to use the information in this book with your co-workers, bosses, friends, spouses, and family.

About This Book

This book will give great ideas for improving the service you offer your customers. However, you must have three basic elements in place in order for those ideas to take root and flourish. Although smiling, saying please, and saying thank you are important, they alone will not lead to good service. But beware! These elements are not necessarily easy to do. (If they were so easy, everyone would be doing them.) The difference between knowing them and living them takes commitment and practice. These three elements are

- ✔ Expand your definition of service.
- ✔ Reconsider who your customers are.
- ✔ Develop a customer friendly attitude.

If you hold the common idea that service is only *giving customers what they want,* you will be in trouble every time a customer asks for something that is impossible for you to provide. But if you expand your definition of service to include fulfilling the multitude of less obvious customer needs, you will *never* be in a situation when you can't provide your customers with some level of service.

How This Book Is Organized

Customer Service For Dummies is organized into five parts, and chapters within each part cover specific topic areas in detail. Each chapter has lists of what to do, what to look for, and how to *go for the gold.*

Part I: Look Before You Leap

In this part of *Customer Service For Dummies,* we explore the basic ingredients that make you and your company winners in the service game. Right from the get-go, you will learn the ingredient that all successful businesses and individuals have in common.

Part II: Simple Actions, Significant Payoffs: Individual Strategies

In this part of the book, we explore those *little things,* those simple actions that lead to significant payoffs in customer satisfaction. We provide you with time tested techniques for dealing with people face-to-face and over the telephone, and we cover a variety of important communication skills that you can use every day at work and at home.

Part III: Six Steps to Service Success: Company Strategies

This part is filled with real world suggestions and solutions that will help you gain a competitive advantage in your business. You learn how to implement a six-step process containing key actions that will make your company a service star — real insights into how to build teamwork, morale, and accountability at all levels of your company.

Part IV: Dealing with Difficult People

In this part, you will learn how to reduce the effects of stress when dealing with conflict situations and how to calm down angry and upset customers (and co-workers!). This part of the book also contains a process that the authors have taught to over 50,000 people in companies and jobs like yours for turning difficult situations into win-win.

Part V: The Part of Tens

We have created a bunch of *cheat sheets* for managers, salespeople, and front-line staff. This part is a quick and easy way for you to brush up on the main points listed in this book — as well as a way to pick up some new tips and techniques.

Icon Guides

Keith Anecdote: These are stories that have happened to Keith.

Karen Anecdote: These are stories that have happened to Karen.

Anecdote: These are stories that have happened to both Keith and Karen, at the same time.

Tip: The tip icon provides you with general recommendations on how you can improve the customer service you offer.

Go For The Gold: This icon alerts you to stellar suggestions that will make you a service star.

Holy Cow: Throughout this book we take on several *sacred cows.* These are popular sayings, beliefs, or folklore held near and dear by service persons and companies alike that we think are misleading or untrue. You may agree or disagree with us, but you will have fun thinking about them.

Caution: This icon flags any potential pitfalls that we think you need to be careful of.

Manager's Moment: These are hot tips, techniques, and suggestions — designed especially for managers — to improve service.

Remember: This is the stuff that we don't want you to forget.

Where to Go from Here

We all love and cherish companies that treat us the way we like to be treated; we'll even pay more to obtain good service. Just look at these recent survey statistics that prove the point:

- ✔ We spend up to 10 percent more for the same product with better service.
- ✔ We tell anywhere from 9 to 12 people when we get good service.
- ✔ When we receive poor service, we tell up to 20 people!

So, how you communicate and establish a relationship with your customers is the *essence* of customer service. This relationship doesn't have to take a long time — it can often happen in an instant. For example, your customers will feel more recognized (and thus more connected) if they are greeted with smiles and are addressed by name. Simple actions such as these keep customers coming back for more.

It certainly pays to please!

Part I
Look Before You Leap

The 5th Wave — By Rich Tennant

"I THINK IT'S GOING TO TAKE MORE THAN FREE PEANUTS TO KEEP THE PASSENGERS HAPPY AFTER THIS ONE, SIR."

In this part...

An ancient Chinese proverb states that the journey of a thousand miles begins with the first step. In this part of *Customer Service For Dummies,* we explore the basic ingredients that make you and your company winners in the service game. Right from the get-go, you will learn the ingredient that all successful businesses and individuals have in common.

Included is an eye-opening questionnaire that helps you evaluate how good a job you and your staff are doing at providing service that delights your customers time and time again while leaving your competitors in the dust.

Lastly, you, like most people, want to receive the same good level of service you provide. So, just to keep things in balance, we include a guideline in this part that helps you get the service you deserve when you are standing on the other side of the counter.

Chapter 1

Back to Basics: The Art of Giving Good Service

. . . .

In This Chapter

▶ Giving more than just lip service

▶ Attitude is everything

▶ The customer chain

▶ Service is more than just saying *yes*

▶ Balancing the functions with the essence of your job

▶ Moments of truth

. . . .

I couldn't care less about my customers!

*I*n all our years of consulting, we've never heard any CEO, manager, or staff person utter this phrase — in so many words. You probably believe, as we do, that satisfied customers are as essential to your business success as healthy profits are to the bottom line. Yet if you look at service from the point of view of being a customer (and we all are), you don't have to go much further than your local mall to see that what companies say about service and how they actually deliver it can be worlds apart.

In our daily dealings with banks, stores, and restaurants, we often feel like service, and even common courtesy, have fallen by the wayside. If, for example, your insurance company really understood the importance of giving personal service, why would it install a voice mail system that does not give you the option of speaking with a real, live person? Or if your local post office realized that it is competing for your business, would the staff be allowed to go on lunch break the same time that you do every day?

Sooner or later we hang up or walk out, scratching our heads and wondering whatever happened to good customer service? Is it impossible to be profitable *and* keep customers happy? Do people *have* to take second place to technology?

As we are forced to do more with less, will service be inevitably sacrificed? We think not. In fact, survey after survey confirms that the companies and individuals whom we like to deal with, the ones who win our business over and over again, are the ones who understand and act upon the *three basic elements* that form the rock solid foundation of excellent service.

Three Basic Elements

This book will give you hundreds of great ideas for improving the service you offer your customers. However, when all is said and done, you must have three basic elements in place in order for those hundreds of ideas to take root and flourish. If not, no amount of smiling or saying please and thank you will lead to good service. You may find yourself looking at these obvious basics and thinking:

> *No big deal, these ideas are Business 101.*

But beware, looks are deceiving. These elements are not necessarily easy to do (if they were everyone would be doing them). The difference between knowing them and living them takes commitment and practice. The three basics are:

- ✔ Expanding your definition of service.
- ✔ Reconsidering who your customers are.
- ✔ Developing a *customer friendly* attitude.

Expand Your Definition of Service

Your definition of service shapes every interaction you have with your customers. If you hold the common idea that service is only *giving customers what they want,* you may well paint yourself into a corner every time a customer asks for something that is impossible for you to provide. If, on the other hand, you expand your definition of service to include *fulfilling the multitude of less obvious customer need*s, you will *never* encounter a time when you can't provide your customers with some level of service.

By addressing less obvious customer needs such as listening with empathy to customers when they have a problem or providing options and alternatives when you can't give customers exactly what they want, you widen the gap between you and your competitors. You can find out more about these less obvious customer needs and how to find and fulfill them in Chapter 8.

Reconsider Who Your Customers Are

Who are your customers, really? Too often we limit our definition of a customer to someone who is outside of our company. Look up *customer* in your *Funk & Wagnall's*. The first definition of customer is *a person who buys*. The second definition is *a person with whom one has dealings*.

In fact, everyone who works in a company has customers regardless of whether they work with external, paying customers or internal co-workers. Customers fall into external and internal categories.

The external customer

These are the people you deal with, either face-to-face or over the phone, who buy products or services from you. They are customers in the traditional sense of the word. Without them there would be no sales, no business, no paycheck. If your definition of a customer stops here, you are only seeing half the picture.

The internal customer

The other half of the picture is the people who work inside your company and rely on you for the services, products, and information that they need to get their jobs done. They are not traditional customers, yet they need the same tender, loving care you give to your external customers.

By expanding your definition of a customer to include your co-workers, you are taking a vital step toward excellent service.

The internal customer chain works both ways. Sometimes you are the customer and other times you are the service provider. For example, a co-worker may come to you and ask for a printout of a report. In this case, you are the service provider because you are giving him what he needs. However, ten minutes later you may turn around and go to that same co-worker and ask for help on a project; now you are the customer.

Many years ago, I worked as a waiter in a restaurant. One of the cooks was moody and had the habit of throwing kitchen utensils at the wall on the far side of the kitchen. The noise of the clattering metal let us all know when the cook wasn't a happy camper and beware! One day, I was taking the order of two dinner patrons. One of them asked to substitute steamed vegetables for the French fries that usually accompanied this meal. As my smile congealed, I immediately thought of the unhappy cook and my desire to live. Eventually, I nervously said, "I'm sure that will be no problem." My trip back to the kitchen felt like walking up the steps to the gallows. I poked my head into the kitchen, quickly threw down the order, and left before the spoons started flying. As I waited on my next table, I noticed that the cook's attitude had put a *wet blanket* on my enthusiasm. His job, as written on his job description, was to prepare food. No mention was made of how his dealings with or attitude toward other employees might indirectly affect the customers' dining experience.

The customer chain

The relationship between internal customers and external customers is what forms the customer chain. If you have a back room kind of job where you rarely see the light of day, let alone a living, breathing customer, you can easily begin to feel that your work has little or no impact on external customers. But if you look at the bigger picture, you can see that everyone in a company plays some part in fulfilling the customers' needs. Barely an hour goes by during the day when you are not, in some form or another, providing something for somebody. Each interaction with an internal customer is an important link in a chain of events that always ends up at the external customers' feet.

About two years ago the *Wall Street Journal* ran an article entitled, "Poorly treated employees treat the customer just as poorly." Boy, does that hit the nail on the head! We have dealt with a frightening percentage of managers who do not realize that their staff are their internal customers. We are convinced that the quality of service that a company provides to its customers is a direct reflection of how the staff of the company are treated by their managers. Make viewing your staff as one of your most important customers and treating them accordingly a priority. Doing so means focusing not on what your staff can do to make your job easier, but on what you can do to make their jobs easier.

Many companies seem to overlook a very important link in the service chain — their vendors. By using the techniques in this book with your vendors, you will not only enhance your relationship with them but also receive better service. In our business, we know that we are dealing with truly customer-focused companies when they treat us as customers even though they are our clients.

We were once invited to present our ideas about service to the senior executives of a large and well-known manufacturing organization. They were puzzled as to why surveys of customers continued to reveal one central weakness: They were not service oriented. We began the meeting and the group became less and less comfortable with our idea about treating co-workers and employees as customers. During an afternoon break at this rapidly deteriorating meeting, the vice president of Human Resources shuffled us into a darkened corner of the board room and said with fear in his eyes, "Are you trying to tell me that the way I treat my staff has an effect on how they treat their customers?" "Yes," we said. He shook his head in dismay, lit his pipe, and wandered off through his own smoke. We were never invited back. Here was a group of educated, experienced professionals apparently unaware of one of the basics of excellent service: treat your staff like customers.

Develop a Customer Friendly Attitude

One thing all companies and individuals who give great service have in common is that they have a genuine *customer friendly* attitude. By *customer friendly* attitude, we mean viewing your customers as the *most important part of your job* and having a sincere appreciation that they choose to do business with you. We don't mean viewing your customers as an interruption of your job and then pasting on a false smile, all the while wishing they would leave so you could get on with your work. In order to understand how to create a *customer friendly* attitude, you need to step back and take a look at what you do during the work day.

One way to easily see what you do during the day is to imagine that you're at work and Oprah Winfrey shows up and says she is doing a special on "The Workers of America." She wants to follow you around with a camera for an entire day and videotape everything you do (with the exception of a few personal moments). At the end of the day, Oprah invites you to view the tape. As you watch, you notice that you are resourceful under pressure, productive, efficient, and very good looking. (That's probably the reason they picked you.)

Seeing yourself on the video has confirmed your suspicions: A day at work is rather like a day in a blender. Once you walk in, everything switches into high gear and is a crazy blur of doing this, that, and the other thing until you leave for the day. The tape demonstrates how surrounded and submerged you are by:

- ✔ ringing telephones
- ✔ memos to read
- ✔ paperwork to process
- ✔ meetings to attend
- ✔ computer data to enter
- ✔ fires to be put out, and so on

Show this videotape to your boss, point out all that you do, and ask for a raise. If you are self-employed, take yourself out to dinner — you deserve it!

Two common threads

These incessant tasks that make up your day are the *functions* of your job. Thinking that all the paperwork, data entry, memos to be written, and meetings to attend are the whole story is very easy. If you look a little deeper, though, you will find two common threads that link together everything that you do at work whether you are a plumber, a teacher, or an IRS auditor.

Communicating with other people

The first of these two common threads is communicating with other people. Plumbers, for example, may spend most of their day alone under a sink — with only a wrench for company — but when they explain to you what the problem is (and what it will cost to fix it) their communication skills will be what count. A teacher's ability to make a subject utterly fascinating or utterly boring has a lot to do with the way they talk about it. What can we say about IRS auditors and their communication skills? We leave that to your imagination. The bottom line is that everyone, regardless of whether he works alone or in a group, uses some form of communication to get his job done.

Communication isn't just talking. It's also body language, writing, and, in today's world, electronic interaction. Chapters 4, 5, and 6 offer you some valuable techniques for enhancing your communication skills.

Establishing relationships

The second common thread is developing relationships with people. When we use the word relationship, we are often describing a personal relationship. But here we mean connecting with another person in order to accomplish something. If you go back under the sink and visit your solitary plumber, you'll find that he or she has relationships with customers, vendors, and fellow plumbers. The same applies to the schoolteacher, who not only has a relationship with the students, but also has relationships with parents, other teachers, and the principal. IRS auditors, in many ways, have the broadest relationships of all because they have a relationship with the government and the entire country.

Instant connections

Communicating and establishing relationships are really the *essence* of your job. They don't have to take a long time and they often happen in an instant. For example, at the department store you feel more recognized — and consequently more connected — if the sales assistant smiles at you and calls you by your name when handing you back your credit card. Simple actions such as these keep the customer coming back for more.

The bad news is that making a customer an enemy for life can take just as little time. When you call a company on the phone and the telephone rings ten times before someone picks it up, what kind of connection has that company made with you? More than likely a negative relationship has been created before any business is transacted. These connections, as simple and quick as they are, are a moment of truth for the customer.

No matter how busy you are, you only get one chance to make a first impression.

Moments of truth

These brief actions or instant connections can be considered moments of truth. Usually no longer than twenty seconds, they have a lasting impact on your customers' perception of the service you offer. Imagine this: A prospective customer comes to see you. She walks up to the receptionist and tells him that she is here for her two o'clock appointment with you. The receptionist (a temp you just hired) is busy working on the computer and doesn't respond or look up for several seconds. When he does look up and speak, he has a go-ahead-make-my-day expression and a get-out-of-my-face tone in his voice. This brief interaction is a negative moment of truth for your potential customer. It doesn't end there. The negative impression she has of the receptionist is unwittingly applied to the rest of your company (including you). We know it isn't fair — but it is the way customers think. We call this type of thinking *customer logic.*

Now imagine the opposite situation. Your customer walks in and the reception-ist immediately looks up, greets her with a smile, and says:

> *Good morning, how may I help you?*

When the customer asks for you, the receptionist tells her you will just be a moment and offers her a cup of coffee or tea. This positive moment of truth gets the customer on your side and paves the way for a successful meeting. Some simple yet high profile opportunities to create positive moments of truth include the following:

- ✔ Answer the phone with a greeting before identifying yourself or your company. Doing so starts the conversation out on the right foot.

- ✔ Become more aware of your facial expression when a customer ap-proaches you. A smile works much better than a grimace. Customers often judge our mood on how we look when they approach us.

- ✔ Don't take it personally when a customer complains. Think of a complaint for what it is, an opportunity to get valuable feedback from your custom-ers. You listen better if you don't feel threatened.

> ✔ Always offer options when you can't give customers exactly what they want. Your customers can live with a *no* if it is softened by alternative recommendations.
>
> ✔ Before transferring a customer to another extension (if you must), ensure that the service provider is available *before* completing the transfer. A dead end transfer creates a negative impression.

For a great story on how one company became a service winner, read Jan Carlzon's *Moments Of Truth* (Perennial Library, Harper & Row). Although written about the airline industry, we've never found a business that couldn't benefit from the advice.

Functions versus essence

Creating positive moments of truth is easy when you are not under pressure.

However, in the face of ringing telephones, messages piling up, reports due, and meetings that run overtime, you can get so caught up in your daily To Do list (your *functions*) that it is easy to forget that the *essence* of your job is serving the customer.

If you forget this principle, the customer becomes an interruption of the job. This attitude of *you're interrupting my job* leaves customers with the feeling that they are unimportant and the company has little or no regard for their needs. Alternatively, when you *create a customer friendly attitude by viewing the customer as the job*, the customer feels valued by your company.

"Creating a relationship with every customer takes too much time." Holy bovine, Batman! If we had a dollar for every time we've heard this statement, we would be writing this book from the warm sands of a tropical beach somewhere. Solving a problem with a partner takes a lot less time than it does with an adversary. In a survey that we conducted for one of our clients, we found that 98 percent of customer interactions were faster and more efficient when the service provider took the time to establish a relationship and create rapport with the customer. When you have a *customer friendly* attitude, you naturally begin to develop a partnership with the other person.

Last year, we took a flight from San Francisco to New York. While about a hundred of us weary travelers patiently waited for our luggage to appear on the carousel, a voice came over the loudspeaker announcing that a loading problem in San Francisco meant our luggage would arrive on the first flight the next morning. Amid quiet moans and louder curses, we were shuffled over to the lost luggage area and asked to form two lines. As we moved closer to the front of our line, we became aware that the other line was moving faster (don't they always). We noticed that the agent in the fast moving line was friendlier than her co-worker who was taking care of our grumbling group of passengers.

Service has a feeling

Think of a company (restaurant, store, bank, and so on) where you enjoy doing business. Why do you like being their customer? Are they friendly, courteous, knowledgeable? Imagine for a moment that you are there right now. How do you feel? OK, now we are going to transport you instantly to a new location. You are standing in line at the Department of Motor Vehicles waiting to renew your driver's license. How do you feel now? If you don't feel any different, you may need psychiatric help!

The friendly agent was really going out of her way to be nice to the passengers. She smiled and apologized, saying that she could understand her customers' frustration and so on. The passengers moved quickly through her line apparently satisfied that everything that could be done was being done. At the head of our line, the story wasn't so pretty. We could tell that our agent was upset because she had a tortured expression on her face, a loud, cranky voice, and an overall bad attitude. Her conversation included phrases like, "What do you expect me to be able to do about it?" "You'll just have to make do until the morning," and the ever popular "The sooner you give me the information I need, the sooner I'll be able to help you . . . ." We started to talk about how each of these agents might go home and talk to her family about her day. We imagined the one with the customer friendly attitude saying, "We had a problem with luggage on the San Francisco flight tonight, but most of the passengers were really understanding." While the other agent's report would be more like, "You can't believe what a terrible evening I've had. There was a problem with the luggage on the San Francisco flight, and the passengers were a total pain in the neck about it. I'm stressed out!" What this agent failed to realize was that it would not have taken her any longer to be friendly to the customers, and it would have been a lot less stressful had she done so.

Are the functions winning?

Following are some clues that you may have slipped into viewing your customers as an interruption of your job:

- Your shoulders hug your neck every time the phone rings.
- Switching on voice mail has become a reflex — even when you are in!
- Every customer or co-worker looks like he or she is out to get you.
- You enjoy saying *no* more and more.
- Every sentence you utter to a customer begins with a sigh.

The functions are important but never more important than the customers they were designed to serve.

Two Types of Companies

In short, you not only have to hold the flame of service high as an individual by having a customer friendly attitude, but if you are a manager, you also have to ensure that all those who work for you do the same. The path to excellent service is not simply a matter of hiring the right people and training the front-line staff. Instead, the path begins with a genuine commitment to create a service-oriented company culture. You will find *two* distinct types of companies.

The in-focused company

If these companies were people, you might be inclined to call them selfish because their main concern is pleasing themselves rather than their customers. In-focused companies are fixated on achieving internal goals that benefit the company, such as cutting costs, earning profits, and budgeting. Customer satisfaction goals are low on the list; they may even be nonexistent (see Figure 1-1). Following are some typical qualities that identify an in-focused company:

- Recognition is usually not given to the staff who provide good service but to those who excel at accomplishing internal company goals.

- Staff have to focus most of their efforts on making their managers, rather than their customers, happy.

- Promotion is based on seniority and favoritism rather than merit.

- Staff, if trained at all, are trained in the functions of the job but rarely in the essence.

- Departments who do not deal directly with the external customer don't see themselves as responsible for customer satisfaction.

- Decisions that affect the customer are made at the top (behind closed doors) and then pushed down without consulting the front line.

- Short-term, bottom-line fixes always win out over long-term solutions.

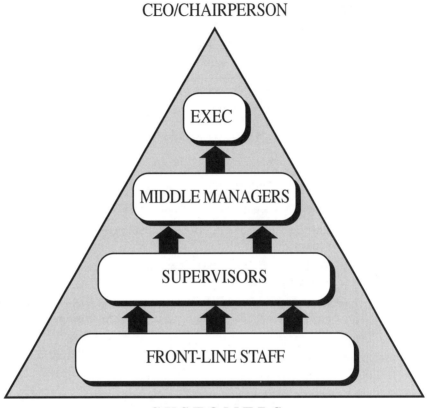

Figure 1-1:
The in-
focused
organization
pleases
itself.

We know of a company that had received dozens of complaints regarding the discourteous handling of telephone calls at corporate headquarters. In response, senior management asked the Human Resources department to design a two-hour training seminar on customer service to resolve the problem. The HR department did so and invited all the upper management to attend. This action would not only underline management support for a new way of thinking, but also provide the opportunity for training the worst offenders — the managers themselves! Their indignant response was that they did not have time to attend such a program; the lower ranks needed the training anyway — not them.

The customer-focused company

A customer-focused company, on the other hand, has one eye on profits and the other eye on how best to serve its customers. This company has learned that profit and market share are the product of listening to customers and acting upon their needs (see Figure 1-2). Following are some qualities that characterize a customer-focused organization:

✔ Recognition is earned by staff who balance job efficiency with customer satisfaction.

✔ Managers focus their attention on supporting staff in doing their jobs well so that the staff can focus their attention on taking care of customer needs.

✔ Promotion is based on good service skills as well as on seniority.

✔ Training staff is a high priority with a focus on both technical and interpersonal skills.

✔ All staff know who their customers are (external or internal) and see how they are part of the customer chain.

✔ A participative management style is common throughout the company, and staff feedback is sought on key customer issues before decisions are made.

✔ Long-term thinking is the rule rather than the exception.

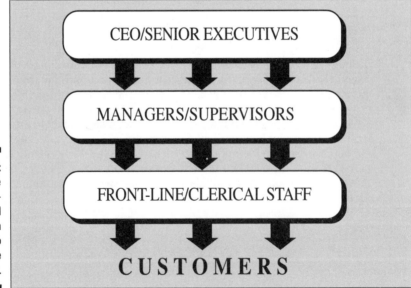

Figure 1-2: The customer-focused organization seeks to please the customers.

An international hotel client of ours does regular guest tracking to monitor customer satisfaction. The results are then forwarded to the general managers at each location. Information such as how one hotel site compares to the others in the same region as well as specific information on each department (front desk, check out, restaurant, and so on) is made available. Management bonuses are based on these guest tracking results, and a yearly achievement forum is held to acknowledge those staff and locations whose guest tracking scores are the highest.

Chapter 3 offers you the chance to evaluate where your company stands.

It pays to please

We love and cherish those companies that treat us the way we like to be treated — we'll even pay more to obtain these services! Here are some recent survey statistics that prove the point:

- We'll spend up to 10 percent more for the same product with better service.

- When we receive good service, we tell 9 to 12 people on average.

- When we receive poor service, we tell up to 20 people.

- An 82 percent chance exists that customers will repurchase from a company if their complaint is handled quickly and pleasantly.

- If the service is really poor, 91 percent of retail customers won't go back to a store.

Chapter 2

Who's Next in Line?: The Art of Getting Good Service

. . . .

In This Chapter

▶ Customer personalities

▶ Getting your server's attention

▶ Making yourself easy to help

▶ Tips for common situations

▶ How to complain

. . . .

*I*t's one thing to know what makes you a winner in the service game, but it's another to know how to get what you want as a customer. In this chapter, we are going to ask you to switch gears and view life from the other side of the counter. We've included a chapter on how to *get* good service in a book on how to *give* good service because we've found that the more you are able to stand in your customers' shoes, the better you will be at providing great service. The other reason is that if you are anything like us, you are equally as interested in getting the best service you can when you are the customer. With this in mind, here are the basics to making life on the other side of the counter less stressful and more successful.

Start Off on the Right Foot

When was the last time you walked into a department store and stood at the counter waiting to be waited on? Two sales associates were in clear view, chatting away about their personal lives. Trying to be patient you stood quietly waiting for them to notice you and offer you a helping hand. After a while you started to think, "Do they see me, or are they still on break? What's going on here?" At a certain point, sooner or later, depending on whether you are a Type

A personality or a Type B personality, you get annoyed. The scene might look something like this:

Type A personality

Being the outgoing, fast moving, and straightforward individual you are, you immediately get the sales associate's attention by loudly announcing: "Excuse me, can somebody help me please? I'm in a hurry!"

This approach would more than likely be greeted with an equally annoyed "I'll be right with you" from the sales associate.

Other Type A tactics include:

- finding the supervisor and registering a formal complaint
- saying "Hey you, haul it over here, I need some help!"
- giving the sales associate your time-is-money lecture
- asking the customer next to you, "How can this store stay in business when they hire such inefficient people?"

Type B personality

Being the laid back, quiet, and patient individual you are, you wait a few minutes for one of the sales associates to help you. Five minutes later, you are still waiting and attempt to nudge things along by clearing your throat a couple of times, hoping they'll notice.

Other Type B tactics include:

- saying "I'm sorry, I don't mean to disturb you, but when you get a chance, can you help me?"
- rustling the wrapper of the item you want to purchase
- sighing out loud
- walking away and finding another sales associate

Three steps

Now you may be congratulating yourself on the fine way your particular personality type handled this situation. While you certainly find pros and cons for both styles, neither of them really works in the extreme. What does work are three simple steps that, regardless of your style, will help you *start off on the right foot* with the person who is serving you.

Step 1: Get them on your side

How you initially approach service providers influences the entire interaction and its outcome. Don't let your time pressures or frustrations run away with you. You want to give the message to the service people that you view them as allies rather than obstacles. Following are some easy and effective ways to convey this message:

- Make direct eye contact as soon as you have their attention.
- Greet the provider by saying *good morning* or *good afternoon*.
- Make a clear and direct request up front, specifically stating what you want (see Step 2).
- Make it clear that you need their help.
- Use the word *please* within the first 30 seconds of the exchange.

Step 2: Ask for what you want

One of the best ways to get what you want is to ask for it! The more clear, concise, and direct you can make your request, the higher the chance that the service provider can deliver it. One of the biggest mistakes customers make is expecting the service provider to be a mind reader. Making clear requests saves you time and lessens the service person's frustration. Following are important elements to include in your request:

- Know the end result you want and don't be afraid to ask for it; don't assume the service person already knows.
- If you have a time frame in mind, let the service person know what it is.
- Make sure the person who is helping you has the authority to do what you are asking.
- Be specific about any details that may vary from the norm.

Step 3: Stand in their shoes

Even if you greet the sales clerks as warmly as you would your best friend and make the world's clearest, most articulate, and understandable request, there may be times when the people helping you cannot deliver 100 percent. The reason may be because they are simply having a bad day, or it might be more complex and be that company rules and regulations have put them in a bind.

We have trained over 30,000 staff in our workshops and find that most people want to provide good service. The problem is that many people work for companies that are in-focused (see Chapter 1). Unfortunately these types of companies don't support, encourage, or empower their staff to do what it takes to give you, the customer, great service. When faced with this situation, the best strategy is not to shoot the messenger. Try to understand the parameters that the person is working within and enlist his help in getting through a system that you both probably feel doesn't work.

If you need help in solving a problem, utilize the resources of the service person by asking:

- ✔ "What do you recommend?"
- ✔ "Do you have any suggestions?"
- ✔ "What would you do if you were in my situation?"
- ✔ "What's a good next step?"

On those occasions when you are dealing with someone who is obviously in a bad mood, try defusing the situation by recognizing her feelings and saying:

- ✔ "You seem like you're having a bad day today."
- ✔ "This situation must be tough for you."
- ✔ "You're doing a great job; I know this is a difficult situation."

You can make life much easier for yourself and at the same time help the service person take better care of you by doing one simple thing: Follow the instructions you are given. Why reinvent the wheel? If you follow the instructions and you still don't understand, ask for clarification. *A minute you spend paying attention now will save you thirty minutes later.*

Express Yourself in Style

In the movie *Network,* Peter Finch's character says, "I'm mad as hell, and I'm not going to take it anymore!" One thing we can promise you is that sooner or later, you will get angry at the individual serving you. The range of your anger may be anything from mild annoyance to outrage. This anger is usually brought on by sheer rudeness, suffocating bureaucracy, complete incompetence, or a combination of all three, in which case you will see shades of red not normally visible to the naked eye. At these times, the normal reaction is to pounce all over the service person (thinking he deserves it) and treat him as badly as you feel you are being treated.

If this approach worked, we would highly recommend it. Unfortunately, as many of you know, it almost never does. More often than not, this method is counterproductive because it puts the service person on the defensive. She becomes more interested in protecting herself than in helping you. The two of you will get further away from problem solving and move closer to taking opposite sides simply to avoid being in the wrong. Sometimes you are justified in feeling angry and expressing that anger. Just be sure to express yourself in style, or as one of our friends says:

> *Stand up for yourself in an elegant way.*

Learn to use "I" messages

Parent effectiveness training teaches that by using "I" messages instead of "you" messages, you can communicate your feelings honestly while minimizing the chance of putting the other person in a defensive posture.

"I" messages state feelings from your point of view and therefore they usually include the word "feel" or "feeling." "I" messages begin, naturally enough, with the word "I." Examples include the following:

- ✔ "I feel frustrated that I can't get the answer I need from your company."
- ✔ "I don't feel comfortable with the way this situation is being handled.
- ✔ "I don't feel I'm getting the help I need."

Major don'ts

At all costs avoid these major don'ts when dealing face-to-face or over the telephone with a service person:

✔ Don't threaten to sue as a tactic.

✔ Don't yell, scream, or shout.

✔ Don't use foul language.

✔ Don't threaten physical harm.

✔ Don't claim you know the owner of the company (when you don't) and say that you will be speaking to him or her about this incident.

"You" messages

By contrast, a "you" message states not what you are feeling, but your opinion of the other person's behavior.

✔ "You are being very rude."

✔ "You are not being helpful."

✔ "You don't seem to know anything about this."

For the flip side, read Part IV, "Dealing with Difficult People." It will give you tips, techniques, and insights on how you can better deal with conflict situations and upset customers.

Mind Your P's and Q's

Certain situations provide more fertile ground for conflict than others. Following is a guide to frequent mishaps and misunderstandings and how you can prevent them. You may think we have exaggerated by making our examples a bit too angelic or devilish, but remember the tone of what you say is as important as the words you use.

When dining out

If you are on a diet — In the '90s, everyone seems to be is on a diet or food program. Phrases that we rarely used a few years ago now dominate our daily conversation. Some of our personal favorites include:

- ✔ no butter or oil
- ✔ on the side
- ✔ steamed not fried
- ✔ hold the mayo

Consequently, many restaurants are prepared to customize your meal and, in fact, have gone one step further by making such items part of their regular menu. However, in those situations where you need to make a change, the best way to approach your wait person is by stating pleasantly:

> *Excuse me, but right now I am not eating any butter. Could you please ask the chef not to put it on the vegetables?*

This statement is a clear but nondemanding way to enlist the support of the waiter who is, after all, the one who has to pass this information along to the chef. Definitely don't state your preference as a demand by saying: "I don't eat butter! Tell the chef to leave it off the vegetables!"

If you have food allergies, high cholesterol, or some other medical condition that requires you to make food changes let your waiter or waitress know this when you first sit down. He or she will usually go out of their way to accommodate medical requirements.

If you want a substitution — Most restaurants have flexible policies when it comes to offering their customers a choice about substitutions. Now and again, though, your harmless request may be viewed as a direct assault on the chef's culinary excellence and artistic freedom. As with food restrictions, a nondemanding request works best:

> *I noticed that potatoes come with the eggs. Would it be possible to have tomatoes with that instead?*

If you don't like your meal — In a good restaurant, sending back a meal you don't like is an opportunity for the establishment to ensure that you get exactly what you want and guarantee a satisfied customer. However, the way some restaurants deal with this predicament can make you vow never to step foot on the premises again. To graciously handle this situation without implying that something is wrong with the restaurant or the chef, try this approach:

I'm sorry, the food here is usually excellent, but I don't like the chicken tonight. Would it be possible to get something else instead?

Avoid putting the waiter, chef, and restaurant in a defensive posture by attacking the quality of the food, saying something like: "Waiter, this chicken is horrible, I can't eat it! Take it back and bring me the salmon."

Asking more than once for an item — When a restaurant gets busy, even the best waiters can forget to bring you something you have asked for. When faced with this problem, ask your own waiter (politely) a second time for the item. If he forgets again, it's okay to stop any passing waiter and say:

Could you please bring me some ketchup? My waiter must have forgotten.

Don't grab the first server who comes along, wrestle her to the ground, defame the other waiter's character, and threaten bodily harm if you don't get your ketchup immediately.

When in a store

Returning an item without a receipt — You may be viewed with suspicion when returning an item without a receipt. A good way to get around this awkward situation is to make the salesperson a partner by clarifying the situation up front. Say:

Hi, I bought this blouse last week, and I seem to have misplaced the receipt. Can you tell me what my options are?

The waiter and the doctor

We heard a joke that goes like this:

A doctor and his wife are sitting in a fancy restaurant when, suddenly, across the room one of the waiters grabs his chest and falls to the ground.

Panicked, the hostess asks, "Is there a doctor anywhere in the room?" The doctor immediately identifies himself, but when asked if he can help, replies, "I'm sorry, that's not my waiter."

This approach can shortcut bureaucracy by getting the sales person to actively help you solve the problem instead of quoting policy.

If you can't find the item you want — At certain stores, finding a specific item is like looking for a needle in a haystack. Take your typical hardware store: a simple item like masking tape can be hidden in any one of a dozen places. Furthermore, directions for how to get to these items are often loaded with code and confusion. For example, a clerk may say, "To find the masking tape, take a left at the caulking materials, a sharp right at lighting, and another right down aisle eight. The masking tape is across from the wrenches." Excuse me? Well, it's Saturday, and you are not in a big hurry, so off you go hoping that your adventurous spirit will be rewarded with one roll of all-purpose masking tape. Sadly, this is not to be. After ten minutes of desperate searching, you go back to the clerk and declare, "Where in the (insert your own colorful phrase here) do you people keep the masking tape? I've been down aisle eight three times already!" A better approach is to garner the clerk's sympathy by saying:

I'm sorry to bother you, but I'm looking for the masking tape. I know it is supposed to be on aisle eight, but I've been there and can't find it. Could you show me where it is please?

With the airlines

If they have no record of your reservation — "I'm sorry, but we have no record of your reservation on this flight." The words we all dread hearing when we fly. Your first thought is to kill the gate agent and hold the pilot hostage until you are given your non-smoking, aisle seat. Recognizing this as a poor strategy, however, you might try another tactic:

I did have a reservation, so I can't image what has happened. Can you still get me on the flight?

If the attendant says yes — no problem. If he says no, ask:

Could you please check to see what other airlines might have space available? Can you book a reservation for me on that flight? Will you call them and let them know I'm coming?

We find that if you ask politely, the gate agents will go out of their way to help (at least 50 percent of the time). We also find that if you ask in a nasty and demanding tone (even though the airline is in the wrong), they will brush you off 90 percent of the time and tell you to contact the other airline yourself on (dare we say it) the *white courtesy phone.*

If your plane's departure is significantly delayed — The best advice if your plane has been significantly delayed is don't panic and run to the gate agent like everyone else. You won't get the service you need. Instead, call your travel agent or the airline's 800 number. They can make travel arrangements on another flight for you by phone. This simple action saves you time and stress and gives the gate agent one less person to deal with.

Create the closest relationship with your travel agent that you can. He or she has the power to get you moving while everyone else is waiting in line to be rebooked on another flight.

If your preassigned seat has been given away — According to airline policy for domestic flights, preassigned seats are not released until 10 minutes before departure time. Once in a while, though, you will get to the airport 15 minutes before your flight and seat 5D, the one you have had preassigned for a month has been given away. Getting angry at this point is understandable: "Look here! I have had this seat reserved for over a month; I'm here in plenty of time. You had no right to give my seat away!" A more effective approach, however, is to take one or two deep breaths and calmly inquire:

Is another aisle seat, close to the front of the plane, available?

If the answer is no and no other acceptable seat is available, ask to speak to a supervisor. She has more authority than the gate agent and can often resolve the problem.

The old adage remains true: "You catch more flies with honey than you do with vinegar."

On the telephone

The telephone is more pervasive in our lives, as customers, than ever before. On an average day, you may find yourself on the phone:

- making a monetary transfer with the customer service representative at your local bank
- getting help from the technical support department of a software company on the new word processing program you purchased
- ordering an item from a mail order catalog
- tracking down the package you sent overnight to Botswana that has not yet arrived
- setting up an appointment with your local cable company for service

Literally hundreds of the business transactions that we used to conduct in person or by mail are now taken care of by phone. The up side is that you can find a phone virtually anywhere, including 36,000 feet in the air, and it's one of the least expensive ways to conduct business.

The down side is that we can spend valuable time tied up on the telephone trying to reach whom we need to reach, when we need to reach them. In order to make the most of your time on the telephone, here are a few hot tips.

When asked to hold — When you call a company and the receptionist asks you to hold, but you don't want to, quickly respond by asking for the name of the person you want to speak with, followed by *please* (of course). Odds are you will be transferred instead of being put on hold.

When you have been on hold for a while — George Carlin, the comedian, used to do a great routine during which he joked that "hold is a lonely place." If you have been on hold forever, consider hanging up and calling back. Tell the receptionist how long you were waiting and ask if he can take a message for the person you are trying to reach.

When you have been transferred around — Occasionally, you get a phone tour of a company by being transferred to all the departments — except the one you need. When this situation happens, ask to be connected back to the operator. Tell her you were transferred to the wrong person, and ask her to stay on the line until the transfer is complete. If she can't do so, ask for the direct number of the person you are calling. If all else fails, have the operator give the person you are trying to reach a message to call you back.

If you get stuck in voice mail — If you can't reach a real person (which happens more and more these days), try calling information and getting the company's main number. Ask for the fax number or e-mail address of the person you want to reach and send him a message. As a last resort, change the last digit of the company's direct dial number and leave a message with whoever picks up the phone (hopefully he or she works in the same company).

Playing telephone tag — If you find yourself playing telephone tag, take advantage of the alternative technologies available. Try sending the person you're trying to reach a fax or, better yet, send a message to her e-mail address online. You can often get a quicker response this way. Another idea is to leave a message on her voice mail system letting her know several, specific times when she can reach you.

The Fine Art of Complaining

Okay, you smiled at the sales clerk when you approached her. You said please and thank you when you asked the gate agent which black hole your flight reservation disappeared into. You politely informed your waiter that you ordered sweet potatoes not sweetbreads. Unfortunately, these approaches have not worked. When all else fails, you may find yourself in a position where making a formal complaint is the next step. Here is how to complain to produce the maximum results.

Complaining on the spot

The first ears that your complaint will reach are probably sticking out of the head of the service person you are talking to. If, after hearing your complaint, the service provider responds with a vacant stare or uncomfortable silence, you may have an overwhelming urge to speak. Don't. Learning to live with that silence will pay off. The server will feel more compelled to respond if you say nothing. This is the point when he is most likely to offer a suggestion, alternative, or run screaming in horror looking for his manager. If he does the latter, you need to move your complaint up the ladder.

Moving up the ladder

If you have gone as far as you can go with the person helping you, ask for a supervisor or a manager. Don't put the person on the defensive by saying, "You are obviously not the right person to take care of this situation, let me speak to someone higher up!" A better approach would be to say:

> *I appreciate everything you have done, but I want to speak with your supervisor so that I can move this situation forward.*

This approach gives the service person a way to turn you over to her manager without losing face.

Be prepared. If the person you are dealing with has a bad attitude, the supervisor or manager may be the same because the manager sets the departmental tone.

You have to walk a thin line when customers come to you and complain about the service they have received from one of your staff. On the one hand, you need to support your staff person, and on the other you need to empathize with the customers. In this situation, *never* criticize your employees in front of a customer and *always* apologize to the customer. Once the customer has gone, use the complaint as an opportunity to educate your employee. Help him see what he did right and how he could improve next time.

How to write a complaint letter

You would like to believe that complaining to a manager is as high up as you have to go in order to solve a problem. Usually it is. When it doesn't pan out that way, you may decide to write the president or owner of the company a complaint letter. Complaint letters can be extremely effective in getting action if they are well written and sent to the right person. The right person is usually the individual that has the power to do something about your situation. If you do not know who this person is, we recommend that you call the company's headquarters or corporate offices. Once you reach a live receptionist, briefly tell him your situation and ask for the person responsible for that area. If he does not know, ask to be transferred to someone who does. Make sure you get the correct spelling of your contact person's name along with his or her title, address, and any necessary mail drop information.

Customers use two main styles in complaint letters.

Style #1: Venting frustration

This getting-it-off-your-chest approach may make you feel better, but it won't produce the best results. In fact, you may be taken less seriously by the person reading a complaint letter that is written for the express purpose of venting frustration.

Figure 2-1 is an example of style #1.

As you can see, passenger Bob does not need to take a class in assertive communications. However, even though Bob may have expressed his true inner feelings and vented his frustration, not much else has been accomplished.

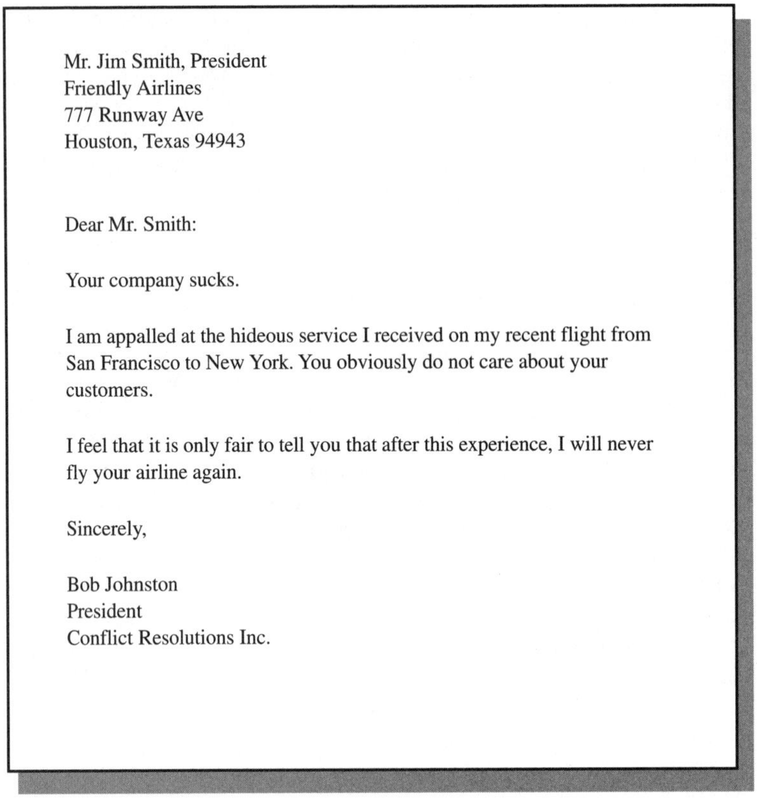

Mr. Jim Smith, President
Friendly Airlines
777 Runway Ave
Houston, Texas 94943

Dear Mr. Smith:

Your company sucks.

I am appalled at the hideous service I received on my recent flight from
San Francisco to New York. You obviously do not care about your
customers.

I feel that it is only fair to tell you that after this experience, I will never
fly your airline again.

Sincerely,

Bob Johnston
President
Conflict Resolutions Inc.

Figure 2-1:
Here is a
get-it-off-
your-chest
complaint
letter.

Style #2: Action oriented

The second style of complaint letter aims not only to express your feelings about the situation, but also to spark some kind of action on the part of the company.

You need to consider eight important items when writing a #2 style complaint letter:

- ✔ date of occurrence
- ✔ time
- ✔ names of those involved
- ✔ your name and contact number
- ✔ specific chronological events

✔ your feelings

✔ specific request for action

✔ benefit to their company

This type of letter reads something like the letter in Figure 2-2.

Mr. Jim Smith, President
Friendly Airlines
777 Runway Ave
Houston, Texas 94943

Dear Mr. Smith:

My name is Bob Johnston, and I am writing to inform you of my experiences on a recent flight with your airline. For your information, the flight was FA #101 from San Francisco to New York on July 3, 1995.

I think that you would be interested to know that this flight did not meet either my expectations for service or the level of service I am sure you wish to deliver. Specifically, the following occurred:

1. The plane was an hour late departing, but the gate agents made no announcement until 30 minutes after the flight was supposed to depart.

2. The ground staff underestimated the number of meals needed on the flight, so there were not enough meals to feed everyone on the plane. I, unfortunately, was one of the passengers who received no meal.

3. The sound on the movie was not working.

While these may seem like trivial occurrences, they made my flight very unpleasant.

As a long-time flier of your airlines, I found this level of service unacceptable and am requesting a ticket refund. For your convenience, I have enclosed a copy of my ticket receipt.

Please feel free to contact me at my office, ext. 7734, if you have any questions. I look forward to receiving a response from you before the end of this month.

Sincerely,

Bob Johnston
President
Conflict Resolutions Inc.

Figure 2-2:
This complaint letter is action oriented.

Friendly Airlines sent passenger Bob two free first-class, round-the-world-tickets as an apology — *NOT!*

Make a point of always acknowledging a service provider that does a good job. We are often quick to criticize when we don't get the service we want and not always as fast to praise when we do. By praising good service, you encourage those delivering it to keep up the good work.

Don't limit your praise to the spoken word only. Putting your praise in the form of a letter and sending a duplicate copy to the service person's supervisor is often beneficial. If you don't know who his or her supervisor is, you can call and find out. Or send them two copies of the same letter with a request that they forward one copy to their boss on your behalf.

Jackpot tipping

Jackpot tipping is a technique that we learned from a friend on how to reward waiters and waitresses who give you extraordinary service. When you get the service that you expect, tip your server the standard 15 percent (or whatever you consider standard). If you receive substandard service, give him a reduced tip, say 10 percent. Now, here's the trick: take the 5 percent difference and keep track of it (either mentally or by jotting it down). For example, if your meal came to $10 and the service wasn't up to par, you would tip 10 percent or $1.

The 5 percent difference (fifty cents) goes into the *jackpot.* Over time you keep adding money to the jackpot until the next time you get extraordinary service. Then the deserving waiter or waitress not only gets his or her 15 percent tip but also hits the jackpot and gets whatever has accumulated in the jackpot account.

You could end up giving someone a $10 tip for a $5 sandwich, but why not? Jackpot tipping is a great way to vote for excellence in a way that will be noticed.

Chapter 3

Mirror, Mirror on the Wall: Taking an Honest Look at Your Service

*R*emember when you were a kid and your parents took you to see *Snow White* for the first time? Snow White's evil stepmother would stand in front of her mirror and ask, "Mirror, Mirror on the wall, who's the fairest of them all?" Now you may only have been a kid, but you knew that if that mirror was smart, only one answer could be right: "You, my queen, are the fairest in the land."

Unlike the wicked queen — who had a hard time facing reality — your survival in today's business world depends on telling the truth about your strengths and weaknesses as a service provider. After all, you have to know where you are before you can move forward. To this end, we have provided you with a paper mirror: two questionnaires highlighting key service criteria that (we have found over the years) mark companies and individuals who are service winners.

The first is an evaluation that will help you discover the quality of service you provide as an individual.

If you are a business owner or a manager, the second questionnaire will help you to assess the customer focus of your company.

Self Evaluation

Use the following ten questions to see if you are delivering bronze, silver, or gold level customer service. Stepping back and objectively assessing yourself will help you see what your personal service strengths are and where you may need to devote some extra attention.

Questionnaire (self evaluation)

Use the following numbers to evaluate each question.

0 = Rarely

1 = Sometimes

2 = Often

3 = Almost Always

____ When having a conversation with a customer, do I give him or her my complete attention and avoid doing other activities (working on the computer, writing unnecessarily, doing a crossword puzzle, and so on)?

____ Do I make eye contact when speaking with a customer to show that I am paying attention?

____ When speaking to a customer over the phone, do I make an effort to use inflection in my voice to convey interest and concern?

____ Do I pick up the telephone by the third ring?

____ When I need to put a customer on hold, do I ask his or her permission and wait for a response before doing so?

____ Do I avoid technical jargon and use language that the customer can understand?

____ When I cannot provide my customer with exactly what he or she wants, do I suggest options and alternatives?

____ Do I sincerely apologize to the customer when a mistake has been made by me or my company?

____ When a customer is voicing a complaint, do I remain calm and understanding — even if I think he or she is wrong?

____ Do I view customer complaints as an opportunity to improve service rather than as a problem that is taking up valuable time?

____ **Total Score**

Scoring your questionnaire

Add together the scores of all ten questions and then look below to see how you did. If you scored:

> 0-12 points: you are at the **Bronze Level**
>
> 13-22 points: you are at the **Silver Level**
>
> 23-30 points: you are at the **Gold Level**

For specifics about what your score means and where to go from here, find your level described below and read on.

Bronze level

Scoring at this level doesn't mean that you don't care about your customers. We find that a score in the bronze level is due to one of the following three reasons:

- ✔ You are a newcomer to the service field and are still learning the ins and outs of dealing with customers. If this statement applies to you, then using the information in this book will help bring you up to the silver level and beyond.

- ✔ You are a seasoned service provider but may have become a little rusty on some of the basics that you once practiced. Refresh yourself on the basics by attending a customer service training program.

- ✔ The last reason has to do with job suitability. Over the years, we have met certain people who just don't enjoy dealing with customers or helping others solve problems. Nothing is wrong with them, they just work better by themselves. If this situation applies to you, you might consider either changing jobs or changing the focus of the job you are now in.

Silver level

You have a solid understanding of the basics, but you are not *using* them consistently. The probable reason for this inconsistency is that you are overwhelmed by the functions of your job. On good days, you give good service, and on bad days, you give bad service. The key is to become more consistent. Remember that regardless of the time you spend with a customer (be it a thirty-second phone call or a one-hour meeting) and regardless of how busy you are, you always have a personal choice about the attitude you project. It takes about thirty days to form a new habit, so make a point of practicing the items covered in the questionnaire every time you deal with a customer — especially when you don't feel like it!

Gold level

Congratulations! You are a professional at providing service. You seem to have the basics down pat and are ready for bigger and better challenges. To continue to grow, consider the following suggestions:

- Once you have finished evaluating yourself, get another perspective by having a co-worker you know and trust evaluate you. He or she may see areas for improvement that are blind spots to you.

- Go beyond the basics of service. Educate yourself in the more sophisticated service skills by learning to take initiative (see Chapter 7).

We suggest you go through the above questionnaire a second time and replace the word *customer* with the word *staff member*. Doing so will help you evaluate how good a job you are doing of treating your staff as customers.

Company Evaluation

Some companies are in corporate denial, the organizational equivalent of personal denial. We can all relate to times in our lives when we had a bit of trouble facing the facts that clearly stood before us. From the surveys and studies we have conducted, it has become strikingly clear that the way many companies work is directly opposite to the service philosophy they put on a banner and hang on the wall. These companies have failed to form a clear assessment of the kind of service they intend to deliver against the kind of service they are really delivering.

This questionnaire will help you discover specific areas in your business where you should be focusing your attention and give you a starting point in your journey toward greater customer service. Be sure to answer the questions from your individual point of view as honestly and objectively as possible. The questions refer to the way things stand now, not how you wish they were or how you think they may be in the future.

Remember that regardless of how good you feel about the quality of service your company offers, there is always room for improvement. Sometimes, though, exactly pinpointing these opportunities is difficult.

Decide ahead of time if you are going to evaluate your individual department or your whole company. You may want to complete this questionnaire twice, once from each respective viewpoint.

In our workshops, we often give an expanded version of this questionnaire to groups of senior executives. We put them into small groups, have them discuss each question, and reach a consensus. Very often their discussions prove to be just as valuable as the answers themselves. After you complete this questionnaire on your own, you may want to give it to some of your co-workers to fill out and then compare results.

Questionnaire (company evaluation)

Use the following numbers to evaluate each question.

0 = Not at all

1 = To a small degree

2 = To a moderate degree

3 = To a large degree

____ Do we survey our customers to find out how satisfied they are with our service/products and ask for their suggestions for improvements?

____ Do we survey our staff to find out how satisfied they are with the working environment and ask for their suggestions for improvement?

____ Do we have a written mission statement or specific long range goals that focus on our commitment to providing our customers with quality products and services?

____ Do we collect information on what poor quality and service costs our company in terms of lost customers, wasted time, and reduced morale?

____ Do we train our front-line staff in telephone and face-to-face customer relations skills?

____ Do we train our managers in the skills they need to support staff in providing excellent service (team building, delegation, coaching, and so on)?

____ Do we put newly hired staff through an orientation process that stresses the importance of customer service in their specific job?

____ Do we have a computer system that supports our staff in providing fast and efficient service to our customers?

____ Do we have a process in place that allows us to make specific changes in our policies and procedures based on customer feedback?

____ Do we go out of our way to reward and recognize staff for their efforts on behalf of the customer?

____ **Total Score**

Scoring your questionnaire

Add the scores of all ten questions and then look below to see which level your company is at. If you scored:

0-9 points — your company is at Level 1: **Bean counting**

10-17 points — your company is at Level 2: **Posters, pins, and plaques**

18-24 points — your company is at Level 3: **Tiger by the tail**

25-30 points — your company is at Level 4: **Bullseye!**

For specifics about what your score means and where to go from here, find your level described below and read on.

Customer service is not a department somewhere in your company. It is, rather, a company culture where every individual at every level is customer oriented.

Level 1: Bean counting

The bean counters are running your company. Your organization probably views customer service as a low priority and focuses most of its attention on financial goals and activities that impact the bottom line, such as cost cutting, budgets, and so on.

Short term results are considered more valuable than long term gains and results are measured by quantity not by quality. At this level, pursuing financial gains to the exclusion of customer satisfaction is like *jumping over a dollar to get to a dime.*

Danger: You will not see the importance of customer service until it is too late and an emergency, such as lost accounts or reduced market share, forces you to make customer service a higher priority. When your company gets to this point, you often face the additional pressures of uncertainty regarding the future, which makes improving service even more challenging. We have witnessed the panicked look on the faces of people in our workshops who realize that they should have been paying attention to their service long before it became an emergency.

Recommendation: Do something about service before it's too late. Examine how important customer service is to the overall, long-term success of your business. You may want to begin by building your company's awareness of the importance of customer service by:

- ✔ conducting a survey to measure current levels of customer satisfaction
- ✔ sending managers and staff to customer service training
- ✔ gathering information that shows the effect poor service is having on your company

Level 2: Posters, pins, and plaques

The walls of your business tell the whole story. Having seen the light, management has put up posters, handed out pins, and designed plaques declaring such popular platitudes as:

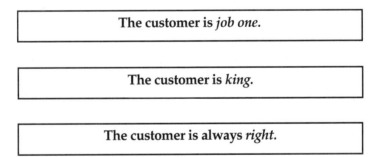

The customer is *job one.*

The customer is *king.*

The customer is always *right.*

Management is now convinced of the importance of customer service but has yet to make customer service a part of everyday business. Management has begun to promote the ideas of customer service and has probably taken one or two highly visible actions to this end. At this level, the attitude of the staff is:

This sounds good, but we'll see if management follows through.

Danger: Your company may get stuck in talk and theory and not go into real changes, thus creating an attitude that customer service is just another *program of the month.* If this issue is not resolved, skepticism is created among the staff that makes any future attempts at improving customer service more difficult. This phenomenon is also known as BOHICA — Bend Over, Here It Comes Again!

Recommendation: Take some highly visible action that clearly demonstrates the company's commitment to customer service. "Put your money where your mouth is" and "Walk what you talk." Your staff should view the actions you take as a benefit to them or a benefit to the customer. Something to think about: What problem can you fix that your staff has been complaining about forever?

A transportation company we know spent a great deal of time telling its staff that customer service was the future of their business. The problem was that the staff had seen very little action from management demonstrating this *commitment* to customer service. The executives eventually realized that they needed to do something to prove to their staff that they were serious about doing whatever was necessary to improve service. For years, staff and customers had complained about the disrepair of one of the service buildings. It needed new carpet and a coat of paint. The executives, in a move that surprised everyone, refurbished the building. This simple, low cost, yet highly visible action said more to the staff than anything else management had done. This step was the beginning of a service improvement process that continues to this day.

Level 3: Tiger by the tail

You've grabbed a tiger by the tail! Good job! Even though you are in the middle of creative chaos and may feel as if you are continually on the brink of being out of control, your company is well on its way to customer service excellence. Your staff are excited by all the positive changes and are cautiously optimistic about the future. A feeling of *we still have a ways to go* permeates throughout the company. Like a trip to the moon, you have achieved lift off, it's too late to go back, and too soon to see exactly where you are going.

Danger: You've opened Pandora's Box and all your company's service weaknesses and problems are laid out before you. Now that you see all that needs to be fixed, you may become overwhelmed, paralyzed, and, consequently, throw in the towel before having accomplished all that you want to.

Recommendation: Keep the big picture in mind and don't try to fix everything all at once. Remember, Rome wasn't built in a day. One way to keep your focus without losing your mind is to select one specific service problem (not necessarily a big one) and completely resolve it before going on to the next. If you follow this routine for six months, you will be amazed at how many indirect problems also get solved. Just remember that there is light at the end of the tunnel, and it isn't the headlights of a train.

A couple on TV has a show about how to remodel houses. In one show, I watched them put in a complete drainage system in three minutes. In the first thirty seconds, they showed how to mark off the trench. In the next sixty seconds, a backhoe arrived and began digging the ditch. Effortlessly and with no mishaps, they next laid in the drainage pipes, all of which fit perfectly. Leaning on their shovels and wearing protective eyewear, they wiped their brows and moved on to replacing the roof! "This is fiction!" I thought. Nobody I know would expect to go out and redo his or her drains so effortlessly. Neither should you expect to remodel a business in record time!

Level 4: Bullseye!

Congratulations! Your company has made service a way of life. You have created a strong focus on customer satisfaction, and this focus influences the way the managers and staff do their jobs every day. The service culture is so strong that it has taken on a life of its own, and you see quick returns on the effort you put into service improvement. Your staff members see customer service as an important part of the job they do and know that the company will back them up in doing what it takes to please the customer.

Danger: When all systems are go, becoming complacent is easy and you may get blindsided by the arrogance of success. In other words, don't read or believe your own press releases. At this level, the biggest danger is the tendency to rest on your laurels thinking that you have arrived.

Recommendation: Look for new ways to innovate. Take a risk and do something that has not been done before in your company or industry. Ask yourself, how can we move our existing services to the next level? As the president of one major airline put it:

> *Our job is to make our existing services obsolete before our competitors do.*

We had the privilege a few years ago of working with an international hotel chain that has a great reputation for service. In meetings with their senior managers, we were continually impressed by their appetite to keep improving service. Even though their customer surveys showed that they were doing an excellent job, they still said things like:

> *We are only as good as the guest's last visit.*

> *We want to continue to be the best.*

> *We can always improve.*

Their ongoing commitment to continued improvement is what set them apart from their competitors and continues to make them winners in their field.

What's Next?

Congratulations, you are at the end of part one. If you have read all the chapters in this section, you know the basics of getting and giving good service. As you move on, remember to put yourself in the customers' shoes. Doing so will help you see how to use the principles, tips, and techniques we offer to your best advantage.

Part II

Simple Actions, Significant Payoffs: Individual Strategies

The 5th Wave   By Rich Tennant

"And *that's* why you're in the back of the store instead of in the front!"

In this part...

Have you ever called a company and been rudely put on hold before you even gave your name? Have you ever waited at the counter in a department store while the sales clerk chatted with a co-worker? Have you ever been informed in a not-so-friendly tone by the waiter/waitress that

Substituting tomatoes for potatoes is against our policy.

If you are like most people, you have, and you usually find yourself thinking how little this person would have to do to turn the situation from a service failure into a service success. In every one of the above situations, some small aspect of the body language, tone of voice, or words used put the customer off.

In this part of the book, we explore those *little things,* those simple actions that lead to significant payoffs in customer satisfaction. We provide you with time-tested techniques for dealing with people face-to-face and over the telephone, and we cover a variety of important communication skills that you can use every day at work and at home.

Chapter 4
A Wink, a Smile, and a Nod: Body Language

*B*ody language is a constant, nonverbal flow of communication. Without saying a word (and sometimes without realizing it), your body language can reveal what you are feeling and thinking. For example, without exchanging a word, you can guess what the service person feels about you — the customer — in the following situations:

- ✔ the bank teller whose eyes roll in exasperation when you bring in the loose change you have collected over the past five years

- ✔ the doctor who ignores you and stares at your chart while you explain your symptoms

- ✔ the painful expression on the "full service" gas station attendant's face when you ask him to put air in your tires (He thought "full service" was Latin for "pay extra for gas.")

A few years ago, a study was done at a major university on how people receive messages from other people (see Figure 4-1). It showed that:

- ✔ 55 percent of what we learn from others comes from their body language.

- ✔ 38 percent comes from the tone of their voice.

- ✔ 7 percent comes from the words they say.

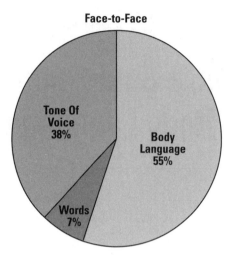

Face-to-Face

Tone Of
Voice
38%

Body
Language
55%

Words
7%

Figure 4-1:
How we
learn from
other
people.

We can all remember a time when we saw a friend or loved one who seemed upset. When we asked what was wrong, we were greeted with teary eyes, a scrunched face, and a cheerful, "Nothing, I'm fine." Clearly, our actions speak louder than our words, and our body language conveys messages that are more believable than what we say. Your ability to read your customers' body language, and project your own in a way that says, "I'm here to help," is one of the least expensive and most powerful skills you have. The primary aspects of body language are:

✔ eye contact

✔ facial expressions

✔ body posture and movement

✔ hand gestures

✔ touching

✔ physical distance

If overdone or underdone, body language can misfire and create a negative impression. Although body language is not an exact science, some general rules do apply.

Eye to Eye

Eye contact is one of the most powerful of all the body language skills. It is called an *attending skill* because it lets customers know that you are interested, receptive, and attentive to what they are saying. Eye contact allows you to listen to customers' feelings as well as to their words. Effective eye contact is achieved by putting a soft focus on a customer's face. For example: The moment a customer walks up to you, regardless of what you are doing, make immediate eye contact by focusing on the whole face, not just the eyes. As the conversation moves on, look away from time to time to avoid giving the impression that you are staring.

Overdone: Students of the Zombie School of Body Language are easy to spot — they stare the person down with a hard gaze and never move their eyes off him. This I've-got-you-in-my-sights approach gives customers the willies and makes them depart before they are zeroed in on for the kill.

Underdone: You walk up to the bank teller and instead of looking up at you, she continues to look down at her paperwork. This lack of eye contact, combined with a clear view of the top of the teller's head, is a negative moment of truth and can be interpreted as lack of interest in helping you. Likewise, when you are talking to someone and he constantly looks around the room and not at you, you get the impression that he has something more important that he'd rather be doing.

Research has shown that people stop making eye contact and look away the moment they sense that the other person will show emotion on his or her face. This natural desire not to be intrusive or embarrass the other person is misplaced when you deal with an upset customer. To give a positive impression that shows you really care, don't look away. Instead, maintain eye contact. Doing so gives the impression that you want to hear what the customer is saying and usually makes him less upset.

In many Asian countries (Japan, Korea, and Thailand, in particular), making strong and continuous eye contact with another person during conversation is considered rude. In fact, in these cultures, children are taught from a young age to avert their eyes and avoid direct eye contact.

About Face

Your facial expression is like a billboard that lets everyone around you know if you are happy, sad, excited, and so on. Be careful not to let the stresses of the day gather on your brow so that you resemble a scrunched up prune. Customers do not care if you have had the day from hell; as far as they are concerned, this interaction is your first of the day. Make sure your facial expression sets a positive tone before you even begin speaking. A relaxed or pleasant facial expression is the ideal most of the time. However, when customers are concerned or upset, you need to adjust your facial expression to suit their state of mind.

Overdone: We were doing a project for a client in England who told us about a bank that had decided to improve its customer service. The bank's good idea for improving service was to slap *happy face* stickers (the big, ugly, yellow ones) up behind each teller's counter with the message `Remember to smile at the customer` written underneath. While not a terrible idea, we thought that this procedure could lead to problems: Imagine how annoyed you would be if your bank teller informed you that you were five thousand dollars overdrawn — and he had a big fat grin on his face! Even a positive facial expression, such as smiling, can be overdone.

Underdone: The daydreaming stare, faraway gaze, and blank look are all classic expressions that can creep over your face without your even realizing it. When customers see you looking this way, they don't want to be the ones to wake you from your coma.

Using a relaxed and pleasant facial expression with your staff is as important as it is with your customers. By using effective facial expressions, you encourage your staff to seek you out for coaching, guidance, and information. To become more aware of your facial expressions, we recommend examining how you look in family snapshots or videos, especially the ones that were taken before you had a chance to "say cheese."

I once worked for a manager who consistently wrinkled his nose whenever I approached him with a question. To me, his expression conveyed a message of, "Oh, no, not you again with another stupid question!" To this day, I don't know what he was really thinking. Regardless, his facial expression stopped me from asking him for the information I needed.

From the Waist Up

Body posture — and body movement in particular — show your energy level and interest in what the customer is saying. You can tell when people are listening impatiently or want to end the conversation by some simple body language clues such as:

- leaning back or stepping away
- turning their bodies away from you
- pushing away from their desks or tables
- gathering up papers
- closing their briefcases while you are still talking
- looking at their watches repeatedly

To show that you are intently listening to and interested in a conversation with your customer, do the following:

- Nod.
- Face the customer.
- Lean Forward.

Nod

One of the best ways to nonverbally show that you are paying attention to what someone is saying is to nod. Nodding is particularly useful when a customer is explaining the details of a situation to you and you don't want to interrupt, but you want her to know that you are following along with what she is saying.

In many parts of the world, a nod up and down means "Yes." However, if you find yourself in Turkey, Iran, or Bulgaria, be forewarned: In these countries when you nod your head up and down, you are saying "No," and when you shake your head back and forth you are saying "Yes." If you understand what we are saying here, say yes with your head, Bulgarian style.

Overdone: While occasional nodding shows that you are listening, continual nodding communicates impatience. We're talking about the distracting nod-nod-nod that people do when they want to hurry the conversation along. This action translates to the customer as, "Hurry up and finish so that I can say what I want to!"

Nodding during a lull in conversation is a clue that you do not have any connection with what's going on around you.

Underdone: The next time you watch a sci-fi movie, pay close attention to the way aliens are characterized by their body language. Their lack of humanness is emphasized by their staring straight ahead with their arms pinned to their sides and their heads locked forward in one position (not to mention their green skin and the one eye sticking out of the middle of their heads). Don't let this phenomenon happen to you. Make a conscious effort to show, with your body language, that you are from this planet.

Face the customer

By turning your whole body (not just your head) toward the customer, you convey the message that she has your full and undivided attention. Facing away from the customer can make her feel that something else is distracting you.

Lean forward

While you don't want to end up in the customer's lap, you do want to lean forward slightly to let the customer know that you are interested in what is being said. When a customer is expressing strong emotions or feelings, leaning forward says, "I really want to hear and understand what you are saying to me."

Hand Gestures

Using your hands when you talk (even on the phone) is a natural way to express your feelings. Some people *talk with their hands* and seem to be conducting an orchestra whenever they speak. There are two varieties of hand gestures to be aware of:

- hands and objects
- hands alone

Hands and objects

The first variety is hand gestures that rely on certain *props* and can give you very clear signals about your customer's state of mind. These gestures can include:

- **placing the cap on a pen and putting it in a pocket**

  This action signifies a readiness to conclude the meeting or conversation.

- **tapping fingers**

  This signifies impatience or frustration.

✔ **repeatedly clicking a ball point pen**

This action can have two different meanings: Either the customer is uneasy or deep in thought. Look for other body language signs to determine which is applicable.

✔ **rattling loose change in a pocket**

This motion usually means, "I'm anxious and ready to move on."

Hands alone

The second variety of hand gestures does not require any props. These gestures can include:

✔ **open-hand gestures (flat hand, palm up, or palm out)**

When used to give directions, they convey an invitation to move or look in a certain direction. Open hand gestures are also a more gracious and softer way to point at a person or object.

✔ **closed-hand gestures (pointing with index finger straight out)**

This hand movement can be construed as a command, rather than an invitation, when used to convey a direction. This gesture is usually considered rude and intimidating when directed at another person. While pointing may be discourteous, even worse is pointing a finger in someone's face at close range. This action will definitely communicate hostility or anger to the customer.

✔ **driving gestures**

You see these gestures in your rear-view mirror when you are stuck in traffic on Friday night. They usually communicate very clearly and need no further explanation.

The key, whether you use your hands a little or a lot, is to be *natural in your movements.* Your gestures should not distract from the conversation.

Overdone: To see overdone hand gestures at their best, watch one of those TV commercials for a car dealership during the late, late movie. Focusing on what the dealers are saying is often difficult because their hands are flying around in big, unnatural, exaggerated, and distracting movements.

Underdone: A noticeable lack of hand gestures can be just as distracting as waving them around like an octopus. Some people are so self-conscious about what to do with their hands that they clasp them behind their backs, in front of their bodies, or pin them to their sides. This lack of motion gives the customer the impression that the service person feels threatened by — or uncomfortable with — what is being said.

Where the hands go, the arms follow. Some cultures, such as the Italians, naturally tend to use big, sweeping hand and arm motions; while others, such as the Japanese, prefer to keep their arm and hand gestures small and infrequent. In fact, moving one's hands or arms in big gestures is considered impolite in Japan.

A Touchy Subject

The most acceptable form of touching in the American work environment is handshaking. In some professions, such as health care, touch can take on a more important role. Nurses and doctors, for example, use touch partly out of necessity but also to convey a caring and concerned attitude. Regardless of your profession, the least threatening place to touch someone (with whom you don't have a personal relationship) is on the arm between the elbow and the wrist.

 You should always be sensitive to the other person's reactions. If you touch someone in a nonthreatening manner on the hand, wrist, or elbow, and he moves his arm away, he's telling you something. Let this reaction be your clue not to touch him again.

Overdone: We do not recommend the *grip of death* handshake used by some people. This type of handshake is overly aggressive and can actually hurt the recipients while giving them the impression that they are being used to strengthen your tennis grip.

Touching can also be overdone by going outside the nonthreatening areas with people you don't have a close relationship with. Some common, easily made mistakes include:

- ✔ putting an arm around the customer's shoulder (unless he is about to faint)
- ✔ slapping the customer on the back (unless she is choking)
- ✔ mussing up the customer's hair (unless you are a hairdresser)
- ✔ hugging him and refusing to let go (unless you are married to him)

Underdone: You go to work for a new company and you are being shown around the office. Your manager introduces you to a co-worker. You extend your hand with certain confidence, prepared to provide her with a nice, firm grip. In return you are offered a weak, dead fish (uggg!) type of handshake. You shudder all over. Offering your hand in a tentative way is almost guaranteed to create a bad first impression.

Touching overseas

As part of his research for *Nonverbal Communication For Business Success,* author Ken Cooper sat in outdoor cafes around the world, observing conversations and counting the number of times the patrons casually touched each other (see Figure 4-2). The results are as follows:

- ✔ San Juan, Puerto Rico came in at first place with 180 touches per hour.
- ✔ Paris, France had 110 touches per hour.
- ✔ Florida, USA had 2 touches per hour.
- ✔ London, England had 0 touches per hour.

Obviously the way we touch, how often we touch, and who we touch vary from country to country almost as much as the languages spoken. Here's a quick look at the role touch plays in different parts of the world:

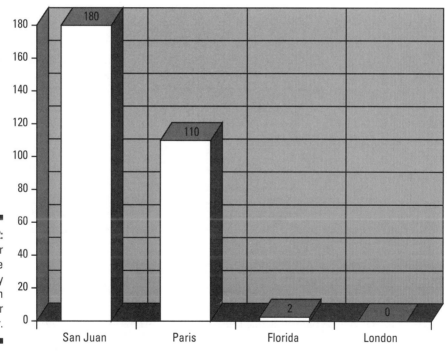

Figure 4-2: The number of times we casually touch each other per hour.

China

In general, the Chinese are not particularly oriented toward touching in public. However, because of the influence of western culture, the handshake is becoming a more widely used form of greeting. Still, the more traditional modest bow or nod is an acceptable way to greet your customers in China.

France

Unlike North America, where a firm handshake is seen as a sign of confidence, in France the handshake is on the light, quick, and frequent side. If you go into a French business meeting, expect to shake the hand of every person in the room. Of course, the French are also well known for the popular *air kiss* on each cheek. If this custom is initiated by a French business associate, go with the flow.

Italy

The Italians are the most *touchy* of all the Europeans. They shake hands often, kiss, embrace, and generally are not shy about expressing physical contact in public. A good guideline is to always follow your host's lead; if your business associate wants to give you a hug, respond in kind.

Latin America

The Latins are probably the most touch oriented of all cultures. Public hugs, pats on the back, and kisses on the cheek are very common. Almost every "hello" and "good-bye" in a Latin American country is accompanied by a warm handshake. If you get to know your Latin American hosts well, they may extend the *abrazo* to you. The *abrazo* is a warm embrace that friends exchange upon greeting each other.

The Middle East

While touching in public between opposite genders is a big *no-no* in the Arab world, touch between same-sex genders is fairly common. For example, an Arab man, as a sign of friendship, may take another man's hand. In Saudi Arabia, one can frequently see men walking down the street hand-in-hand.

What to know before you go

If you are planning a business trip or vacation to a country you have never visited before, you may want to do some research first. Several excellent books are available that will help you understand cultural differences and customers throughout the world. For more information on body language and other important things to know about a country, try the following resources.

Culture Shock Series (Times Books International): This series of books is wonderful. Each book focuses on a specific country within Asia (*Culture Shock Malaysia*, for instance). They are full of detailed information and cover most business and social situations. They are different from most other travel books because they don't just tell you the rules of behavior, they explain the thinking and mind set behind them. We have found them extremely useful, especially for doing business in Southeast Asia.

Gestures by Roger E. Aztell (John Wiley & Sons, Inc.): This book provides a broad look at how body language is used around the world. One thing we like about this book is its coverage of over 86 different countries. The tips are well written, clear, and to the point. Note that this book focuses its attention on the specific do's and don'ts of body language and does not go into great detail regarding the psychology of the culture.

Japan

The traditional greeting in Japan is still the bow, although the Japanese will make accommodations to westerners and shake hands. In general, however, touching is considered to be a private matter. Public displays of affection are thought to be impolite, and we have never seen a hug or kiss take place publicly between a foreign businessman and his Japanese customer.

Excuse Me, You Are Standing in My Space

Personal space is the distance that feels comfortable between you and another person. If another person approaches you and invades your personal space, you automatically move back without a thought.

If you see customers moving away from you, they may be doing so in an attempt to create more space for themselves. If this is the case, step back and keep your distance. By maintaining a safe personal zone, you facilitate communication, comfort, and trust. Three distinct spatial zones exist:

- intimate
- personal
- social

Zone One: Intimate (0 – 2 feet)

This zone is reserved for romantic partners, family members, close friends, and children. Entering this zone when you don't belong is embarrassing and/or threatening to the other person. That's why standing close to people in a crowded elevator is so uncomfortable. The small space forces us to be closer to other people than we would like. Most of us deal with this feeling by staring up at the floor numbers as if they hold the meaning of life.

Zone Two: Personal (2 – 4 feet)

Most of our conversations with customers will take place in this range. The personal space creates the privacy necessary for a confidential discussion while maintaining a safe and comfortable distance between you and the customer.

Zone Three: Social (4 feet or more)

This *on stage* range is mainly used by teachers in the classroom, the boss at a company meeting, or the instructor at a training class. However, just as you can get too close for comfort in the intimate zone, it is also possible to get too far for comfort in the social zone.

Overdone: The personal zone is most commonly overdone when you are waiting in line at places such as:

- ✔ customs at the airport
- ✔ the pharmacy
- ✔ the checkout stand at the grocery store

Because people are usually impatient in these places, they tend to stand closer to you in hopes that doing so will move them to the front of the line faster.

Underdone: I once had a meeting with a prospective client. I was shown into his office and asked to take a seat. In the room was a giant desk with a large chair behind it. In the corner of the room were two very small chairs about six feet away from the big desk. I sat in one of the two chairs and waited. When the client came in, I expected him to sit down next to me. Instead, he walked behind his giant desk and sat down in his large chair. The distance between us made it hard for me to pay attention to what he was saying. I left the meeting feeling that the physical distance between us had stopped us from having an in-depth conversation.

Cultural differences

As with touch, personal space is different throughout the world. In general, most Asians, especially the Japanese, tend to stand farther apart than Europeans and North Americans. Latin Americans and Middle Easterners, on the other hand, stand much closer together.

A friend of ours was at an embassy cocktail party where a South American gentleman was talking with a Japanese gentleman. Our friend reported that the two of them never stood still the whole evening. They waltzed around the room as the South American kept moving closer — trying to close the gap between them — while the Japanese gentleman kept backing away — trying to increase the gap.

Neatness Counts

Another part of body language is neatness. Being neat and organized plays an important role in two areas:

- ✔ how we look
- ✔ how our work areas look

How we look

Personal grooming has a big impact on your customers. Dirty hands and fingernails, messy hair, and body odor are all delicate items to discuss, but the cost of not dealing with them can mean the loss of otherwise happy customers.

Similarly, incomplete or dirty uniforms create a negative impression. If most of the employees are wearing complete uniforms, but one employee is missing a cap, jacket, or tie, that person sticks out like a sore thumb. This wardrobe snafu is seen by customers as a sign of sloppiness and inconsistency.

Our customers expect us to look appropriate for the job we do. Don't try to have clean hands and fingernails if you are an auto mechanic — customers will probably get the impression that you have never lifted the hood of a car.

How our work area looks

The neatness of our work environment is especially important if our customers have access to it. Customers will make decisions about how organized and competent you are by the way your desk or work area looks. If your desk is piled high with papers, files, messages, and memos, making the excuse, "I have a system, I know where everything is..." impresses only the gullible and is a negative moment of truth for everyone else.

Customer logic has its own rules. One of these rules is that the customer is allowed to make what seems like an unreasonable connection between things. A classic example of customer logic at work is the airline executive who once noted that his passengers assumed that if their seat pockets or trays were dirty, they could not be sure that the airline did a good job of servicing the airplane engines.

I was once in a preliminary meeting with a financial planner whom I was going to use to help me organize my finances. (This was before *Personal Finance For Dummies* was published.) Toward the end of the meeting, he crossed his legs and I caught a glimpse of the bottom of his left shoe where he had a hole in the sole. I couldn't help but think of this sloppiness as a bad sign for someone whose job was to promote financial sufficiency; I ended up not hiring him. Whether this decision was fair or not took second place to the impression that the hole in his shoe had left on me.

Small Things Mean a Lot

The information in this chapter is summed up for us by an article we read. A university library wanted to study the effect that simple, interpersonal actions had on students' perceptions of the services they received.

They divided the librarians who checked out the books into two groups. The first group was instructed to be efficient and help the students check out their books with no added interpersonal skills, such as eye contact, smiling, or physical contact. The other group of librarians was instructed to be efficient and to add some interpersonal skills such as looking the customer in the eye, using his or her name (written on the library card), and causally touching the customer on the wrist when giving the book back. Customers were interviewed as they left the library and asked to share their feelings about the service they had received.

Not surprisingly, the customers who received efficient service and nothing else all agreed they received poor to fair service. The customers who received the added interpersonal skills reported that they received *good to excellent* service. The point being that the little things we do with body language often have the biggest impact.

The next time you are a customer in a restaurant, hotel, or bank, take a moment to evaluate how well the service person uses his or her body language. The better you get at observing other people's body language, the more aware you will become of your own.

Chapter 5

It's Not What You Say, It's How You Say It: Tone of Voice

• •

In This Chapter

▶ Two keys to good inflection

▶ Volume control

▶ Pace the customer

▶ How is your tele-tone?

• •

*T*he minute you pick up the phone, body language disappears and your tone of voice becomes 86 percent of the story (See Figure 5-1).

Face-to-Face

Over the Phone

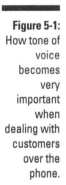

Figure 5-1:
How tone of voice becomes very important when dealing with customers over the phone.

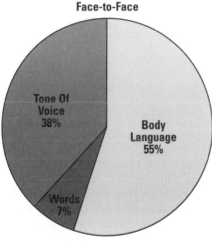

Tone Of Voice 38%

Body Language 55%

Words 7%

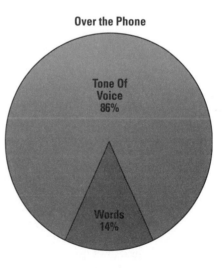

Tone Of Voice 86%

Words 14%

Almost the entire message you project to a customer over the telephone is communicated through your tone of voice, and it doesn't take long for your customers to pick up on your attitude. In fact, your customers know within ten seconds of the call whether they are talking to beauty or the beast! Some people you speak to only have to say "hello," before you find yourself thinking, "I don't want to deal with this person." So you hang up and call again, hoping somebody with a more compassionate tone picks up the phone.

No matter what words you use, the tone of your voice reveals what you think and feel. For example:

- ✔ A monotone and flat voice says to the customer: "I'm bored and have absolutely no interest in what you're talking about."
- ✔ Slow speed and low pitch communicates the message: "I'm depressed and want to be left alone."
- ✔ A high pitched and emphatic voice says: "I'm enthusiastic about this subject."
- ✔ An abrupt speed and very loud tone says: "I'm angry and not open to input!"
- ✔ High pitch combined with drawn out speed conveys: "I don't believe what I'm hearing."

Developing your telephone tone (tele-tone for short) is one of the most valuable business skills you can acquire. Three things will help you to be a winner over the telephone:

- ✔ inflection
- ✔ volume control
- ✔ pacing the customer

Inflection

If you have ever read a story to a child, you know that the words of the story are far less interesting than the inflection you put in your voice. In fact, if you get lazy and don't make a ruff, grumbling sound when you say, "I'll huff and I'll puff and I'll blow your house down!" your child will more than likely stop you and say, "Read it like you mean it." Inflection is the wave-like movement of highs and lows in your pitch. It's the peaks and valleys in your voice that let your customer know how interested (or uninterested) you are in what they are saying. Inflection also reflects how interested you are in what you are saying to the customer. When inflection is missing, your voice can sound monotone. The dictionary defines monotone as a series of words or sentences in one unvaried key or pitch — *a tedious sameness.*

If I've said it once, I've said it a hundred times

When you are saying the same thing over and over again, slipping into the habit of speaking in a monotone voice is easy. The operator who says, "Good morning, law offices of Smith, Smith, and Smith" one hundred times a day can forget to put any life into the greeting. Even if you have said something a thousand times, your customer may be hearing it for the first time. So remember, using inflection is as important with the first call of the day as it is with the last.

Improving your inflection

Some people are born with naturally interesting voices and seem to effortlessly use inflection to sound warm and friendly. Others of us, who are not so fortunate, need to practice. If you feel that your vocal inflection needs polishing, you can do four things to improve the quality of inflection in your voice:

- ✔ Smile when talking on the phone.
- ✔ Practice stressing words.
- ✔ Breathe (deep, long, and slow).
- ✔ Exaggerate your tone.

The disk jockey

Too much inflection is just as bad as too little. Don't scare your customers away by unleashing your hidden desire to be a disk jockey on them. Answering the phone with a resounding have-we-got-a-deal-for-you tone of voice creates instant distrust. These are the people, usually from the phone company or the local paper, who call as you sit down to dinner and excitedly say, "HELLO!" as if you are a long lost friend. This tone, as you know, is your cue to hang up.

Smile when talking on the phone

One way to positively affect the inflection in your voice is to smile, especially when you first answer the telephone. The reason for doing so is not psychological but physiological. When you smile, the soft palate at the back of your mouth raises and makes the sound waves more fluid. For those of you who have ever sung in a choir (or in the shower), you know that the wider you open your mouth and the more teeth you show, the better tone you get. The same applies on the telephone. Smiling helps your voice to sound friendly, warm, and receptive.

Some telemarketing companies are so convinced of the value of smiling when talking on the phone that they install mirrors above the telemarketers' desks to remind them to smile. These are the same people, by the way, who call you when you are about to sit down to dinner.

Change the stress on the words

Another way to improve your inflection is to be aware of how stressing certain words changes the feeling of what you are saying. The following sentence "What would you like us to do about it?" changes in feeling, meaning, and tone when you:

- ✔ say it defensively (emphasizing the words "would you")

  "What *would you* like us to do about it?"

- ✔ say it with curiosity (emphasizing the words "like us")

  "What would you *like us* to do about it?"

- ✔ say it with apathy (not emphasizing any of the words)

  "What would you like us to do about it?"

Breathe

Believe it or not, the inflection in your voice can be greatly increased by learning to take long, slow, deep breaths. Most people become *shallow breathers* when they're under pressure. The next time you are in a stressful situation, try to notice what happens to your breathing. The more upset you become, the shallower and quicker your breath will be. When this breathing pattern happens, your vocal cords tend to tighten, making your voice go up and sound strained. By being aware of your breath, especially under stressful situations, you can slow down your breathing, thereby relaxing your vocal cords, bringing down your pitch, and creating a calmer tone of voice.

Exaggerate your tone

Whenever we are asked to help someone with a monotone speaking voice improve his inflection, we have him start by practicing exaggerating his tone using the following three steps:

1. **Take a short and uncomplicated sentence like, "Bill isn't here right now," and say it out loud with your normal level of inflection.**

2. **Think of inflection on a scale of one to ten, with one being monotone and ten being a disk jockey. Now say the same sentence over, but this time exaggerate your inflection all the way up to a ten.**

   Sometimes we ask people to visualize themselves as circus barkers under the big top announcing to a noisy crowd of a thousand people, "Bill isn't here right now." Practice this step and stop only when you sound really obnoxious and embarrass yourself as well as everyone around you.

3. **Now say the same sentence again, this time taking your inflection down a couple of notches to a level eight. Say the sentence one more time taking it down to a level five or six.**

   Level five or six is a good level at which to keep your inflection over the phone. If you find your inflection slipping over time, go back to step one and repeat the process.

Volume

Imagine you are at a party talking to a close friend when she leans toward you and starts to tell you something private. She begins speaking in a very soft voice, almost a whisper. Invariably, as soon as your friend's tone lowers, the people standing near by will strain their heads in your direction trying to hear what is being said.

Such is the power and uncanny magnetism of volume control.

 If a customer is angry and speaking loudly, don't yell back at the same volume (even though your instinctive reaction may be to do so). Instead behave like a professional and start out by speaking at a somewhat lower volume than the customer, gradually bringing the customer's volume down to yours. With a confused customer, speaking a little louder than usual helps give him something to focus on and helps you to control the conversation more easily.

Pacing

Pacing is approximately matching your customer's *rate of speech* and *intensity of feeling*. Pacing is the best single tool you have for creating rapport with your customer.

By focusing on the similarities (instead of the differences) between you and your customer, you meet the customer at her level and make her feel at ease.

Rate of speech

The average American speaks at a rate of 100-150 words per minute. The average listener, on the other hand, is *capable* of listening up to a rate of 600-650 words per minute. By pacing a customer's rate of speech, you can close the gap and have more hits than misses in your telephone communication. One factor that significantly affects a person's rate of speech is where he or she comes from.

Geographic location

Geographic location can influence the speed at which you talk. Take two extremes: Native New Yorkers generally talk a mile a minute while Southerners are known for their slow drawl. If you put a Southerner and a New Yorker together (we've seen it happen and it's not a pretty story), the New Yorker is always trying to get the Southerner to speed up and the Southerner is always trying to get the New Yorker to slow down. In order for any ground to be gained, either the New Yorker or the Southerner has to pace the other.

As a service provider, your job is to pace the customer — not the other way around! If you notice that you are thinking bad thoughts about your customer, wondering why he is not slowing down or speeding up to your rate of speech, quickly shift gears and move into a pacing mode.

If you are a fast talking New Yorker on the phone with a customer from Texas, remember to use the conversation as an opportunity to bridge the gap by practicing your pacing skills and *slooowing* way down.

Slow down little lady

I was once leading a customer service workshop in Texas. Because I grew up in Los Angeles, I tend to speak at a fairly quick pace. About an hour into the workshop, a man in the back row (wearing a big, ten-gallon hat) raised his hand, stood up, and said politely (with a perfect Texas accent), "Little lady, you need to slooow down, you are just going tooooo fast. We're not goin' anywhere, take your time." Once I got over the shock of being called "little lady," I realized I was not pacing them. I forced myself to slow down and learned a good lesson about the importance of pacing my customers!

Intensity

Intensity is the strength of emotion that is projected along with the words you are saying. Your level of intensity changes with your level of concern. For instance, saying, "I'm not ready yet" would have a very different level of intensity if you were getting dressed for a party than if you were next in line to jump out of the plane on your first skydive.

How your customers feel determines their level of vocal intensity. If they are calm and relaxed, their level of intensity will probably be fairly low. If they are upset or angry, their level of intensity will rise. Imagine leaving your wallet, keys, or date book at a restaurant. What level of intensity would you be projecting when you call the restaurant on the phone? Probably very high. In this situation, the service provider's job would be to increase her intensity in order to show you, the customer, that she understands your concern by reflecting your intensity back to you.

Reflecting back intensity

Back to the missing wallet. When you call the restaurant, you will probably be panicked and want quick action. The hostess, wanting to calm you down and thinking your problem is no big deal (because it happens all the time), may respond to your high intensity by being casual, low key, and very calm. The hostess believes this strategy is excellent for keeping the situation under control. She is wrong. This action will have the opposite effect because she is not reflecting back to you the intensity of your concern. You will only feel that you are both on the same wavelength when she paces you by stating strongly:

> *I will look for it immediately!*

To improve tele-tone, try the following exercise: Tape record yourself while on a telephone call and then listen to your voice on the tape. Don't record your customers without asking their permission first. (It's impolite — and illegal. Remember Watergate?) If you don't feel comfortable taping a real conversation, try taping a role play situation with a co-worker. As you listen, use the following list to evaluate your tele-tone:

- ✔ Did I speak with inflection to show interest and concern?
- ✔ Did I use a level of volume that gained the customer's attention?

✔ Did I pace the customer by adjusting my rate of speech to match his or hers?

✔ Did I pace the customer by adjusting my intensity to match his or hers?

You can support your staff in improving their tele-tone by periodically listening in on their conversations and coaching them afterwards. Be sure to tell your staff when you plan to listen in and why. Tell them that you view this exercise as a positive opportunity for them to improve their skills, not as a way for you to catch them doing something wrong.

Chapter 6

Help, I'm Stuck in Voice Mail:
Telephone Etiquette

● ●

In This Chapter

▶ Test your telephone etiquette IQ

▶ The five basics

▶ The pros and cons of voice mail

▶ The cursing caller

● ●

*T*he essence of dealing with people, politely and efficiently, over the phone can be boiled down to one simple thing: telephone etiquette. Being nice on the phone isn't difficult if you follow some simple guidelines about how to:

✔ answer the phone

✔ put callers on hold

✔ transfer a call

✔ take a message

✔ end a call

Unlike body language, which can vary from culture to culture, telephone etiquette has a universally agreed upon set of rules that pave the way for smoother, faster telephone calls with customers. Even small things, such as how long it takes for your phone to be answered or the words you use when you answer a call, can create a lasting impression. In many businesses, the telephone is the customer's *first* contact with a company, so being telephone friendly is one of the least expensive ways to immediately upgrade your service. Telephone etiquette helps take the guesswork out of what to say and when to say it.

Good telephone etiquette is one way that you can help ensure that a customer can call any department within your company, in any city, on any day, and be dealt with in a uniform way. Customers love consistency, and they expect to receive the same level of service that they received today when they call tomorrow, next month, or next year.

Test Your Telephone Etiquette IQ

Before we give you the ins and outs of basic telephone etiquette, you may want to test your current knowledge by rating each of the following scenarios as true or false.

Scenario one

The time is 11:45 am and Cindy is at her desk putting the final touches on last quarter's sales figure report, which is due to her boss by noon. She is on the final page of the report when the phone rings. Cindy tries to ignore it for a few moments (hoping the person will go away), but the ringing continues. Eventually, she picks up the phone and says with a smile, "This is Cindy, how may I help you?"

Cindy is demonstrating good telephone etiquette:

_____ True   _____ False

Scenario two

Mary Jane is a sales assistant at a large hardware store. Her supervisor, Debara, is having a brief meeting with her about some new stock that has just arrived. Mary Jane's telephone rings. She immediately picks it up, greets the customer on the other end of the line, and politely says, "Let me put you on hold for just a moment."

Mary Jane is demonstrating good telephone etiquette:

_____ True   _____ False

Scenario three

Jim is a travel agent who works for a large national travel agency. His area of specialty is domestic travel. His phone rings and on the line is a customer who needs help booking an overseas trip to Morocco. Jim explains to the customer that he does not deal with foreign travel by saying, "I'm sorry, you've reached the domestic travel department, you need to talk to international. Hold on for a moment, and I will transfer you."

Jim is demonstrating good telephone etiquette:

_____ True _____ False

Scenario four

Alex is the assistant to the vice president of marketing for a clothing manufacturer. She receives a call for her boss — from a person whose voice she doesn't recognize — and says, "May I ask who's calling please?" The customer on the other end of the line gives her name and Alex replies, "I'm sorry, he isn't in right now, may I take a message?"

Alex is demonstrating good telephone etiquette:

_____ True _____ False

Okay. How did you do? If you marked any of the scenarios as true, think again. All of the above scenarios are *false* because they broke some cardinal aspect of telephone etiquette and could, consequently, give the customer a negative impression. Following is the rationale behind why each scenario is false, along with the basics that will make you an expert in each area.

How to Answer the Phone

In Scenario One, Cindy let the phone ring for too long and forgot to greet the caller.

The time is 11:45 am and Cindy is at her desk putting the final touches on last quarter's sales figure report, which is due to her boss by noon. She is on the final page of the report when the phone rings. Cindy tries to ignore it for a few moments (hoping the person will go away), but the ringing continues. Eventually she picks up the phone and says with a smile, "This is Cindy, how may I help you?"

We have found that the way a company answers the phone tells the whole story about the kind of service you can expect to receive from them. How you answer the phone sets the tone of the entire call. The correct phrases said in the right order can give a positive first impression and convey an immediate message about your company. The basic rules are as follows:

- ✔ Pick up the phone within three rings.
- ✔ Greet the caller.
- ✔ Give your name.
- ✔ Ask the customer if you can help.

Pick up the phone within three rings

Three rings is the generally accepted standard for picking up the phone. After the third ring, our tolerance as customers starts to waver, and little seeds of doubt begin to form because we interpret an unanswered phone to mean all sorts of nasty things, such as the following:

- ✔ Your company is too out of control to deal with the basics — such as picking up a ringing telephone.
- ✔ Your company is understaffed and doesn't have enough people to answer the phones.
- ✔ Your company has gone out of business.

In Scenario One, Cindy made the mistake of letting the phone ring for too long before picking it up. She seemed more concerned with finishing the work she had in front of her than answering the phone. In Chapter 1, we talk about how the functions of your job can sometimes make the customer seem like an interruption of your job. This scenario is an example of the function (finishing the report) getting in the way of the essence (being responsive to the customer).

 If you hear a phone ringing in your department and no one picks it up, make it your business to do so. Remember, a person expecting a prompt response is on the other end. Even if you personally cannot help him or her, you can at least take a message and further the cause of good customer relations.

Greet the caller

A greeting should always be the entry point of a phone conversation because it instantly indicates your friendliness and openness to the other person. When answering the phone, say *hello, good morning, good afternoon,* and so on before you identify yourself or your company. Your customers want to be greeted even if they are in a hurry. In Scenario One, Cindy left out this important step and may have given the caller the impression that she was in a hurry (which she was) by not including a greeting.

"Howdy," "Hi," and "Yo" are also greetings, of a sort, but they are not on our preferred list. We recommend avoiding them because they are too casual for all but surf shop clientele.

Don't make your greeting too long or over the top. One annoying trend that we are trying to stamp out is the greeting that tells us stuff we really don't want to know. This kind of greeting usually goes something like: "Hello. It's a beautiful day here at Spatula Cosmetics. How may I help you?" This greeting is guaranteed to annoy even the most positive of customers and invites mockery and sarcasm (especially in our office).

Give your name

This basic act of courtesy lets the caller know that she has reached the correct person, department, or company. Although obviously not rocket science, identifying yourself to the caller can save both parties a lot of time and frustration. How you identify yourself to the customer varies depending on the circumstances.

Answering your own phone or direct dial line

Usually, in this situation, the caller knows the company he has reached and you only need to identify yourself by giving your name.

Answering the phone for the entire company

Receptionists and switchboard operators, for example, would normally answer the phone and give the company name rather than their own name.

Answering the phone for a department

Usually saying only the name of the department is sufficient, followed by your name. However, if the call is coming directly from outside (not through a switchboard or auto-attendant), say the company name before you identify the department and yourself.

Ask the customer if you can help

Saying, "How may I help you?" completes telephone answering etiquette by demonstrating that you and your company are ready and available to assist the customer with his or her needs.

This step applies primarily if you are answering a department phone and especially if you are in a customer service or technical support department. If, on the other hand, you are answering your own phone or the company phone, this step is probably optional (although it doesn't hurt in either case).

Early on in the conversation, write down the customer's name and use it at least three times during your conversation with him or her.

Putting it all together

Using the guidelines outlined above, three typical ways your company might want to answer the phone are:

✔ **Direct Line**

"Good morning, this is Andrew, how may I help you?"

✔ **Company Phone**

"Good afternoon, Pine Box Productions, how may I help you?"

✔ **Department Phone**

"Good morning, Technical Support, this is Andrew, how may I help you?"

Remember to train any temporary staff you hire in telephone etiquette for customer contact positions such as a receptionist or customer service representative. Some companies forget that this person, no matter how temporary, is a key member of the front line staff that creates a first impression when customers call into the company.

Call into your own company or department anonymously and see how well you are dealt with. How do your staff rate at answering the telephone, transferring you, taking a message, and so on? If you think your staff will know your voice, try having your spouse call.

Last name grunt

Some people believe that because they only deal with internal customers, they don't need to use good phone etiquette and answer their phones in a short, curt, or gruff manner. A typical example is the *last name grunt,* where the caller hears nothing but the quickly blurted last name of the person picking up the phone. Regardless of who is calling you, your phone tone has an impact on how much rapport you create with the caller.

Scenario One Revisited: The time is 11:45 am and Cindy is at her desk putting the final touches on last quarter's sales figure report, which is due to her boss by noon. She is on the final page of the report when the phone rings.

Cindy immediately stops what she is doing and picks up the phone by the second ring. She answers with a smile and says:

Good morning, this is Cindy, how may I help you?

How to Put a Customer on Hold

In Scenario Two, Mary Jane didn't ask the caller if she could put him on hold — she told him.

Mary Jane is a sales assistant at a large hardware store. Her supervisor, Debara, is having a brief meeting with her about some new stock that has just arrived. Mary Jane's telephone rings. She immediately picks it up, greets the customer on the other end of the line, and politely says, "Let me put you on hold for just a moment."

Most of the questions that we get from people in our seminars about putting customers on hold revolve around dealing with many different things at once (several people on hold, people in your face needing your attention, and so on). We have found that the biggest problem is the stress level of the service provider. Without knowing the following steps, you can easily lose control and stop thinking clearly. The etiquette for putting your customers on hold will help you avoid becoming confused and befuddled and thereby avoid the many negative moments of truth that customers associate with the telephone.

The main points of telephone etiquette for putting customers on hold are as follows:

- ✔ Ask customers if you may put them on hold.
- ✔ Wait for a response.
- ✔ Tell customers why they are being put on hold.
- ✔ Give a time frame.
- ✔ Thank customers for holding after returning to the line.

Ask customers if it's okay to put them on hold

Because it is an inconvenience to your customers (or anybody) to be put on hold, you should *always* ask the caller's permission before putting them on hold.

Think of putting a customer on hold as parking them in a dark closet with the door locked. At any time this black hole of the telephone world must be filled with thousands of poor souls wondering:

- ✔ Does anybody know I'm here?
- ✔ Have I been forgotten?
- ✔ Why is this taking so long?
- ✔ I've been waiting so long — who was I waiting for?
- ✔ Should I hang up and lose my place in the queue?

If you are going to subject your callers to this netherworld, no matter what the length of time, the least you can do is ask their permission.

In our scenario, Mary Jane missed the boat at this point. She told the customer she was putting him on hold, rather than asking his permission and then waiting for an answer.

Wait for a response

The second part of asking the customer's permission to be put on hold is waiting for a response. Situations where the service provider doesn't wait for a response ("Can you hol——" *click*) are all too common, so don't be surprised if your customers are so shocked that you are waiting for their response that they don't answer. If this situation happens, you can assume that their silence means *yes,* and you can go ahead and put them on hold.

As soon as the customer agrees to hold, say "Thank You" before clicking off the line.

Tell customers why they are being put on hold

We have found that most customers are very patient if they are politely informed as to why they must hold. Most people find it easier and more comfortable to wait on hold if they have a mental picture of what the service provider is doing while away from the phone. Be sure to provide whatever information is pertinent, such as:

- ✔ "The answer to your question will take a few moments because I need to consult my manager."
- ✔ "I need just a minute to get the correct file."
- ✔ "I need a moment or two to check with another department."

Some confusion exists about the difference between keeping the customer well informed with pertinent information and making excuses for poor service. For example, imagine that you receive a call from a customer who has not received a delivery. An informative response would be: "May I put you on hold for a moment while I call the dispatch department?" An excuse response would be: "I don't know why that happened . . . I know that we've had a few people out sick this week and things have been a little backed up, but these circumstances shouldn't have affected your delivery. Let me put you on hold while I call them to see what's going on."

Give a time frame

Giving the customer a time frame helps diminish the I've-been-forgotten factor and has a calming effect. How specific the time frame needs to be depends on the length of time you think your customers will have to be on hold. If the time is short, then accuracy isn't so important. If they will have to wait a longer time, then an honest estimate works much better. Following are three examples:

Short wait time (up to 60 seconds)

If you know, prior to putting the customer on hold, that his wait time will be brief, you can say something as casual as:

> *This will take a few moments.*

Long wait time (1-3 minutes)

This amount of time is an exceptionally long period for the caller to be on hold. It is a good idea in this situation to not only give an accurate estimate of the hold time but also to double check that the wait will be acceptable:

This question could take me two or three minutes to sort out with my supervisor. Would you like to hold, or do you want me to call you back?

Eternity (over 3 minutes)

At this point, customers really start to get their undies in bunches over how long they have been waiting. Let's face it, how long can you listen to Greensleeves played over and over again before you begin thinking of exotic ways to vent your frustration and anger on the service provider?

If you have to put the customer on hold for any significant period of time, it is better to ask for their phone number and tell them you will call them back when you have the information. Don't have people holding for so long that they turn on their speakerphone and forget who you are by the time you get back on the phone with them.

When dealing with a customer who is on a long hold pattern, return to the line every thirty seconds or so and inform him of your progress in dealing with his particular situation.

Thank the customer for holding

What can we say? Saying *thank you* when you return to the line is good, old-fashioned, common courtesy. This action nicely rounds off the on-hold sequence and acknowledges the customer's understanding and patience.

Scenario Two Revisited: Mary Jane is a sales assistant at a large hardware store. Her supervisor, Debara, is having a brief meeting with her about some new stock that has just arrived. Mary Jane's telephone rings.

She immediately picks it up, greets the customer on the other end of the line and politely says:

I am just finishing off a meeting. May I please put you on hold a minute?

Mary Jane waits for a response and when the customer agrees, Mary Jane says:

Thank you.

Mary Jane returns to the line within the minute and says:

Thank you for waiting. How can I help you?

A trend we love

If you are on hold and have called a company that has installed one of the newer, more sophisticated, auto-attendant technologies, you are given an approximate wait time and told how many callers are waiting ahead of you. This information, at least, gives the customer some control over whether she chooses to wait and helps eliminate the I've-been-forgotten factor that we addressed earlier.

Sometimes holding is inconvenient for callers, so don't automatically assume that they will. If they respond with a "no," ask them if they would like a return call, if they would like to leave a message, or if they would like to be transferred to someone else?

Silence can be golden

In our experience, most customers prefer to have silence or soft music while in the holding mode. Our hate list for *on hold* strategies is as follows:

1. **Prerecorded advertising.**

   Absolutely hands down the worst! Apparently leaving us on hold for an hour or two isn't sufficient for some companies — they want to add insult to injury by subjecting us to endless advertising slogans promoting their entire product line and the superiority of their service!

2. **Weird computer music.**

   Some companies take a classical or popular piece of music, usually Greensleeves, and play it on something that sounds like an electric hairpin. Then the music is reconfigured for the high tech world we live in. This type of music is annoying and only serves to irritate customers even more while they are waiting.

3. **Local radio station tuned in to the Heavy Metal Retrospective program.**

   Any music that is loud, aggressive, or hurts the ears is not what you want to play for customers while they are waiting on hold.

How to Transfer a Call

In Scenario Three, Jim neither asked the caller if she wanted to be transferred nor waited for the call to go through before hanging up.

Jim is a travel agent who works for a large national travel agency. His area of specialty is domestic travel. His phone rings and on the line is a customer who needs help booking an overseas trip to Morocco. Jim explains to the customer that he does not deal with foreign travel by saying, "I'm sorry, this is the domestic travel department, you need to talk to international. Hold on for a moment and I will transfer you."

We have found that customers have the least telephone tolerance when being transferred over and over again. To customers, being shuffled from department to department can mean that the staff are too overwhelmed to care or that the company just isn't interested in what they, the customers, need.

The main points of telephone etiquette for transferring a customer are as follows:

- ✔ Explain why the caller is being transferred and to whom.
- ✔ Ask the customer if he or she minds being transferred.
- ✔ Make sure someone is there to pick up the call before you hang up.
- ✔ Tell the person to whom you are transferring the call the caller's name and the nature of the call.

Explain why the caller is being transferred and to whom

This feeling is called *telephone destiny*, and the customer's basic questions are "Where am I going, and who will greet me when I get there?" By telling customers to whom they are being transferred and why, you are answering one of the existential questions of telephone life. Besides, if the customer inadvertently gets disconnected, he can call back and ask for that person by name.

Ask the customer if he or she minds being transferred

Customers get angry if they are transferred when they don't want to be. Sometimes, after being transferred several times, a customer may just want to leave a message. If the person is calling on a cellular phone, holding may just be too expensive a proposition. As with putting a caller on hold, the customer should always be asked if she minds being transferred. Jim, in Scenario Three, did not do this. Bad Jim.

Make sure someone is there to pick up the call before you hang up

This simple, yet elusive, step saves the customer the frustration of being transferred to someone who isn't available. By staying with the call until the recipient picks up, the service provider is being responsible for connecting customers to a living, breathing person who can help them. In Scenario Three, Jim transferred the caller without waiting on the line to see if someone from the International department was available to pick up the call. If no one had answered, imagine how angry the customer would be when (or if) he called back a second time.

Tell the person to whom you are transferring the call the caller's name and the nature of the call

Once the person to whom you are transferring the call picks up, briefly give her the customer's name and the nature of his call. When the person receiving the call gets on the line with the customer and already knows the customer's name and basic circumstances, the customer feels well taken care of and gets a sense of being known by — and thus important to — your company.

In the event that the caller does not want to be transferred, offer to take a message and assure the customer that you will personally see to it that the message gets into the hands of the right person. Then, after you hang up, see that the message gets safely to its destination.

Scenario Three Revisited: Jim is a travel agent who works for a large, national travel agency. His area of specialty is domestic travel. His phone rings with a customer requiring help booking an overseas trip to Morocco.

Jim explains to the customer that he does not deal with foreign travel and says:

> *I'm sorry, this is the domestic travel department. You need to talk to Bob in international; would you like me to transfer you to him?*

The customer agrees, and Jim says:

> *All right, I will transfer you now.*

When Bob picks up Jim says:

> *Bob, I have Mrs. Jones on the line; she needs some help booking a trip to Morocco.*

The transfer is complete and Jim clicks off the line.

How to Take a Message

In Scenario Four, Alex should have asked the caller's name *after* telling him her boss' availability.

Alex is the assistant to the vice president of marketing for a clothing manufacturer. She receives a call for her boss — from a person whose voice she doesn't recognize — and says, "May I ask who's calling please?" The customer on the other end of the line gives her name and Alex replies, "I'm sorry, he isn't in right now, may I take a message?"

If you have ever received a hastily scribbled message with the caller's name misspelled and the phone number missing an area code, you know how frustrated you can feel as a service provider. As a customer, you know how you feel when you leave a message with someone whose sloppy attitude leaves you feeling as if *this message will never see the light of day.* Poorly taken messages produce uncertainty and worry for the customer and put the person receiving the message at a disadvantage when she calls the customer back. To take messages that provide the customer with a sense of confidence and empower your co-workers, incorporate the following steps in your message taking routine:

- ✔ Explain your co-worker's absence in a positive light.
- ✔ Inform the caller of the availability of the person he wants to talk to *before* asking his name.
- ✔ Give an estimated time of your co-worker's return.
- ✔ Offer to help the person yourself, take a message, or transfer her to another party.
- ✔ Write down all important information and attach any pertinent files.

Explain your co-worker's absence in a positive light

Customers do not want to hear the gruesome details as to why the person they're trying to reach is unavailable. Likewise, your co-workers do not want their private lives discussed over the phone with complete strangers. Explaining to a customer that a co-worker is not available because he is having his gall bladder removed is unnecessary, insensitive, and unprofessional. Phrases that can create a negative impression and should be avoided include the following:

- ✔ "Nan hasn't come in yet today."

  This statement infers that Nan is late.
- ✔ "I don't know where Nan is; she was here a minute ago."

  This remark says that Nan is a loose cannon and we can't keep tabs on her.
- ✔ "Nan had an emergency and isn't here."

  This statement says that she is having personal problems.
- ✔ "Nan is out sick."
- ✔ This remark may prompt the customer to ask Nan personal questions when she returns the call.

The best example of the worst explanation for a person's absence was when a secretary informed me that her boss (the person I was trying to reach) was not there because he and his wife were getting a divorce, and they were at the lawyer's office finalizing the divorce papers. Believe me when I tell you that I did not want to know this.

You can always explain a co-worker's absence in a positive light by using general phrases that convey the message, yet don't reveal too much personal information, such as:

- ✔ "Nan isn't available at the moment."
- ✔ "Nan stepped away from her desk."
- ✔ "Nan is out of the office today."
- ✔ "Nan is in a meeting."

Inform the caller of the availability of the person he wants to talk with before asking for his name

Screening is the practice of filtering out the calls that are not considered important enough for the manager, vice president, or boss to take. Customers can sniff out a screening when they are asked for their name (as well as the purpose of the call, in some cases) before they are told the availability of the party they are trying to reach.

In Scenario Four, Alex messed up and probably offended the customer by conveying the idea that the customer was being deliberately avoided. Customers, for good reason, are very sensitive to being screened by secretaries or assistants. Stating the availability of the person does not mean that she is necessarily available to speak to the caller. For example, an assistant may tell a customer that the person for whom they are asking is in the office but tied up in a meeting right now.

If you have a policy of asking for the caller's name before announcing a person's availability, we recommend you change your policy. If you don't know how your assistants deal with this situation, find out and, if necessary, coach them to do it the right way.

Give an estimated time of your co-worker's return

When possible, give an approximate return time for the person the customer is trying to reach. Doing so gives the customer some control by allowing him to reschedule the call for another time. Also, if the customer chooses to leave a message, he will have a realistic expectation as to when he can expect a call back.

Offer to help the person yourself, take a message, or transfer her to another party

In companies where a general lack of teamwork exists, the employee answering the phone may find it very easy to tell the customer that the person she is trying to reach is not in and leave it at that. However, doing so is poor telephone etiquette. Once you establish the unavailability of your co-worker, immediately offer to take a message or ask if someone else can help the caller. If, after the customer explains why she is calling, you can help her, by all means do so. If you know another person who can help, transfer her (using the telephone etiquette you learned earlier in this chapter). If you cannot help or transfer the customer, be sure that you take an accurate and detailed message containing all pertinent information including:

- correct spelling of the customer's first and last names

- correct phone number, including area code — be sure to repeat the number back to the customer to ensure accuracy

- brief message explaining why the customer called

- name of the person the customer wants to reach

- time and date the customer called

Scenario Four Revisited: Alex is the assistant to the vice president of marketing for a clothing manufacturer. She receives a call for her boss — from a person whose voice she doesn't recognize — and says:

Ms. Lapert isn't in right now, but I am expecting her back later this afternoon. May I ask who is calling please?

After the customer gives her name, Alex goes on to say:

Mrs. Smith, can I take a message for Ms. Lapert, or can I help you with something myself?

Ending the Call

Even if you practice letter perfect telephone etiquette throughout the call, don't underestimate the importance of ending the call on a positive note. Some key actions for ending calls this way include the following:

- Repeat any action steps you are going to take to ensure that both you and the customer agree on what is going to be done.

✔ Ask the caller if you can do anything else for him or her.

Doing so gives the customer a final chance to tie up any loose ends that may not have been discussed during the call.

✔ Thank the customer for calling and let him know that you appreciate his bringing the problem (if there was one) to your attention.

✔ Let the caller hang up first so that she doesn't accidentally get cut off in the middle of a sentence.

✔ Write down any important information as soon as you get off the phone.

Doing so prevents you from getting caught up in other things and forgetting pertinent information.

Using Voice Mail

No chapter on telephone etiquette would be complete in this day and age without a discussion of voice mail. At this point, the fact that voice mail is here to stay is pretty clear, and its use is spreading throughout the business world like weeds in a well-watered yard.

The idea of voice mail — the corporate and more sophisticated version of an answering machine — is to provide you with a means of being *available* to receive messages, even when you aren't. We find two opposing views on the subject of voice mail, and no other topic can divide a room faster. Basically, some people see voice mail as a great time saver, while others view it as a customer relations killer.

Voice mail adversaries

The main objections raised by service providers who dislike voice mail center around the customers' reactions to its use. Issues that we've heard expressed, include the following:

✔ Will our customers object to talking to a machine?

✔ Won't it remove the personal touch that we've always considered so important?

✔ What if people don't return their voice mail messages promptly?

From the customers' point of view, the negatives of using voice mail include the following:

✔ **Being given a choice of eight different numbers to press, choosing one, and then finding out that they made the wrong choice.**

Some ill-designed voice mail systems can trap you in a loop with no way to reach a live receptionist. You sometimes get caught in this trap when you press "0" and get a recorded voice telling you:

> *This is not a valid option.*

The only way out is to hang up and call back.

✔ **Leaving several voice messages and never receiving a call back.**

This problem has convinced some customers that voice mail is just another obstacle in the way of getting the service they need.

Last year I received a call from my car lease company. Apparently, I had been sending my payments to an incorrect address. When I picked up the phone, the person on the other end asked if I was Mr. Bailey. Once I confirmed that I was, she said, "I have a very important message for you." I listened and after a few seconds, a recorded message stated that my payment had not been received and asked if I was planning on sending it. I just wasn't in the mood to have a conversation with a machine, so I hung up. A week or so later, I received another call — same company, same person, same important message for me. This time, determined not to be trapped in a one-sided conversation, I said that I didn't want to talk to a machine...there was silence while my service agent regrouped after such an impudent request...she then continued, "You have to listen to the recording!" I refused again. She retorted, "If you don't listen to the recording you are going to have to talk to a real person!" Is it me or is something very wrong with this picture? I, like most customers, want the option of dealing with a person.

Always give your customers a way out of voice mail so that they have the option of talking to a real person.

Voice mail advocates

Undoubtedly, voice mail has a big *up* side. Three important benefits that service providers who are fans have voiced are as follows:

✔ Voice mail saves time. The customer can leave detailed information that the service person can act upon before calling the customer back.

✔ Service providers who check their voice mail regularly get messages faster than if they have to depend on getting them from a co-worker who may not be readily available or who may be available but takes incomplete messages.

✔ Voice mail increases productivity by allowing you to switch it on when you are having a meeting or discussion in your office. This way, you're not interrupted during your meeting, and you can give your undivided attention to the customer when you return his or her call.

The cursing caller

Once in a while, you will get someone on the phone who is so angry that they hurl words at you that we can't print. What to do with the cursing caller? We hear this question in almost every seminar we lead. Telephone etiquette dictates that you handle the situation with the following three steps:

1. **Give the customer the benefit of the doubt and politely say, "I really want to help you, but I'm having trouble with the kind of language you're using. Could you please refrain from using that kind of language?"**

   The customer may be so carried away with emotion that he may not even realize he is cursing. After hearing the above statement, most customers will stop, apologize, be a little embarrassed, and a lot better behaved. For the few who are more thick-headed, move on to Step 2.

2. **Give a second warning and restate what you said in Step 1.**

   For example: "As I have said, I really want to help you, but I'm having trouble focusing on the problem because of the language you're using. Would you please stop!" Most people, after the second warning, will refrain from cursing. If the customer does not stop at this point, your only alternative is to catch him off guard by countering with your own barrage of foul language.... Just kidding. If all else fails, move on to the final step.

3. **Let the customer know that you are no longer the person who can help him, and inform your supervisor of the problem.**

   Say, "As I have said, I really want to help you, but I am having trouble with the language you are using. What I am going to do is have my supervisor call you to discuss the problem." Hang up and immediately inform your supervisor of the situation. You should only have to use this step on very rare occasions.

   If a caller starts threatening you physically (he or she is going to come to your office and search you out, and so on) go immediately to Step 3. While you are paid to provide service, you are not paid to be abused or threatened.

From the customers' point of view, the positive side of voice mail includes the following:

> ✔ **Being able to leave a detailed and personal message for the specific person they want to speak to.**
>
> This option is impossible if another person takes the message.
>
> ✔ **Knowing that a service provider, although not immediately available, will receive their message and call back as soon as possible.**
>
> Customers perceive this system as providing increased availability of the service provider.

Use voice mail to enhance your communication with your customers by:

> ✔ returning all voice mail messages within 24 hours
>
> ✔ always answering your own phone (when you are sitting at your desk and not in a meeting) rather than letting voice mail do the job
>
> ✔ changing your voice mail message if you are going to be out of the office for more than one day (don't forget to change it back when you return, either)

Voice mail is just a tool, and it isn't inherently good or bad — it's all in how you use it. Are you using voice mail to avoid dealing with your customers or as a way of making you more accessible to them?

What's in a name?

What salutation should you use with your customers? Mr., Mrs., Ms., Bill, (if that's his name), Sir, Madame, Your Highness...? The possibilities are endless, and negotiating the shark infested waters of remaining service oriented and politically correct at the same time can be difficult.

1. **Listen to your customers — they will tell you how to address them.**

   "This is Dr. Smith." (Call him Doctor)

   "This is Mrs. Simon." (Call her Mrs.)

   "This is Carol Cransbee." (Call her Carol or Ms. Cransbee, to be safe)

2. **When in doubt, play it safe and address your female customers as Ms. rather than Mrs. or Miss.**

   If she wants to be called something else, she will let you know.

3. **Ask permission to use his or her first name.**

   "May I call you Bob?"

   Good luck and remember, if customers don't like what you call them, apologize and call them by what they prefer.

Chapter 7

It's Never Crowded along the Extra Mile

*A*t one time or another, all of us have had a service person take initiative and show us such exceptional customer care that we couldn't wait to tell our friends and family about it. As customers, we remember the companies that go the extra mile on our behalf or take the extra step to ensure that we are delighted with the service we receive.

The difference between good service (which, in our opinion, is not so easy to find) and "I-can't-believe-I'm-still-on-this-planet" excellent service, is the amount of *initiative* you take. Service initiative is the top-of-the-line, gold brand of service that goes beyond meeting your customers' expectations to exceeding them. It is the service person's willingness and ability to provide customers with something that they will appreciate and don't expect.

I feel that most department stores do a pretty mediocre job of service these days. Having to hunt the clerk down, tie him up, and teach him how to use the cash register is not unusual. So when I get the kind of service I received recently, I am blown away! I was shopping at the local mall where there are two main department stores, one on each end. I went to the first department store and immediately found what I was looking for: the perfect belt, in the perfect color, and, wouldn't you know it, the wrong size! I asked the salesperson if the store had any more stock in the back. She said no and added that this was the last of those belts. Disappointed, I turned to leave. "Wait a minute," she said. "Let me call some of our other stores and see if they have the belt in stock." I thought that was nice of her. She came back a few minutes later and told me she had had no luck locating the belt. I turned to leave again. "Hold on," she said. "Let me call the buying office and see if they can get the belt from the manufacturer." I thought this offer was exceptional. Once again, she came back and said no luck. Finally, I turned to leave, satisfied that this woman had gone beyond the call of duty and done everything she could for me. "Don't leave yet," she said. "I think they carry this line of belts across the mall at the other department store. I'll go over on my lunch hour and see if I can find it for you. I'll call you later to let you know." What? Was I still on planet earth? I felt like I was in the movie *Miracle on 34th Street* where Santa Claus sends the customers from Macy's to Gimble's. While extreme, this example of initiative proved to me that going out of your way for the customer creates a powerful and lasting impression.

Goodwill Initiative

Of course, Karen's belt experience, as described in the preceding anecdote, is a dramatic example of initiative where the service person went way beyond the call of what anyone would have expected. Other, more simple everyday examples of initiative include:

- ✔ the cab driver who gets out of the taxi and goes around to open the door for you
- ✔ the store clerk who offers to let you use the store's phone instead of the pay phone
- ✔ the local computer consultant who calls back a week after he sets up your computer system to make sure everything is working okay
- ✔ the car dealership who calls you one month after you purchase your new car to see if you need anything
- ✔ the hair salon that sends you a greeting card each year on your birthday
- ✔ the restaurant that provides free, valet parking
- ✔ the gas station attendant who washes your windows — even though you are in the self-serve lane
- ✔ the dry cleaner who puts a little tag on your shirt or blouse informing you that she has replaced a button or two as part of the store's complimentary service

All of these examples have one common quality: they reflect initiative that is taken out of pure *goodwill* toward the customer.

The service provider or company is not required to take the action: it is extra, unasked for, and has a pleasing impact on the customer. Unfortunately, this type of goodwill is usually reserved for the holidays when we expect to get free calendars and other giveaways that show a company's appreciation of our patronage. Although this effort is praiseworthy, goodwill initiative has less of an impact at this time of the year because it is more common and therefore more predictable. Goodwill initiative has the most impact when it is unexpected.

Goodwill initiative is only as good as the goodwill with which it is given. Going into your local bank and being thrown a free ball point pen by a grouchy, impolite, and impatient teller just doesn't cut the mustard. Especially when the message on the barrel of the pen reads `The bank that cares.` About what? That's what we want to know.

We were consulting with a company who had conducted a survey with their customers and had received a *good* rating for the quality of service they provided. A short while later, they lost about one-third of their customer base to a new competitor. Confused and concerned as to why they had lost so many customers, they conducted another survey, this time with lost customers, and the response they received was pretty much unanimous:

Your service is good, but your competitor's is excellent.

The lesson they learned was that good customer service is not necessarily enough in a tough market. Goodwill initiative helped the newly arrived competitor elevate their service beyond good to excellent.

Hold a meeting with your staff and brainstorm ways to show goodwill to your customers. Many of the ideas you come up with will be easy to implement, inexpensive, and enjoyable.

Bounce Back Initiative

Goodwill initiative is, by definition, something that you or your company does out of a genuine desire to show appreciation to your customers and enhance their experience of doing business with you. Putting it plainly, however, giving good customer service when everything is going right is easy. The real test of how good your service is, is how you handle things when the going gets tough.

How you handle a problem situation with a customer can make the difference in her decision to use your company again. When you or your company makes a mistake with a customer, bounce back initiative helps you recover any respect, confidence, or faith that has been lost by your actions. Situations that require bouncing back are often the result of simple mistakes or oversights that hurt the customers' perception of your company. For example:

- ✔ The chef cooks your steak well done instead of rare, the way you ordered it.
- ✔ Your car isn't ready by the time the auto shop said it would be.
- ✔ You are assessed a late charge on a bill that you paid on time.
- ✔ You have to wait for over an hour at the doctor's office.

When these types of incidents happen, the service provider should promptly bounce back by taking three specific steps.

Three Steps to Bouncing Back

Imagine it is Monday and a customer is on the phone screaming at you because that special order he was supposed to receive Friday still has not arrived. Simple enough to resolve this problem (you think). You will just send him his order by overnight delivery. He'll get it by Tuesday morning.

Although this action may quickly fix or correct the problem, it does not necessarily get the customer back on your side. He may get the delivery on Tuesday, but what impression will he keep at the back of his mind about the way your company conducts business? A fair assumption would be that the customer would be relieved to get his package on Tuesday but may be a little wary about any delivery promises your company gives in the future. That is why only taking corrective action is insufficient and does not, on its own, demonstrate initiative.

You need to do three things to help the customer feel good about doing business with you in the future:

- ✔ say you are sorry
- ✔ fix the problem
- ✔ give the customer a care token

Say you are sorry

So simple, yet often overlooked. When standing in front of an upset customer, an apology can calm the fires of wrath. Apologize even if you are not the person who made the mistake because a customer relates to you as representing the company that messed up.

Don't be stingy with apologies. Remember that an apology is not an automatic admission of guilt. For example, if you are talking to a sick friend, you most likely say how sorry you are. Both of you know that the illness is not your fault, but you can still be sorry that your friend is having such an unpleasant experience. Apologizing is a way of letting the customer know that you care and want to right the wrong.

 Some staff resist the idea of apologizing to customers because they don't want to make the company look bad by admitting the mistake. This thinking is false logic because customers already believe that you (or the company) blew it. Denials just agitate them more and make them even angrier.

 One of the big sacred cows of customer service is the idea that *the customer is always right.* Well, we don't want to shock anyone, but we disagree. Sometimes the customer is downright wrong. But, really, what difference does it make if the customer is right or wrong? Your job as a service provider is to make customers feel valued and important and to solve their problems. Too many companies spend too much time trying to figure out who is at fault — who cares? The solution ultimately comes down to *fixing the problem,* not assigning the blame.

Fix the problem

This step requires you to listen to the customer's assessment of the problem. She will explain the situation from her perspective, and your job is to fully absorb what she is saying about her unique set of circumstances. Once you identify the customer's problem, the next step, obviously, is to fix it. Sometimes you can easily remedy the situation by changing an invoice, redoing an order, waiving or refunding charges, or replacing a defective product. At other times, fixing the problem is more complex because the damage or mistake cannot simply be repaired. In these instances, mutually acceptable compromises need to be reached. Whatever the problem, this step begins to remedy the situation and gives the customer what she needs to resolve the source of the conflict.

 Don't waste time and effort by putting the cart before the horse and trying to fix the wrong problem. It's easy to jump the gun and think that you know what the customer is about to say because you've heard it all a hundred times before.

Doing so loses you ground on the recovery front and further annoys the customer. More often than not, what you think the problem is at first glance is different than what it becomes upon closer examination.

Give the customer a care token

Many service providers miss the opportunity to score really big points once they have fixed the problem. They need to take one last, but critical, step: giving the customer a care token. A *care token* is a specific action that you take as a way of letting customers know that you consider the mistake you made (whatever it is) unacceptable, that it won't happen again, and that you care about keeping their business. Care tokens say so much, and we are surprised that companies seem so stingy with them. Here are a few examples of care tokens that responsible companies might offer:

- ✔ An airline gives you a $25 certificate off your next flight because they didn't board enough meals and you were unable to eat (for some people, this problem would be a blessing in disguise).

- ✔ A restaurant buys you a glass of wine because you don't like the way they prepared your meal.

- ✔ The garage gives you a loaner car because your car isn't fixed on time.

- ✔ The one-hour photo shop gives you a free role of film when they take longer than an hour to process your holiday snaps.

What the care token costs is not important. It certainly doesn't have to be expensive, but it does have to show, in a tangible way, that you are sorry.

Bounce back initiative is only effective if your basic services are in order and working. Customers find bounce back initiative unacceptable when it replaces competent and expected services.

A new copy shop recently opened near our office. Modern and full of new, streamlined, state-of-the-art copiers, I just couldn't wait to use them. The first time I went over, I waited forty-five minutes to get served because of a shortage of trained staff. They *bounced back* by apologizing, explaining the situation, and giving me a care token coupon that was worth a hundred free copies. Okay, I thought, fair enough, they're new and getting their act together, no big deal. A week later I went back and waited thirty minutes for service. They apologized, explained the situation, and gave me a coupon for a hundred free copies. This time I was a little less understanding. Two weeks later I went back and the same thing happened again. I didn't want another free coupon! They had bounced back just once too often! My opinion of their service was so soured that I began looking for another copy shop.

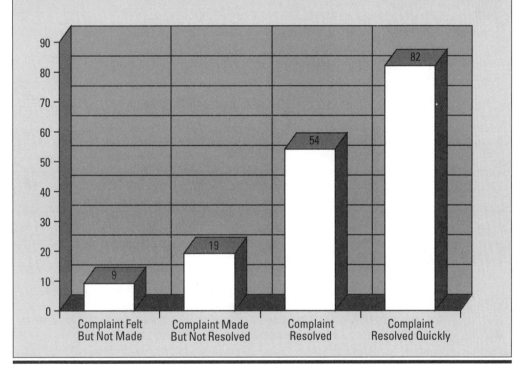

Too many bounces

A well-known study was done by the TARP (Technical Assistance Research Project) Institute, a customer service research and consulting organization, in Arlington, Virginia that revealed the power of handling complaints well and bouncing back. This graph shows (by percentage) how likely customers are to repurchase from your company in the event that they have a complaint.

What have you done for me lately?

Taking initiative is most effective when it adds value to the customer experience by going above and beyond the core services your company provides. Some airlines, for example, think they are giving you great service when they deliver you to your destination in one piece! This service is only the ticket into the game. It is not initiative because it is a fundamental expectation that all customers have about all airlines. Therefore, it is a basic core service.

Core services are not static and they change with time. New innovations and ideas that your company adopts to show initiative today will eventually be copied by your competitors and become so widespread that the customer will begin to consider them to be normal and therefore a core service that no longer separates you from the crowd. Some examples include:

- hairdryers and TV remotes in hotel rooms
- power windows in cars
- frequent buyer or traveler programs
- 800 numbers for catalogs or other mail order products
- ATM machines at supermarkets, gas stations, and so on
- telephones on airplanes

Companies that stay on the cutting edge of customer service are always taking a leadership role by looking for ways to improve their own services, rather than playing catch up with their competitors.

When to Bounce Back

Getting good at recovering from service blunders and breakdowns is about knowing not only how to bounce back but when. While we can't tell you every potential situation where you may need to do bounce back, at least five basic service breakdowns exist where bounce back initiative is critical:

- a deadline is missed
- an order is incorrectly filled
- the customer is treated rudely or unprofessionally
- the customer is given incorrect information
- the customer is unhappy with the product or service

A deadline is missed

When you fail to deliver your goods or services by the expected time, the result is more than likely going to be an upset customer. Situations include:

- being late for appointments with your customer (and not calling)
- giving a specific date or window of time for a service to be delivered and not meeting it
- promising delivery of a product by a certain date and not meeting the deadline
- telling your customer he will be on hold for just a few minutes and returning to the phone 30 minutes later
- telling the customer you will call her back tomorrow and not calling back until the day after tomorrow — if ever

The closer you cancel to the agreed upon deadline time, the more upset your customer will be. The reverse is also true: the farther away from the deadline time you cancel, the less upset your customer will be.

For example, if you call at noon to let your customer know you will be late for your 4:00 p.m. appointment, he will react differently than if you call at 3:59 p.m. to tell him you will be an hour late.

An order is incorrectly filled

When a customer places an order (for a meal in a restaurant, goods from a mail order catalog, and so on) she has a natural and understandable expectation that she is going to get *exactly* what she ordered. If, upon delivery, the customer's expectations are not met, she will be upset for several reasons. First, she has the disappointment of not receiving what she expected. Second, she has the inconvenience of returning the wrong item; and third, she has the wasted time of waiting for the correct order to be redelivered.

The customer is treated rudely or unprofessionally

The root of this situation is poor communication and the customer's negative perception of the way he is treated by one or more service providers. Some typical situations include:

- being put on hold abruptly and with no choice in the matter
- a service provider arguing with a customer
- customer phone calls not being returned
- customer being accused of doing something wrong or lying
- customer being ignored by the service provider

The customer is given incorrect information

Your customer relies on you for accurate information. Even little mistakes can cause the customer big problems. Imagine the following scenario: You receive a letter from the IRS stating that your tax return is inaccurate and inconsistent with their records. They are demanding an explanation with accompanying paperwork. You call your accountant who says he must look into the matter. He calls you back and explains that he made a mistake and accidentally omitted an important document from your return. Without bounce back initiative, your faith in your accountant may diminish to the point of desertion. As customers, we have very little tolerance for inaccuracies from professionals whose sole job it is to eliminate them. This is also true of our internal customers — co-workers expect a consistent level of professionalism and competency from us. If they do not receive it, a weak link is created in the customer chain. Other examples that often require bouncing back are:

- wrong or poor directions on how to reach your place of business
- mistaken invoicing, billing, and so on
- incorrect dates or times for specific events
- incorrect information about company policy or procedure

The customer is unhappy with the product or service

Perception is everything. If, in the customer's mind, she has been wronged by your company, it's up to you to do what you can to fix it. It's not fair and life is tough, but the *reality* of your customer service exists only in your customers' perception of it. If a customer is unhappy with your product or service, bouncing back will work much better than excuses, reasons, and hard-luck stories. (We know that you — like every other business — have limits to what you can do for your customers. For tips on how to say *no* in a customer-oriented way, see Chapter 8.)

MANAGER'S MOMENT

Two types of problems

Two distinct type of service problems require bounce back initiative:

Predictable problems

These problems will happen as long as you are in business and to a large degree can be planned for. For example:

✔ running out of stock

✔ misunderstanding a customer's request

✔ computer or technology breakdowns

Surprise problems

These problems are unique to the situation, the client, and your business. They are not predictable and therefore cannot be planned for. These instances are where the service provider who uses initiative can save the day.

One way you can help to encourage your staff to take bounce back initiative in your department is to meet with your staff to discuss predictable service breakdowns and come up with a plan on how to deal with them.

Ideas for Taking Initiative

The following list shows some key ways that you can go the extra mile with your customer when taking goodwill and bounce back initiative.

Goodwill give aways

Give aways are the free stuff that you give to your customers to show your appreciation for their business. Many companies have done this effectively by creating the club concept. You might belong to the pantyhose club (buy twelve get the thirteenth free); the yogurt club (buy ten get the eleventh free); or the overeater's club (buy one entree get two more free). As a club member, you have a card that is stamped or punched each time you make a purchase.

Bounce back give aways

These give aways usually involve giving away the items, goods, or services (at no charge) that were incorrect or messed up to start with.

Goodwill discounting

When a customer purchases over a certain amount, he or she is offered a discount on the set or list price.

Bounce back discounting

Because of a service failure, the company gives a customer a coupon authorizing a discount (usually anywhere from 10 to 25 percent) on his or her next purchase. This policy also helps ensure that the company will have a repeat customer.

Goodwill absorption of extra costs

When you have a good customer, don't be penny wise and pound foolish. It costs five times more in energy, resources, and money to get a new customer than it does to maintain a current one.

Take care of loyal and regular customers by absorbing extra costs when appropriate. For example, if a customer places an exceptionally large order, you may offer to waive the delivery charge.

Bounce back absorption of extra costs

When mistakes result in inconvenience to the customer, any extra cost involved in putting things right as soon as possible should be absorbed by your company.

For example, the refund check that the customer was promised by Tuesday did not arrive, so you offer to send it by overnight courier at no cost to the customer.

Goodwill personal touch

Personal touch goes a long way in letting the customer know that he or she is valued and appreciated. Making a personal call or writing a personal note says "thank you" to a customer who has just used your services. This gesture also provides customers with your name and a personal contact if they need assistance in the future.

Bounce back personal touch

In this situation, calling works a lot better than writing because it is more immediate and allows faster follow up. Calling a customer after a service breakdown has occurred helps ensure that the problem has been completely resolved to the customer's satisfaction and that no other action is required. This personal touch helps reestablish your company's credibility while confirming your sincere concern about the problem being resolved.

Service Heroism

Every once in a while, if you are lucky, you will have the good fortune to be on the receiving end of this type of service. While the term *service heroism* may evoke notions of an overnight delivery courier pushing through waist-deep snow to deliver a package by 10:30 am, in reality service heroism is often one person going out of his or her way to make the customer's life easier.

Service heroism has a "wow" quality to it. When customers experience it, they say "Wow!"

On one of my many visits to the San Francisco airport, I checked in at the airline club desk. Without realizing it, I left some important documents on the counter top. Later that evening, I was ripping my luggage open looking for the documents. Of course, they were nowhere to be found. So I did what I usually do when I am being resourceful — I called my wife. She calmly informed me that the airline club counter agent who had checked me in had noticed the documents, seen my name on them, looked up my records in the membership files, and called my home number to let somebody know that the documents were safe. The agent also confirmed that she had my correct address and mailed the documents to me so that I received them the next day. Wow!

In order for your staff to take initiative, they must feel confident that they will not be punished if they make a mistake. Don't reprimand them for taking actions that deviate a little from the straight and narrow. The nature of initiative requires that staff may often need to take actions that are not written down in the company policy manual.

Chapter 8

What to Do When You Can't Say *Yes*

● ●

In This Chapter

▶ Reasons for saying *no*

▶ Your customers' six basic needs

▶ Two basic truths about *no*

▶ Saying *no* with service

▶ The sandwich technique

● ●

No! Nein! Non! Nyet!

*N*o matter which language you say it in, customers don't like to hear the word *no*. Regardless of whether you are in England, Germany, France, or Russia, your customers want what they want, when they want it, and how they want it. If they don't get what they want, they are likely to be disappointed, frustrated, or upset.

Imagine how you would feel in any of the following situations:

✔ Your dentist tells you that he has unexpectedly run out of nitrous oxide, and you cannot have the gas you requested for the root canal scheduled for this appointment.

✔ While out with some friends, you offer to pay for dinner. A few minutes after giving the waiter your credit card, he returns with an apologetic facial expression and tells you that your card was declined.

✔ You return from lunch and realize that you left your wallet or purse at the restaurant. You call the restaurant and the host or hostess tells you that nobody has handed anything in.

✔ You arrive late at the airport and after running three miles to the gate, you discover your flight has already departed. The service agent tells you that no other flight is leaving tonight.

Like it or not, you, and every other service person, will from time to time have to say *no* to your customers (whether you want to or not). Many companies tout the belief that service is *giving customers what they want,* and when you can, you should. The problem is that service providers often have this belief so etched in their minds that when they cannot give the customers what they want (in other words they have to say *no*), they feel helpless and often fail to use other techniques that might bring about a satisfactory conclusion to a difficult situation. When it comes to saying *no*, three facts are important to keep in mind:

- Sometimes circumstances force you to say *no*.
- Saying *yes* does not guarantee a happy customer.
- Saying *no* does not mean that you have to end up with an unhappy customer.

Circumstances That Make It Impossible to Say Yes

No business in the world can say *yes* to every customer request and stay in business. Like it or not, circumstances exist that require you to say *no* to your customers. These include the following examples:

- federal regulations
- the law
- company policies and procedures
- out of stock
- just not possible

Federal regulations

Certain rules and regulations may be imposed on your business (depending on the industry you are in) by an outside government agency. For example, if you work in a bank, you would have to say *no* to a customer who wanted to open a business account that paid interest (Federal Regulation Q prohibits banks from paying interest on business accounts).

The law

Companies must comply with federal and state laws. For example, if you are a car rental agent and a customer can't produce his driver's license, you can't rent him a car, even if you know him personally. (A friend of ours is a vice president at a car rental company, and he was unable to rent a car to a friend when she visited from out of town because she had an expired driver's license.)

Company policies and procedures

These are the type of restrictions that are imposed, not because of a legal requirement, but as part of the _company's rules_ regarding how it conducts its business. For example, if you work as a salesperson in a retail store, you may not be able to refund a return item that a customer brings in because she was unable to find the sales receipt.

Out of stock

For whatever reason, the item the customer wants is temporarily unavailable. For example, you work in an ice cream parlor and a customer comes in salivating with excitement as he orders a chocolate fudge, double-malted shake with whipped cream — and you have just sold the very last scoop of chocolate fudge.

Just not possible

Sometimes a customer makes a request that is just not possible to fulfill. For example, you are a hairdresser and one of your clients who has very short hair asks for a style that would require her to grow another three inches of hair while she is sitting in the chair!

Yes is not enough

The belief that saying _yes_ and giving your customers what they want will automatically make a happy customer is an easy trap to fall into. It doesn't always work that way. You can see how this theory works by thinking about your last trip to your local post office. In general, the post office is well-stocked and rarely, if ever, runs out of stamps, money orders, and so on. Almost everyone who goes to the post office leaves having received exactly what he went in to get. If getting what you want is the only criteria, then the post office should be the greatest service provider on the planet. Yet, in our office, we toss a coin to see which one of us has to go. One reason is the guaranteed long line, another is the somber attitude of the clerks, and so on. The point is that we get what we want (that is stamps, packages mailed, and so on), but we do not necessarily end up with that *I can't wait to go back for more* great service feeling!

No isn't necessarily bad

The opposite is also true. You can, as a customer, end up not getting what you want and still feel like you received good customer service. Imagine you are in the ice cream parlor again asking for that chocolate fudge, double-malted shake with whipped cream. The counter person apologizes and tells you that, unfortunately, he is out of chocolate fudge ice cream. However, he does not leave it at that. Instead he invites you to try a sample of their new flavor, Decadent Coco Overload. You try it and swoon! The counter person makes you a Decadent Coco Overload double-malted shake, and adds a big, extra blob of whipped cream. You leave in sugar shock — but happy.

Learning to fulfill other needs

In the preceding ice cream parlor example, the service provider had to say *no* to the customer but knew that when he couldn't give the customer what he wanted, his job was then to fulfill as many of his other needs as possible:

- ✔ By apologizing, he showed empathy towards the customer's disappointment.

- ✔ When he offered the customer a taste of a second type of ice cream, he provided an alternative to the customer's first choice.

- ✔ By putting extra whipped cream on the malt, he provided the customer with a care token as part of bounce back initiative. (Care tokens and bounce back initiative are powerful service tools that are explained in Chapter 7.)

In Chapter 1, we said that the ability to change how we define and think about service is one of the secrets used by excellent service providers. These providers are aware of all the other unspoken requirements that our customers have.

Six Basic Needs

By talking to thousands of customers and service providers over the past few years, we've found that customers seem to carry around a sort of invisible report card in their heads. Every time they do business with you they are, without fully realizing it, scoring you on how well you are doing, not only at giving them what they want, but at fulfilling six basic customer needs. Following is a list of these needs along with scenarios told to us by people in our workshops:

- ✔ friendliness
- ✔ understanding and empathy
- ✔ fairness
- ✔ control
- ✔ options and alternatives
- ✔ information

Friendliness

Friendliness is the most basic of all customer needs, and it is usually associated with being greeted politely and courteously.

Cliff, a San Francisco building contractor, always stops at the same coffee shop for breakfast, even though it is out of his way. He says that the food is good, yet pretty much the same as he can get closer to home. He keeps going back because he loves the way the waiters and waitresses are always friendly and upbeat. They all call him by name and usually have his coffee poured as he is walking in the door. By adding this extra value to Cliff's breakfast eating experience, the coffee shop separates itself from other cafes and competes on more than just the ham and eggs level.

Understanding and empathy

Customers need to feel that their circumstances and feelings are appreciated and understood by the service person without criticism or judgment.

Gayle, vice president of a public relations firm, got an unexpected promotion and had to relocate within two weeks from Charlotte, North Carolina to Atlanta, Georgia. To help her find a new home, she called Peachtree Realty (located, incidentally, in the Peachtree Shopping Center on the corner of Peachtree Road and Peachtree Avenue). Susan, the real estate agent at Peachtree Realty, understanding the time pressure Gayle was under, faxed Gayle a description of the various neighborhoods within 30 minutes of Gayle's new office (including houses for sale and prices). This action made Gayle feel that Susan was able to stand in her shoes and empathize with her situation.

Fairness

The need to be treated fairly is high on most customers' list of needs.

Donna, a telephone receptionist, was waiting in line at the supermarket when a checker opened up the next check-out lane. The person in line behind Donna pushed his cart past hers and made a mad dash to the check-out stand that had just opened. The check-out clerk, to his credit, politely asked the pushy customer to allow those who were in the front of the line to go first. By standing up for what was fair, the clerk impressed everyone (except the pushy customer) and fulfilled Donna's need for being treated fairly as a customer.

Control

Control represents the customers' need to feel as if they have an impact on the way things turn out.

Richard, a software engineer, planned to leave work early one day to meet the cable company at home for a repair. About an hour before he was supposed to leave work, the cable company called him to let him know that they were running about 30 minutes behind. This gesture on the company's part gave Richard control. He was able to reorganize his schedule so that he could stay and finish the project he was working on rather than waiting around at home getting more angry and frustrated with each passing minute, wondering what was going on.

Options and alternatives

Customers need to feel that other avenues are available to getting what they want accomplished.

Rona, a lawyer with a Washington, D. C., law firm, was preparing an important case for a court appearance at the end of the week. As part of her research, she needed a recent report from a large U.S. car manufacturer. When she called the car manufacturer, they informed her that the report had not yet been published. She explained why she needed the report and the urgency of the situation. The car company came up with a solution by sending Rona, via electronic mail, a draft copy of the report.

Information

Customers need to be educated and informed about the products, policies, and procedures they encounter when dealing with your company.

Milton, a human resources director, is a novice tennis player who went to buy his first tennis racquet at a local pro shop. The manager of the store, understanding that Milton needed to be educated about the fine points of buying a tennis racquet, took the time to explain the differences between the many types of strings and such and why prices varied from racquet to racquet.

By the time Milton left the shop, he not only had a tennis racquet he felt good about having purchased, but he also had a better understanding of how a racquet can affect the game.

A popular piece of customer service folklore states that if you give customers what they ask for (just say *yes*), then you will end up with satisfied customers. This folklore is false. Customers *do* ask for what they want, but they usually *don't* ask for the six basic needs outlined in this section. When did you last go into a pizzeria and say, "I'd like one slice of pepperoni pizza, please," and then add, "Could you please be understanding, friendly, and fair?" Customers don't ask for these other needs, but they miss them when they are not provided. To really provide top quality customer service, you need to move beyond the *yes* folklore to fulfill all your customers' needs.

Different Strokes for Different Folks

The needs of your customers not only vary according to their individual personalities but can also change depending on the nature of your business. A trip to Disneyland, for example, is remembered for the *fun* and *safety* of the park and rides. These two service qualities are part of what makes a day with the mouse so enjoyable and memorable. Compare this excursion with a visit to your accountants. In this situation, your needs are more in the realm of *accuracy* and *certainty*. We would be suspicious if our accountant was having fun — when we weren't — and started to laugh uncontrollably during a meeting.

Along with the six basic service qualities we have covered, dozens more exist that are specific to different businesses and occupations. See the sidebar "A multitude of customer needs" for a list of some of the many customer needs we have discovered over the years.

Using the needs listed in this sidebar, check off the top six that you consider the most important to your customers. Ask your staff to do the same. Compare lists and report back to your staff with the results. Then in a brainstorming session with your staff, evaluate how well you think you are doing at fulfilling these needs and how you can improve those that need more attention.

A multitude of customer needs

accessible	dependable	industry leaders	respectful
accurate	discreet	influential	responsible
after sales service	easy to do business with	innovative	responsive
alternatives	easy to locate	interesting	reputation for excellence
attentive	easy to use	intimate	safe
attractive	effective	knowledgeable	serious
authentic	efficient	large in size	sincere
available	elegant	leading-edge technology	skilled
available inventory	empathic	listens	small in size
careful	entertaining	low cost	special
caring	exciting	medium in size	stimulating
cheerful	expensive	moderate in cost	technical support
clean	experienced	modern	timeliness
comfortable	experts	on time	tranquil
committed	extra amenities	personal	trustworthy
competitive	fair	pleasant	understanding
concerned	fast	pleasurable	unique
consistent	flexible	private	up scale
convenient	friendly	professional	warm
cost effective	healthy	quick	well known
courteous	helpful	quiet	well planned environment
creative	homey	relaxing	well stocked
customized	honest	reliable	
dedicated			

Two Ways to Say No

Given that saying *no* is a fact of life and that sooner or later you will have to deliver bad news to the customer, your choice is not whether you say no but how you say it. You can say no in two different ways:

- ✔ the hard *no*
- ✔ the service *no*

The hard no

Nothing turns an uncomfortable *no* situation into a heated argument like a service person who thinks that her job is to be the brick wall that stands between the customer and what he wants. This way of saying *no*, without empathy or any expression of desire to help, is infuriating to the customer. The underlying attitude of the *hard no* is "no way, no how, never in a million years!"

You can always tell you are facing a hard no as a customer when you ask the service person if any other easy solution is available to whatever situation you are dealing with and she says, "No!" Then you ask for a recommendation about what to do next and she says, "I don't know!" Finally, *you* come up with some possible options and she systematically shoots them down, one by one. Get the picture? You are facing a *hard no*!

From observing customers and service providers over the last ten years, we are convinced that a hard no approach takes more time and effort than the service no approach.

How to drive a customer crazy

Nothing drives customers crazier than not getting what they want from a service provider who treats them like an adversary and isn't interested in looking for ways to help the customers resolve their situations. From observing customers and service providers over the last ten years, we are convinced that a *hard no* approach takes more time and effort than the service no approach. Some of the one-liners (said, of course, in a monotone voice) that clearly reflect this "I don't care," *hard no* attitude are:

- That's not our policy.

- That's not my job.
- I'm not allowed to do that.
- I have no idea.

The body language that accompanies these responses can be:

- a blank stare
- head held down
- look-away eyes
- distracted fidgeting

The service no

While giving customers a hard *no* clearly doesn't work, we are not suggesting that you somehow try and make a *no* sound like a *yes*. No technique can accomplish this feat — except lying! We have seen many service providers who, not wanting to confront the situation honestly, tried to keep customers happy by bending the truth. Doing so gives customers the unrealistic expectation that they are going to get what they want and, sooner or later, when they discover that they have been misled, they are even more upset! Manipulating customers into thinking you're saying *yes* when you're really saying *no* is not the answer. Nor is the answer hoping that a *no* will be received with joy and understanding.

The *service no* sandwich

We have used this sandwich technique for years when we have to say no, and it works with most customers — except the one percent who wouldn't change their attitude even if you levitated in front of them! It is called a sandwich technique because the bread (so to speak) is two phrases that are wrapped around a filling of recommended actions. The two phrases are:

• What I will do is . . .

This phrase tells customers that you want to help them, along with the specific actions you will take to get their problem(s) resolved. The alternative actions you offer may not be exactly what the customer wants but will usually help create an acceptable resolution to the problem and reduce the customer's feelings of frustration.

• What you can do is . . .

This second phrase tells customers that they have some control over the outcome of the situation and that you consider them your partners in getting the problem resolved. Possible suggestions for customers may involve recommendations for a temporary fix to the problem or actions that the customer can take in the future to prevent this occurrence from happening again.

Following are two common scenarios where using this technique turned a potentially hard no situation into a service no success.

Situation one: A customer calls into the insurance office where you work, concerned and upset about the monthly bill he just received, which shows no record of last month's payment being made. In addition, he has been charged a late fee. Since the customer says he paid the bill on time, he wants you to waive the late charge immediately.

After sincerely apologizing for the inconvenience this problem has caused him, you whip out your ever-handy service no sandwich technique and say, "*What I can do is* see if we have received the check since your bill was sent. If we have, then I will waive the late fee. If not, I can't remove the late fee today, but *what you can do is* fax me a copy of the canceled check, and as soon as I receive it, I can waive the late fee. "

Situation two: A customer calls the store where you work to order a product that your company sells. You are temporarily out of stock and therefore have to say no. After apologizing to the customer for the inconvenience and empathizing with her disappointment, you say, "*What I can do is* put the item on back order and ship it out to you by two-day mail when it comes in. *What you can do is* give me a credit card number over the phone so that I can complete the paperwork now and ship the product out as soon as it arrives."

The solution is a technique that we teach our clients called the _service no sandwich_. This technique requires no culinary training and helps ensure a successful outcome with a customer who cannot get exactly what he or she wants.

The key to scoring high marks with the customer, whether you say _yes_ or _no_, is always asking yourself the question: "What does _this_ customer _need,_ and how can I provide it to the best of my ability?"

Part III

Six Steps to Service Success: Company Strategies

In this part...

*I*f you are a business owner or manager, stop dead in your tracks, grab a pen and paper, a cup of coffee (regular or decaf), and get ready. Filled with real world suggestions and solutions, this part of the book helps you gain a competitive advantage in your business. You learn how to implement a six-step process containing key actions that will make your company a service star.

You also get real insights into how to replace the corporate gremlins that hamper change with effective methods for building teamwork, morale, and accountability at all levels of your company.

By following the specific exercises and assignments in this part of the book, you are guided in taking a step back and looking at your business as a whole. The exercises help you create a working blueprint of the service improvement process within your company and assist you in creating a foundation upon which your company can grow with distinction.

Chapter 9

Taking Your Company's Pulse: How to Survey Your Customers

*B*efore you invest any time, money, or effort in developing an overall strategy for service improvement, we strongly suggest that you first take steps to understand what your customers want and expect from your company. Then clarify how well you are doing at meeting or exceeding those expectations. Without a doubt, we feel the best way to gather this information is by surveying your customers *and* staff.

An initial survey helps you to identify the starting point for the journey ahead. Think of it as the **You Are Here** sticker that locates you on your future's floor plan. It not only provides you with a pulse on the current state of your service quality but also:

- ✔ enables you to get specific feedback about how satisfied your customers are with the level of service they are receiving

- ✔ gives you a basis for open, nonjudgmental, and constructive discussions about your service weaknesses and strengths

- ✔ provides you with an initial benchmark measurement that you can use to assess your future progress

Some companies have the attitude that surveying is unnecessary or even a waste of time. They believe that they are so close to their customers that they have an innate sense of what their customers' want. Being Californians, we understand this psychic connection to your customer base; however, general assumptions are not a substitute for hard facts. Developing a strategy based on untested (or worse, inaccurate) assumptions is like coming up with a good answer for the wrong question. To avoid this type of situation, it is essential to take your company's pulse before you begin any quality service improvement program.

This we-know-better attitude was exemplified by a company we know that spent thousands of dollars developing a service strategy and then invested several millions more implementing it with 50,000 of their staff, world wide! The problem was they did all this *before* asking their customers what they wanted. About a year later, it became obvious that their strategy, which seemed like a good idea at the time, was way off base. Faced with this reality, they decided to revamp the strategy by asking their customers for feedback. Another few million dollars and several years later, they had a new strategy that fit the customers' criteria as well as their own.

Your Survey Game Plan

A consultant from a market research firm once started his conversation with us about surveys by saying something like:

> . . .and you will probably need a cross-stratification of each diverse population in order to get a statistically significant . . . .

What the heck was he talking about? Our eyes rolled back into our heads and we decided, then and there, that there must be an easier way of understanding the subject of surveys (that did not require holding a Ph.D. in statistics).

So in the hopes of removing some of the mystery, we have created a simple, step-by-step guide to the essential elements you need in order to come up with a game plan for creating and conducting an effective survey.

Keep in mind that your company's game plan will be unique and should be tailored to your own specifications depending on the why, who, and what of the feedback you want. For this reason, *borrowing* a survey developed by another company and using it, without modification, with your customer base would be difficult.

You must answer the following four questions when putting together your survey game plan:

✔ Whom should we survey?

✔ What type of survey should we conduct?

✔ Who should conduct our survey?

✔ What survey method(s) should we use?

Whom Should We Survey?

If you have already decided to survey your customers and are reading this chapter to find out the next step, don't stop there. The importance of surveying customers is obvious to most companies. However, we believe that, in addition to surveying your external customers, a staff survey is also an essential part of the surveying process.

We recommend that you survey your customers and staff simultaneously (or at least not too far apart) because often the issues that come to light in your customer responses will directly correlate to situations described by your staff.

For example, in a survey we conducted for a software company, the majority of customers reported dissatisfaction with the way they were treated when they called into the technical support department. In the corresponding staff survey, several technical support representatives complained that their call times were so closely monitored that they felt pressured to give incomplete answers to the customer so that they could move on to the next caller. By seeing both sides of the problem, the company was able to make some immediate changes for the better.

What Type of Survey Should We Do?

The type of survey that your company chooses depends on your purpose for doing the survey. Are you looking for some insight into why you've lost market share? Are you interested in getting a general idea of how your customers feel about your company? Maybe you have been experiencing high staff turnover and want to get to the bottom of the problem. Following are some of the most basic types of surveys that you may want to consider:

✔ random customer survey

✔ company-wide attitude survey

✔ lost account survey

✔ target account survey

✔ customer exit survey

Random customer survey

This is the tried-and-true, good, old-fashioned, all-around survey that is used by companies who want to measure overall customer satisfaction and highlight any widespread service problems. A random survey involves selecting a percentage of your customers, contacting them by phone, mail, or in person (or a combination of all three), and asking them to evaluate the service they receive from your company. If your company has never done a survey, or has not done one in a long time, a random survey is a good place to start.

In the written customer surveys we have conducted, the response rate is usually between 40 and 60 percent. Remember to take these numbers into account when deciding how many customers you need to survey to in order to get back the number of responses you want.

Company-wide attitude survey

This survey helps you assess three areas critical to forging strong links in the chain that determines the service your customers will receive. They are

- How satisfied are your staff with their jobs?
- Do you have open channels of communication?
- Do employees feel a sense of teamwork throughout your company?

How satisfied are your staff with their jobs?

Nothing can tarnish the service your customers receive faster than coming face to face with an employee who has a resentful attitude about his job or your company.

This attitude can be caused by many things, but we find the most common are:

- not feeling listened to or appreciated
- feeling overwhelmed by an ever-increasing workload
- inadequate job training and/or support
- lack of teamwork between departments
- poor supervisors or managers

Although none of these situations can be corrected overnight, a survey can help highlight common problem areas and put them on the table for discussion.

Do you have open channels of communication?

We've yet to deal with a company that didn't have communication problems. The question is, how serious are those problems? If, for example, your staff feel disenfranchised because they have no formal avenues for giving feedback to upper management, then their frustration will be taken out on customers. A staff survey can help you assess how good a job you are doing at establishing open channels of communication and where room for improvement exists.

Do employees feel a sense of teamwork throughout your company?

Is each person within your company an island unto him or herself? If the coffee pot runs dry, does the last person using it brew another pot? If a customer calls in and reaches the wrong person, is she treated with care and concern or is she transferred randomly into telephone hyperspace? A staff survey can help a great deal in identifying and correcting teamwork deficiencies throughout your company.

This type of survey is almost always implemented through a confidential written questionnaire that is sent out to all staff and managers. If your company has never done a staff survey, or has morale problems such as high turnover, we strongly recommend that you do a company attitude survey.

Lost account survey

This type of survey is excellent if your company wants to know why you have lost a particular customer or group of customers. With this survey, interviews are conducted (usually by telephone or in person) with customers who no longer do business with your company.

Let the lost customer know that you are sorry that he is no longer doing business with you and that you are interested in learning from your mistakes. Understanding the customer's reasons for leaving will help you make improvements for future customers. One of the greatest benefits of this type of survey is that you are often able to discover the specific reason a customer left.

Because you are catching the customer at a critical moment, you may have the opportunity during the interview to use bounce back initiative (see Chapter 7) and save the account.

Depending on your industry, isolating the customer's actual moment of departure is not always easy. This fact can make recovering a customer before it's too late difficult because you may miss your window of opportunity to take timely and effective actions. If you are able to catch the customer in time, we recommend that you do not have the person who was originally involved with the customer contact him or her. To maintain objectivity, have someone who has had no previous contact with the customer conduct the interview.

Target account survey

Rather than doing a random survey of your customer base, you may want to do a more targeted and focused survey of a particular customer group. For example, if 80 to 90 percent of your business comes from ten customers, you may want to create a survey that is specifically targeted to them. The advantage of a targeted survey is that it is limited in scope, precisely focused, and can be specifically designed for a particular group. We recommend this type of survey especially if you want to improve your service to a particular segment of your customer base.

If you have more than one target group and you are asking them all the same questions, one easy way to separate the responses is to print the question-naires on a different shade of paper for each group. High volume customers can be printed on white paper, medium volume on buff paper, small volume on light blue, and so on.

Customer exit survey

These are on-the-spot interviews conducted with customers as they exit from your place of business. For example, you have probably, at one time or another, been stopped by someone with a clipboard in hand as you left the supermarket. He or she probably asked you if you had a moment to answer a few questions about the service you received at the store that day. Customer exit surveys are the cousin of random customer surveys, with one important exception: they catch the customer immediately after he or she has received the service. Doing so provides you with specific, accurate, and immediate feedback while the experience is still fresh in the customer's mind.

We recommend this type of survey if your customers physically visit your place of business to use services or purchase products.

Who Should Conduct Our Survey?

Should you use the services of an outside resource or conduct the survey using in-house talent? That is the question! The answer is not unlike deciding whether or not you should fix your own car.

The main advantages of doing it yourself are that you can save money and learn from the experience. The main disadvantage is that because you are probably not an expert in this area, you may encounter unexpected problems that can cost you additional time and money to fix.

Many companies choose to use an outside resource such as a consulting company or market research firm to conduct their survey because they have the expertise on hand to deliver a top notch product in the most efficient way.

In either case, conducting a survey requires varying amounts of resources (mostly time and money) depending on the scope of your project. You should consider three things when deciding whether you should conduct the survey using in-house talent or whether you should employ the services of an outside agency that specializes in service surveys.

The size and composition of your customer base

If your customer base runs into the thousands and you have various groups (based on buying patterns, geographic location, or industries) that require separate review and analysis, then you should probably consider using an outside company to conduct your survey.

For example, suppose your customer base is made up of three thousand accounts that break down into two distinct groups. One group buys your services or products in small quantities, yet they buy frequently. The second group buys infrequently, but they purchase large amounts when they do. In this case, you may want to ask each group different questions and then compare the responses.

The number of customers you want to survey and the complexity of how you want to divide them up are important factors to consider when deciding who conducts your survey.

The availability of your resources

The major resource issues that need to be determined prior to conducting the survey are:

- Can you afford to pay an outside firm to do the work for you?
- Do you have staff who are qualified to do the job?
- Assuming you do have the staff with the expertise needed to design and conduct the survey, do they have the time to do it?

For most any company that we deal with, the ultimate decision has more to do with time than money.

The openness and honesty of your staff

Another thing to consider when conducting your staff survey is how easy — or difficult — getting honest feedback will be. We find that most employees are reluctant to write down what they really think when they know the results are going to be scrutinized in-house. Even if you insist that they fill out the survey anonymously, they may still worry that you will recognize the color of the ink they used to circle their answers! Issues about confidentiality (and paranoia) can undermine in-house staff surveys even when they are conducted with the best of intentions.

We once conducted a survey for a company who had long ago forgotten to treat their staff like customers. Not surprisingly, the low staff morale was taking its toll on the service customers were receiving. After we mailed out the staff questionnaires, we received several personal phone calls from various staff members who wanted to know if this survey was truly confidential. Could we really be trusted not to leak their identity to their bosses? Because we were an outside consulting company and had no ax to grind, we were able to reassure the staff and get some insightful feedback. This feedback, we are sure, would not have been forthcoming if the company had been collecting the information itself.

If you choose to use an outside consultant, a list of hiring criteria is found in Chapter 23. If you own a small business and can't afford to hire an outside company to conduct your surveys, don't fret! By following the tips and techniques in the rest of this chapter, you can create and conduct a basic survey that will work fine. If you do decide to conduct your own survey, we recommend that you set up a small task team of three or four people who are responsible for designing and implementing the survey.

What Survey Method Should We Use?

Survey methods are simply the different ways that you can use to collect feedback from your customers and staff. The four main methods are:

- ✔ written questionnaires
- ✔ telephone surveys
- ✔ focus groups
- ✔ face-to-face interviews

Written questionnaires

This method involves a one- to four-page document that poses a series of specific questions tailored to the needs of your company and addressing specific concerns of the customer or staff group that you are surveying. The questions asked in the survey are usually phrased in one of three ways:

- yes/no questions
- poor/excellent questions
- degree questions

Yes/No questions

These are *closed-ended questions*, meaning that they are phrased in such a way that they prompt a simple yes or no answer. These questions are most commonly used to gather general information about the respondent. The respondent simply circles or checks the yes or no boxes. Following is an example from a customer survey conducted by an insurance company:

Have you created an estate plan in the last five years?	❏ Yes	❏ No
Do you have children still living at home?	❏ Yes	❏ No
Would you like to be contacted more frequently by your agent?	❏ Yes	❏ No

Because yes/no questions are black and white and offer no shades of gray to choose from, they tend not to yield the type of rich feedback necessary for a survey to be really useful. Therefore, they should only be used to gather basic information and in combination with other styles of questions.

Poor/Excellent questions

These are usually open-ended questions that begin with the words *How* or *What* and are answered either by circling or checking a number or word that best reflects the respondent's opinion. For example:

How would you rate the overall service that you receive from our counter staff?

    ❏ Poor   ❏ Fair   ❏ Good   ❏ Excellent

Or, if numbers are used, the questions might look like this:

> What is your overall evaluation of our billing department? (Circle one)
>
> 1   2   3   4   5   6
>
> (Poor)   (Excellent)

Although not immediately apparent, the more numbers you have in the scale, the more work and tabulation you have to do when processing the responses. Say that you decide to make graphs from the answers you get from your customer questionnaire. If your questionnaire has a rating scale of 1 to 4, then your graph only has to chart four categories. If you have a scale that goes from 1 to 8, then the graph requires twice as many sets of numbers in order to chart eight categories. We recommend that you never have less than four rating categories (numbers or words) or more than eight.

Degree questions

These are open-ended questions that usually start with the words *Did, Does, Do,* or *To what degree.* They usually refer to specific experiences or events and are rated by circling one of four specific words. For example:

> To what degree does our newsletter keep you informed on important trends? (Circle one)
>
> Not at all   To a Small Degree   To a Moderate Degree   To a Large Degree

A variation on this theme are statements that offer a scale of possible answers that range from *Strongly Disagree* to *Strongly Agree.*

The person answering the questionnaire is asked to circle the number or words that best reflects his or her opinion. For example:

> The accounting department provides accurate and timely billing. (Circle one)
>
> Strongly Disagree   Disagree   Agree   Strongly Agree

Or, if numbers are used, it might look like this:

> The salesperson I deal with is very knowledgeable about the product.
> (Circle one)
>
>   1   2   3   4   5   6
>
> (Strongly Disagree)   (Strongly Agree)

If you are using a numbers format and want to avoid middle-of-the-road answers, use an even series of number, such as 1 to 6 rather than an odd series of numbers, such as 1 to 5. By circling a 3 in the odd series, the respondent hasn't indicated a preference of any sort, and his sitting on the fence may not give you the kind of data that you are looking for. By using an even series of numbers, you remove the middle number option, and the respondent has to get off the fence and express a preference in one direction or another.

Don't forget about the shortened version of the full questionnaire, the quick response card. These are the short, one-piece, postage-paid questionnaires that you find included with products you purchase, at your hotel bedside, or sitting between the pepper and salt shakers on restaurant tables. This option is a good one if you can't conduct a full survey or the nature of your business lends itself to this method. Beware however, customers who fill out response cards are at either end of the spectrum — those who are very happy or very unhappy with your service.

Telephone surveys

Sometimes geographic distance, time constraints, or other factors make a telephone survey the ideal way to go. Telephone surveys come in two basic styles:

- ✔ ask and answer
- ✔ discussion

Ask and answer

These surveys follow a pre-designed set of questions that are not meant for improvisation or embellishment. The interviewer, after explaining the type of rating scale she is using, reads each question to the respondent and makes a note of the answers. Because ask and answer telephone surveys are basically written questionnaires that speak, they do not necessarily require an interviewer who has any familiarity with the industry she is surveying. For example, an interviewer who has no knowledge of cars could ask the following question as easily as a seasoned mechanic could: "Using a scale of one to six, where one means poor and six means excellent, please rate the following question: 'How would you rate the courtesy of the service technician who checked in your car?'"

Discussion

These telephone surveys ask more spontaneous and exploratory questions and can only be effectively conducted by an interviewer who has a good understanding of the nature of the business being surveyed. A good interviewer in this situation will pick up on part of an answer and then probe the respondent for more details. This discussion format allows for greater depth and often the discovery of issues that were not identified prior to speaking with the customer. For example:

Interviewer — What was your impression of the service technician who checked in your car?

Customer — He was okay.

Interviewer — Was there something that he could have done better?

Customer — He seemed to be in a bad mood.

Interviewer — Was it something he said?

Customer — Not exactly, it was more the way he said, "Good morning." He sounded kind of gruff, as if he'd just had a fight with his boss.

Focus groups

Focus groups are groups of eight to ten of your customers who come together, at your invitation, to answer service-related questions that are prepared by you and then presented by your moderator. Because of the group dynamic, focus groups usually provide a lot of rich feedback in a relatively short period of time. The average focus group usually lasts between an hour and an hour and a half.

Customers are invited, by letter (usually followed with a confirmation phone call), to participate in a focus group. Breakfast or lunch is often served as a courtesy if meetings take place during the working day. Some companies invite their customers to participate in the evening and serve light refreshments.

The success of any focus group depends largely on the moderator's skill. The moderator can be an external consultant or someone from inside your company. Armed with a few predesigned questions, the moderator's main role is to:

✔ ensure that everyone around the table has an opportunity to speak

✔ keep the group on track

✔ probe for the most in-depth information possible

✔ take detailed notes that will be transcribed later

The initial questions asked by the moderator are usually simple conversation starters such as:

✔ How is the overall level of service of this company?

✔ What is one thing you would like to see this company improve or change?

✔ How is the company's response when you have problems?

Invite 50 percent more customers than you want to attend. Doing so allows for about a one third no-show rate, which is fairly normal. Several different venues are available from which you can choose to hold your focus groups. The three main choices regarding locations and facilities are:

✔ market research facility

✔ hotel meeting room

✔ onsite meeting room

Market research facility

These are facilities that are designed specifically for collecting feedback from small groups of customers. The rooms contain a large meeting table, microphones for recording customer feedback (for later transcription), and often a video camera so that the session can be shown to appropriate in-house groups.

One unique feature of a market research room is the one-way mirror that lets representatives of your company view the focus group inconspicuously as the meeting takes place. Your customers are told ahead of time that they are being observed and that the mirror allows for privacy and a minimum of distraction.

One advantage of a focus group is that seeing and hearing your customers praise and criticize your service, in person, has more impact than just reading comments on a questionnaire.

If you think that you may want to use the focus group videotape for future promotional purposes, be sure that all the attendees sign a video release form. Figure 9-1 is a generic example of a video release form.

Video Release Form (Sample)

(*Your company name*)   Date:

(Focus group date and time)

I hereby give and grant (*your company name*) unlimited right and permission to issue and authorize publicity to use, reproduce, transmit, broadcast, exploit, publicize, and exhibit my name, likenesses, transcriptions, films, and other reproductions thereof in connection with the distribution, exhibition, and exploitation including specifically video, film, sound recordings, and/or still photography by (*your company name or video production company name*) made during the filming of the (*focus group name*) with or without any advertising statements or testimonials made by me which you may, in your discretion, prepare for use in connection therewith, throughout the world, and in perpetuity.

I agree that I will not hold you or your production company or anyone who receives permission from any of you, responsible for any liability resulting from the use of my name, statements, or testimonials.

NAME (sign in ink) _____

NAME (print) _____

ADDRESS _____

CITY _____ STATE _____ ZIP _____

PHONE _____

SOCIAL SECURITY NUMBER _____

Figure 9-1:
A video
release
form.

Hotel meeting room

The same procedures used for the market research facility apply here, except that you won't find any built-in mirrors, and bringing in your own tape recorder is a good idea. In lieu of a recording device, the moderator takes comprehensive notes that will later be transcribed or written up as a report. Using a video camera in this situation is awkward because it cannot be hidden easily and may make customers self-conscious. Only the moderator and customers should be in the room during the focus group because customers tend to open up more slowly and be less frank if they are talking directly to a group of representatives from the company they are being asked to assess.

Many hotels will offer you a meeting room for free or at a reduced rate if you have them cater a breakfast or lunch for your attendees.

Onsite meeting room

This location is the least expensive but also the least desirable in which to hold a focus group. Focus groups can be easily interrupted and participants seem to be less talkative when the focus group is held on the service provider's territory. If you have no other choice but to use a room within your place of business, at the very least make sure that no one interrupts the group and that you use the most private room possible, preferably with a door that can be closed.

We recommend using the focus group as the preliminary method of surveying. Because issues that may have been previously hidden come to light in a focus group, they can then be turned into questions that are incorporated into a written questionnaire, which goes out to a broader group of customers.

Usually you can get a good idea of the main areas to focus on in your questionnaire by conducting two or three focus groups for each group of customers that you are interested in surveying. For example, you may want to divide customers by volume, frequency, geographic location, and so on.

Focus groups with staff

In addition to using the focus group method with customers, focus groups with your staff can be an effective part of your staff survey. These sessions are usually held on-site (unlike customer focus groups) and last about one hour. They usually require an experienced, *outside* facilitator who can listen objectively to the staff comments without getting sidetracked by current hot issues that are not necessarily pertinent to current service issues. Areas that are usually worth exploring in a staff focus group include:

- ✔ Are employees empowered to take initiative with their customers?
- ✔ Are employees rewarded or recognized for providing excellent service?
- ✔ Do supervisors, managers, and senior executives listen and act upon feedback from staff on how to improve service to the customers?

After several staff focus groups, an experienced facilitator should be able to identify the key internal service issues within the company or department.

An experienced, strong facilitator is necessary for staff focus groups because they can easily and quickly get out of hand. The facilitator must be able to let the group vent on hot issues while still having time to address key service questions.

Face-to-face interviews

When you want to get the most anecdotal information from your customers in the most personal format, use the face-to-face interview method. These are one-on-one meetings that are useful when dealing with issues such as:

- ✔ finding out why a customer has stopped doing business with you
- ✔ getting feedback from customers who deal with competing companies
- ✔ approaching senior executives for whom a group setting would be inappropriate

We recommend that you do not use tape recorders or video cameras when you are in a face-to-face meeting. This equipment is far too obtrusive. The only acceptable method of recording your customer's feedback in this type of setting is by taking notes.

Although it takes a little more work and coordination, you get the best survey results by using a combination of different survey methods to poll your customers (and staff). We find that combining focus groups with written questionnaires, combining one-on-one interviews with telephone interviews, or employing any other combination of methods, provides the best mix of general and specific feedback, as well as qualitative and quantitative data.

Communicate the Results

The benefits of gathering feedback can be negated if you do not follow through on the results. Once your company has taken the initiative to actively invite feedback, you must take actions to correct at least some, if not all, of the problem areas highlighted. Doing so is vital.

Going to the effort of gathering the information and then not doing anything about the problems identified is not only a waste of time and money, but can also increase the likelihood that future service improvement efforts will be viewed with skepticism.

For this reason, you must close the loop on the surveys you have conducted by getting back to the people who provided you with the feedback. Doing so benefits your relationship with your staff and the customers because you not only confirm that you heard what they said but that you are making changes accordingly.

After conducting an extensive company attitude survey, one of our clients took the report findings, which were some fifty pages long, and condensed the information into a four-page synopsis that was sent out to every staff member. This action was taken several weeks before the beginning of a large customer service training program was launched. As a result, participants entering the workshops were more aware of current service issues and the reasons for the training program. Forwarding the survey results also helped confirm that employee feedback was being heard and taken seriously by senior management.

One of our clients conducted an extensive external customer survey of their mass merchandising customers. After digesting the survey feedback, they invited those customers who participated in the survey to attend a luncheon. The event was sponsored to thank the customers for their feedback. The luncheon was followed by a meeting, the purpose of which was to present to them the overall survey results and conclusions. Almost all the customers invited attended. As a by-product of conducting the survey and sharing the results — both good and bad — with their customers, our client enhanced their image, prestige, and credibility among the customers who had participated in the survey.

Sample Questionnaires

For your convenience, we have concluded this chapter with some sample customer and staff questionnaires along with a selection of cover letters. You can use these as a guideline for developing your own surveys.

If you are starting from scratch and have never conducted a survey before, you may want to modify the questionnaires we have provided and use them as a basis for getting your own survey underway.

Sample Customer Questionnaire – General Survey (A)

Please circle one rating for each of the following questions.

1. How do you rate the overall service that you receive from us?

    (Poor) 1   2   3   4   5   6 (Excellent)

Comments: _____

_____

_____

_____

(continued)

2. How do you rate our overall systems capabilities?

(Poor) 1   2   3   4   5   6 (Excellent)

Comments: _____

_____

_____

_____

3. How do you rate the overall quality of our sales representative?

(Poor) 1   2   3   4   5   6 (Excellent)

Comments:_____

_____

_____

_____

4. How do you rate the consistency of service among our different offices?

(Poor) 1   2   3   4   5   6 (Excellent)

Comments:_____

_____

_____

_____

5. Generally speaking, does our company:

Check one

a. exceed your expectations   ❏

b. satisfy your expectations   ❏

c. not live up to your expectations   ❏

Comments:_____

_____

_____

_____

(continued)

6. What are your recommendations for improving the quality of service/
   services we offer you?

Comments:_____

_____

_____

_____

7. Given your business and industry, how do we need to change in order
   to continue to be your partner five years from now?

Comments:_____

_____

_____

_____

8. How do you rate our overall computer capabilities?

   (Poor) 1   2   3   4   5   6   (Excellent)

Comments:_____

_____

_____

_____

NAME AND ADDRESS (Optional): _____

_____

_____

Thank you.

Sample Customer Questionnaire – Specific Survey (B)

1. What type of insurance policies do you hold with us? (Please check appropriate boxes.)

Personal Insurance

    ❏ Auto   ❏ Health   ❏ Home Owner's   ❏ Life   ❏ Dwelling/Fire

    ❏ Renter's   ❏ (Other) _____   ❏ (Other) _____

Have you ever made a claim?

    ❏ Yes   ❏ No

Business Insurance

    ❏ Rental Property   ❏ Business   ❏ Trucking   ❏ Farming

    ❏ Employee Benefits   ❏ (Other) _____   ❏ (Other) _____

Have you ever made a claim?

    ❏ Yes   ❏ No

2. How do you rate the speed with which your claims have been settled?

Personal

(Very Slow) 1   2   3   4   5   6   (Very Fast)

Business

(Very Slow) 1   2   3   4   5   6   (Very Fast)

Comments: _____

_____

_____

_____

3. Would you like to be contacted more frequently by your insurance agent?

    ❏ Yes   ❏ No

If "Yes," how often would you like to be contacted?

    ❏ Prior to renewal   ❏ Quarterly   ❏ Semi-annually   ❏ Annually

(continued)

4. How often does your insurance agent review/update your policies to ensure the best coverage for your particular circumstances?

Personal

❏ Never   ❏ Sometimes   ❏ Often

Business

❏ Never   ❏ Sometimes   ❏ Often

5. How would you rate the overall quality of your XYZ insurance agent?

Personal

(Very Slow)   1   2   3   4   5   6   (Very Fast)

Business

(Very Slow)   1   2   3   4   5   6   (Very Fast)

Comments:

_____

_____

_____

6. How do you rate your XYZ insurance representative in the following areas:

Understanding your needs

(Poor)   1   2   3   4   5   6   (Excellent)

Shops for best price

(Poor)   1   2   3   4   5   6   (Excellent)

Notifies of premium increases

(Poor)   1   2   3   4   5   6   (Excellent)

Responsiveness

(Poor)   1   2   3   4   5   6   (Excellent)

Knowledge

(Poor)   1   2   3   4   5   6   (Excellent)

(continued)

Concern

    (Poor) 1   2   3   4   5   6 (Excellent)

Follow up

    (Poor) 1   2   3   4   5   6 (Excellent)

Speed

    (Poor) 1   2   3   4   5   6 (Excellent)

Flexibility

    (Poor) 1   2   3   4   5   6 (Excellent)

(Other) _____

    (Poor) 1   2   3   4   5   6 (Excellent)

7. How do you rate the overall quality of our insurance staff?

    (Poor) 1   2   3   4   5   6 (Excellent)

Comments: _____

_____

_____

_____

8. When compared with our competitors, how do you rate the premiums charged for the insurance services you receive from us?

    (High) 1   2   3   4   5   6 (Low)

Comments: _____

_____

_____

_____

(continued)

9. When compared with our competitors, how do you rate the quality of service you receive from us?

(Poor) 1   2   3   4   5   6 (Excellent)

Comments: _____

_____

_____

_____

10. How do you rate our billing in the following areas:

Accuracy of invoices

    (Poor) 1   2   3   4   5   6   (Excellent)

Speed of billing

    (Poor) 1   2   3   4   5   6   (Excellent)

Invoices easy to understand

    (Poor) 1   2   3   4   5   6   (Excellent)

Timely corrections to invoices

    (Poor) 1   2   3   4   5   6   (Excellent)

Follow up

    (Poor) 1   2   3   4   5   6   (Excellent)

(Other) _____

    (Poor) 1   2   3   4   5   6   (Excellent)

Sample Staff Questionnaire (A)

On a scale of 1 to 4, with 1 being "strongly disagree" and 4 being "strongly agree," please indicate your response by circling the number that most accurately reflects your feelings about the following statements.

(A space is provided after each question for you to write down any examples, suggestions, or comments you have that relate to the question.)

1. The management of our company genuinely believes in the importance of providing an excellent level of service to customers.

       1   2   3   4

Comments: _____

_____

_____

_____

2. My manager sets a good example of satisfying customer needs by his/her actions at work.

       1   2   3   4

Comments: _____

_____

_____

_____

3. When I go out of my way to help a customer, I am usually supported and acknowledged by my manager for doing so.

       1   2   3   4

Comments: _____

_____

_____

_____

(continued)

4. I have been provided with the training, support, and equipment that I need to perform my job effectively.

      1   2   3   4

Comments: _____

_____

_____

_____

5. I understand the policies and procedures of my company and have flexibility to alter them as necessary to get my job done to the best degree.

      1   2   3   4

Comments: _____

_____

_____

_____

6. My manager gives me regular, constructive feedback on both the positive and negative aspects of how I am performing my job.

      1   2   3   4

Comments: _____

_____

_____

_____

7. Our company does a good job of recognizing and rewarding staff for excellence in job performance.

      1   2   3   4

Comments: _____

_____

_____

_____

(continued)

8. My manager supports and encourages us to create teamwork between our department and other departments within the company.

       1   2   3   4

Comments: _____

_____

_____

_____

9. My manager makes a habit of asking me and my co-workers what support we need and/or what suggestions we have to do our jobs with the highest degree of excellence.

       1   2   3   4

Comments: _____

_____

_____

_____

10. In my opinion, our company's strongest points are:

Comments: _____

_____

_____

_____

11. In my opinion, our company's weakest points are:

Comments: _____

_____

_____

_____

Sample Staff Questionnaire (B)

Please rate your manager's ability regarding the following statements (check the appropriate response). Please write any comments you have in the space provided below each question.

Department _____   Region _____

1. Overall, my manager gives me the support and encouragement I need in order to best service my customers/co-workers.

    ❏ Poor   ❏ Fair   ❏ Good   ❏ Excellent

Comments: _____

_____

_____

_____

2. My manager encourages me to view other departments, those to whom our unit provides services and products, as internal customers.

    ❏ Poor   ❏ Fair   ❏ Good   ❏ Excellent

Comments: _____

_____

_____

_____

3. My manager "walks what he/she talks" when it comes to satisfying customer needs.

    ❏ Poor   ❏ Fair   ❏ Good   ❏ Excellent

Comments: _____

_____

_____

_____

(continued)

4. When I go out of my way to help a customer, I am usually supported and acknowledged by my manager for doing so.

❏ Poor   ❏ Fair   ❏ Good   ❏ Excellent

Comments: _____

_____

_____

_____

5. My manager makes me feel that what I do makes an important contribution to the customers' overall level of satisfaction.

❏ Poor   ❏ Fair   ❏ Good   ❏ Excellent

Comments: _____

_____

_____

_____

6. If I express an idea on how services can be improved within our unit, my manager appreciates the idea and is responsive to implementing it if appropriate.

❏ Poor   ❏ Fair   ❏ Good   ❏ Excellent

Comments: _____

_____

_____

_____

7. My manager makes a habit of asking the people in our unit what support they need and/or what obstacles are in the way of our providing excellent service to our customers.

❏ Poor   ❏ Fair   ❏ Good   ❏ Excellent

Comments: _____

_____

_____

_____

(continued)

8. My manager rarely reverses decisions I make without consulting with me first.

❏ Poor   ❏ Fair   ❏ Good   ❏ Excellent

Comments: _____

_____

_____

_____

9. My manager has an open mind when it comes to trying out new ideas and ways of doing things suggested by our unit.

❏ Poor   ❏ Fair   ❏ Good   ❏ Excellent

Comments: _____

_____

_____

_____

10. My manager promotes people based upon merit rather than favoritism.

❏ Poor   ❏ Fair   ❏ Good   ❏ Excellent

Comments: _____

_____

_____

_____

(continued)

11. I understand the policies and procedures in my unit well enough to know how much flexibility I have in altering them in order to provide the best service for a customer.

❏ Poor ❏ Fair ❏ Good ❏ Excellent

Comments: _____

_____

_____

_____

12. I believe that the way I do my job has an effect on the quality of service our external customers receive.

❏ Poor ❏ Fair ❏ Good ❏ Excellent

Comments: _____

_____

_____

_____

Sample Cover Letters

In addition to the sample questionnaires, we have included some sample cover letters to customers and staff inviting them to participate in the surveying process.

These cover letters give you an idea of the flavor and content you may want to include in your own cover letters to your customers and staff. Make sure that you let your customers and staff know how much you appreciate their participation in the survey.

Sample Cover Letter - Customer, Written Questionnaire

October 25, 1995

Dear Customer:

We are committed to serving you, our customer, to the best of our ability. To this end, we have asked an independent consulting company to assess our customer orientation and commitment to the provision of quality service.

Obviously, such a study requires that we measure the perceptions of our customers. We would very much appreciate your taking a few moments to complete the enclosed questionnaire. It is designed for your candid feedback and evaluation of our company's service orientation.

Please return the completed questionnaire in the postage-paid envelope to the following address by Wednesday, November 8, 1995:

Sterling Consulting Group
180 Harbor Drive, Suite 212
Sausalito, CA 94965

Thank you very much for your participation. We look forward to receiving your response.

Sincerely,

Sample Cover Letter - Customer, Focus Group

Dear Customer:

We at (*your company name*) are committed to providing the best service we can to our customers. Part of this commitment is understanding how we can build on those areas where our service is strong and improve in those areas where our service is weak. We also want to identify new services that we can provide to meet your future needs.

It is to this end that I am inviting you to be part of a customer focus group. This group will consist of approximately eight of our valued customers. The entire process will take about ninety minutes and a light breakfast or lunch will be provided.

The details are as follows:

Location:

Time:

Date:

We would very much appreciate your attendance at the focus group. We will be contacting you by phone soon to see if you are available and willing to participate. Should you have any questions, please feel free to contact me at (*your phone number*).

Sincerely,

Sample Cover Letter - Staff, Written Questionnaire/Focus Group

To: Company XYZ Staff
From: Bob Smith, President
Date: November 1, 1995
Re: Survey Questionnaires

Dear Company XYZ Staff Member:

In the near future, we will be conducting a confidential survey for the purpose of getting recommendations on how Company XYZ can improve the level of service we offer to our customers and enhance teamwork within the company. We have hired an outside consulting firm, Company ABC to conduct the survey. Company ABC is a management consulting company specializing in helping companies improve teamwork and customer service.

In addition to these survey questionnaires, Company ABC will be interviewing some of you in focus groups. They will also be interviewing selected customers to get their perception of the service Company XYZ provides.

This questionnaire is confidential, and you will be one of many people asked to fill it out. Please do not write your name on the enclosed survey so that we can maintain your confidentiality. Once you finish filling out the questionnaire, please return it directly to Company ABC in the attached prepaid envelope.

Thank you in advance for taking the time and effort to complete this questionnaire. We look forward to receiving your feedback.

Sincerely,

Bob Smith
President
Company XYZ

enc.:

Chapter 10

Putting the Puzzle Together: Creating an Action Plan

• •

In This Chapter

▶ The importance of overall strategy

▶ Getting your team together

▶ How to create a mission statement

▶ The six key strategy areas

▶ Continuous improvement is the key

• •

*1*n the immortal words of Will Rogers:

> *Even if you are on the right track, you'll get run over if you just sit there.*

Standing face-to-face with the inevitable task of coming up with a plan for improving service can be paralyzing. Many companies know that customer service is important and genuinely want to improve the quality of service they offer. Unfortunately, few realize that doing so requires developing an overall strategy that translates this desire into day-to-day reality.

Think of putting this plan together as akin to doing one of those really big puzzles of New York's Manhattan skyline. At first, you excitedly open the box and dump the contents onto the dining room table. As you begin to work on the puzzle, you are amazed at how easily things fit into place. After a while, though, you hit the hard spots and become frustrated because you just can't find the top of that darn Empire State Building. Eventually you arrange all the pieces perfectly, and the completed puzzle is proudly displayed on your dining room table.

Creating an overall strategy for making your company more service oriented is like doing a puzzle. It takes patience, careful attention to detail, and diligence to get the end result. However, when the strategy is complete, the clarity about where you are going and how you will get there, not to mention your sense of satisfaction, will have been well worth your efforts.

Assemble the Key Players

Now that you have decided to embark on this journey and have done your customer research, you are ready to move forward. The first critical step in putting together a strategy is to assemble the team of key players who will be responsible for writing the strategy and then seeing it implemented throughout the company.

If you haven't done your customer research, stop dead in your tracks, go no farther, turn back the pages of time, or at least the pages of this book, and review Chapter 9. Don't waste your time by moving on to developing a strategy before you *really* know what your customers and staff think.

Who should be on the team?

Because this process will affect your whole company (not just the more obvious customer contact departments such as sales, marketing, and customer service), all areas including accounting, production, and information services should be represented on the team.

Keep in mind that the members of this team will be the people who lead your company through its transformation from in-focused to customer focused. As such, they should have the *authority* to design an overall service strategy and the *power* to implement it.

Occasionally, we have worked with companies where executives have tried to clone themselves by delegating their position on the service improvement team to middle managers within the company. This scenario is especially common in larger companies where the executives consider themselves too busy to sit in yet more meetings.

This procedure almost never works because while these middle managers are often well intentioned, intelligent, capable people, they do not have the political weight or authority to actually implement the plan they have created. Not only does this tactic undermine the implementation process, it also undermines the managers' morale. The managers come up with a great idea and get excited about the possibility of change only to have their hopes dashed when they discover that the very executives who put them on the team form the road-blocks to getting anything done. For this reason, the senior executives of your company should be the ones who spearhead the process and take their place as the key players on the team.

If you are the owner of the company or the president of your organization, show your sincere commitment to quality service by making it a priority to be on the team and show up at every meeting enthusiastic about the process. This kind of top-driven commitment does more than anything else to inspire the rest of your company to get on the service bandwagon.

How big should we be?

If you are a small business, your core team will probably be composed of yourself (assuming you are the owner) and your top two or three people. If you are a manager in a larger company, the team will need to include the top key players within your organization. We have found that having too many people on the team makes it cumbersome to schedule meetings. To make the group as efficient and productive as possible, have no more than eight people on the team.

When does the team meet and for how long?

The single most important factor in the success of your team is consistency. In order to achieve this, the team should meet for two to four hours, every four to six weeks.

Each member must then make attending the meetings a priority. At the beginning of the process, most team members are excited. However, as time goes by, the functions of the members' jobs can start to dampen their enthusiasm as short-term, everyday concerns tug at them for attention. If you are not careful, the meetings can become one more item on a never-ending to do list and the bigger purpose of what you are trying to accomplish will be lost.

Also keep in mind that a key player missing at a meeting can create havoc down the road because any major decisions made will affect the whole company. Think of this process as similar to climbing a mountain. You and your teammates are standing at base camp looking up at the peak you want to reach. You all get attached to one another with ropes and harnesses and off you go, up the mountain. If, half way up the mountain, a team member says, "Sorry, but I changed my mind, I don't want to be here anymore," you have a big problem.

You can help ensure consistent attendance by setting the dates for the next six meetings at the initial gathering. Doing so allows all team members to schedule the meetings well in advance and make plans to attend.

Details make the meeting

One way to help you make your meetings successful is to ensure that all the logistics are taken care of. A meeting that is well planned and free of distractions will go a long way in making things run smoothly and efficiently. A few essential items that you may want to put on your checklist are as follows:

✔ Prior to the meeting, make sure that all members understand that no interruptions, barring emergencies, are acceptable.

✔ Use a well-lit room. There's nothing like a bat cave to squash enthusiasm, dampen discussion, and encourage sleepiness and boredom.

✔ Use a large conference table (round or oval is best) so that all the participants can see each other from wherever they are sitting.

✔ If you use a hotel conference room, make sure the public address system and/or piped-in music is turned off.

✔ If you are meeting over lunch, make sure that all the arrangements for food are taken care of ahead of time. If you choose to bring lunch in, then set time aside for eating because we have found that listening and speaking with a mouth full of food is difficult at best.

Have the supplies on hand that you need including:

✔ water and glasses

✔ pen and paper for each member

✔ two flip charts with markers

✔ roll of masking tape or thumb tacks for displaying flip chart pages on the wall

You may want to consider using an outside facilitator for these meetings. A good facilitator helps keep the meetings on track, provides coaching on how to implement the action items, and acts as the nonpolitical mediator when disagreements arise.

Where do we go from here?

Your team is assembled and you have all agreed on the direction you are heading in. The next three major jobs to accomplish are:

✔ writing a company mission statement

✔ assembling a plan for service improvement

✔ communicating the strategy to your company

Write a Company Mission Statement

A mission statement is a one- to four-paragraph statement that stresses the importance of quality service and spells out your company's basic commitments. It can include:

- ✔ a definition of the business you are in
- ✔ what markets you serve
- ✔ what principles or beliefs you are pledging to adhere to with regards to your customers and employees

Remember, the words *mission statement* mean different things to different people. In your company, it may be called a vision or values. Whatever the name, a mission statement is a declaration of purpose, values, and direction. It is long term, and, by necessity, general in nature. A mission statement has an enduring quality because it is always being fulfilled yet never over and done with.

When did you last see your mission statement?

Corporate mission statements, until recently, were very fashionable and in the rush to keep up with the Dow Jones', companies held off-site retreats, wrote their mission statements, and then … did nothing! Most of these statements ended up in a drawer gathering dust or etched in brass, mounted on an expensive walnut plaque and hung in the company lobby for all to see. In short, their missions were missing in action.

Only by translating the general mission statement into a specific strategy and set of tactics does it become part of the everyday reality of how your company does business.

We find that even among those who enthusiastically applaud mission statements, confusion often exists. If you look into the darkened corners of corporate life, many business people (although they'll rarely admit it) still don't know why mission statements are such a big deal, and most importantly, often don't know how to write one. So if you don't already have a mission statement, here's our crash course on how to write your own.

If you already have a company mission statement, you may want to check to make sure that it addresses your commitment to both customers *and* employees. You may even want to take this idea one step further and spell out your commitment to your shareholders and community.

How to write a mission statement

Over the last ten years, we have facilitated hundreds of companies in writing their mission statements. We have tried to demystify the process by breaking it down into four simple steps:

- ✔ Brainstorm customer comments.
- ✔ Find the basic values and themes.
- ✔ Turn the list into a statement.
- ✔ Don't forget your employees.

Brainstorm customer comments

To begin the process of developing a mission statement, you must imagine that you are sitting in a restaurant two years in the future. At the next table, but out of sight, you overhear a group of people chatting. After a short while, you realize that one of the people speaking is a customer of yours and he is talking about what doing business with your company is like. He does not know that you are at the next table eavesdropping (you know it's wrong, but you can't help yourself). What kinds of things would you *want* to hear him say?

All members of the task team should picture themselves in this situation and write down, on their own individual sheet of paper, the exact comments that they would want to hear. For example:

- ✔ "They are really helpful."
- ✔ "The quality of their work is second to none."
- ✔ "They fixed my problem in no time flat."
- ✔ "The staff are always courteous."

After ten minutes, go around the team and have each member read aloud what he or she wrote down. Have a selected team member, or the facilitator, write each item on the flip charts.

Since the rules of brainstorming apply to this first step, no comments, evaluations, or long discussions should happen at this time. The group should just listen to each person read his or her list and bite their tongues if needed!

Find the basic values and themes

Because several pages of comments will be written on the flip charts, tape the pages up in the front of the room where everyone can see them. Then, as a group, examine all of the comments written on the displayed pages. Look for the common threads by separating out those values, words, and ideas that keep recurring. Some examples of themes would be comments relating to the courtesy of your staff, the top notch design of your product, or the efficiency of your systems.

Begin a new flip chart that lists just the common themes that emerge from the combined lists.

Turn the list into a statement

Once a master list of themes has been created, the next step is to begin molding them into a one- or two-paragraph statement that expresses the company's commitment to quality service.

Have each member of the team write his or her version of the mission statement based on the themes list.

After 15 minutes, go around the team and have each member read aloud what he or she wrote down while a selected team member, or the facilitator, writes each mission statement up on a separate flip chart page. Put the mission statements up on the wall in the front of the room. Your team now has the task of discussing the individual statements, picking the best from each, hashing out any differences of opinion, and slowly developing one mission statement upon which you all agree.

You may find it easier to write this statement if you have a lead-in sentence. Sentences that we have used with clients include:

- ✔ The purpose of XYZ company is . . .
- ✔ The mission of XYZ company is . . .
- ✔ Our commitment to our customers is . . .
- ✔ At XYZ, we are committed to providing our customers with . . .
- ✔ XYZ believes in providing . . .

Don't forget your employees

Remember that a mission statement has two parts, one that spells out your company's commitment to your customers and the other to your staff.

The final part of the process involves repeating the first three steps but changing the focus to your employees. For example, imagine overhearing a group of your staff talking about your company, what would you want to hear them saying? List their comments on a flip chart and go through the same process as before.

Once completed, these two separate statements join to become your company mission statement. Following are some examples.

Sample mission statements

Mission Statement A

Our mission is to conduct a successful enterprise providing service and value to customers while maintaining a profit and return consistent with peak performance levels within our industry and reflecting the risks inherent in our business.

We will deliver superior service to all of our customers, consistently fulfilling our commitments to them by providing:

- friendly, courteous service
- efficient service
- desirable products
- competitive prices

We will take the initiative to help each customer fulfill his or her immediate needs and expectations by our extra effort.

We will accomplish our mission in a manner that develops and maintains our reputation for quality and integrity within our industry and community.

Mission Statement B

Our Purpose

The purpose of XYZ is to provide, by example, the opportunity for ourselves and others to accomplish satisfaction and success through a value system of service, commitment, expansion, quality, and contribution.

Our Values

1. To provide excellent service and value for the money.

2. Trust in each and every person's ability and commitment to do his or her job and support the company.

3. Provide an ongoing opportunity for each individual to continually achieve and expand his or her potential.

4. Place an emphasis on generating satisfaction from quality and integrity throughout the company.

5. The recognition that each and every person's contribution makes a difference toward the achievement of the company's goals and values.

Writing a mission statement always takes longer than you think it will because, in order for every team member to take ownership of the statement, every word needs to be scrutinized and discussed.

Mission Statement C

XYZ believes that we can best serve our clients by investing in two important resources: people and technology. These investments enable us to go beyond the traditional role of our business to create intelligent partnerships.

We commit to an organization that shares the following principles:

- ✔ understanding our clients' businesses and striving to exceed their needs
- ✔ creating a rewarding and enriching environment for our staff
- ✔ providing innovative solutions for business growth
- ✔ expanding our leadership role in the industry
- ✔ approaching our business with enthusiasm and a sense of humor

---

Hold a one- or two-day off-site retreat where the only task before you and your team is to develop the mission statement. By going off-site, you avoid distractions that can get in the way of this important process.

Put Together the Plan

Having conducted a survey and written your mission statement, your management team now has the information and foundation they need to spell out an effective customer service strategy. There are six critical areas which must be included in your strategy:

- top-down commitment
- ongoing feedback
- training
- improving processes
- service standards
- rewards and recognition

Top-down commitment

Without a doubt, the single biggest difference we have seen between companies that are customer focused and those that are not is the degree to which executives and managers *walk what they talk*. In the final analysis, it is not what your team says about service, but the actions that they take that tells the rest of your company what is *really* considered important. Said another way:

Fish stink from the head down.

The attitude of your front-line staff toward customers is a direct reflection of the tone set by your management. The quickest way for your team to hinder a customer service improvement effort is to promote service excellence with their words yet express mediocrity with their actions.

You and your team members must figure out, as part of the overall service plan, what actions you will take to show the rest of the company that you are serious about customer service. Some of the benefits of doing so are:

- setting the tone for the entire service process
- helping to establish credibility with the staff
- providing the momentum required to change the company culture
- inspiring the staff to give their best in support of the service improvement initiative

Talk is cheap. When this vital, up-front commitment is missing, what invariably follows is an endless cycle of blame, increased staff skepticism, and frenzied activity that goes nowhere fast.

The CEO of a financial institution we once worked for appeared in a videotape that was shown to employees to underscore the importance of providing excellent service and taking care of customers. The video was a complete failure and did more to set the company back than to move it forward. The reason for the failure was that the CEO had a long-standing reputation for hurling objects across his office when he was unhappy with his staff. Not surprisingly, any grain of respect that remained for the CEO was dashed by the hypocrisy of his not *walking the talk* when it came to service. The CEO's lack of credibility proved to be a significant roadblock to improving service.

Be a role model

Perhaps one of the most significant jobs your team has to accomplish is to learn to be a model for the service you are trying to create in your company. By jumping in and helping out with customers, modeling the same good service skills you ask your staff to use, and by taking high profile actions that stress the importance of customer service, your team establishes their credibility in deeds as well as words. Following are some examples of actions that managers have taken to show their commitment to quality service:

- ✔ Executives at a well-known communications company take complaint calls in the customer service department once a month and follow up on all complaints until resolved.

- ✔ Executives at a rental car company take a weekly trip riding the bus from the rental location to the terminal to speak with passengers and get their impression of the service offered.

- ✔ The owner of a large building supply company once went to a job site and personally laid carpet to ensure that a rush job was finished on time.

- ✔ A general manager in a transportation company started holding informal lunch gatherings where the employees could ask him questions or make comments and suggestions related to improving the conditions at work and the service offered.

- ✔ A vice president from a consumer credit company was on a plane and talked to a passenger with a complaint regarding a different division of the company. Even though the area did not fall under the VP's area of responsibility, he apologized and took responsibility for seeing that the problem was brought to the attention of the appropriate people and subsequently resolved.

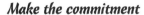

Make the commitment

The biggest resource requirement for this part of the strategy is a substantial commitment of time on the part of the senior management group as well as a willingness to make personal changes in the way they work. Gruff attitudes and curt responses are a luxury that you can no longer afford; they have no place in a truly service-focused environment. Being willing to discover and change your own personal habits (those that are perceived as negative by your staff or customers) will say more to your staff about your commitment to quality service than any amount of memos, e-mails, letters, or videotapes ever could.

Ongoing feedback

Assuming that you have conducted an initial survey, your management team now needs to put a method for gathering ongoing feedback into the service plan. Without a system for regularly measuring your service effectiveness, you really have no way of knowing if you are improving or not.

How often you take your company's pulse depends on the size of your company and customer base:

- ✔ If you are a small business, you should aim for surveying your customer base once or twice a year and your staff once a year.

- ✔ If you are a large company, you may want to survey segments of your customers once a quarter or twice a year and your staff once a year.

Any of the surveying methods described in Chapter 9 can be used for gathering ongoing feedback.

Training

As we mentioned earlier, there is a misconception that training is the panacea that will cure all your corporate ills. Some business owners have the sad belief that if they just train *those people out there* (in other words, their *staff*), the level of service their company offers will improve. It never does.

The enthusiasm generated by participants in a training workshop is fragile and easily extinguished by the environment that they return to. We've seen a lot of companies where the staff have been trained, for example, in empowerment (current business buzz word). They get excited about the concept of being able to make more local decisions themselves and being more flexible and responsive to their customers. Yet as soon as they leave the training and get back to work, they are squelched by a manager or supervisor who is uncomfortable with the idea of giving away a little authority.

Training, while an essential part of service improvement, can do more harm than good when no infrastructure in the workplace is in place that allows your staff to actually practice what they learn.

For specific ideas about how to use training in a positive way, see Chapter 11.

Improving processes

Processes, while obviously indispensable, can help or hurt your customers and staff depending on how they are designed. Some procedures may work favorably for your company but unfavorably for the customer. Usually these procedures were created to protect your company in some way, but because of changing values, technology, work practices, or markets, they have been made obsolete and no one has noticed — except the customers and staff who have to continually do battle with them.

Your strategy must address how you will build a system into your business that lets you periodically evaluate your policies, procedures, and processes. As someone once said:

> *You can take super people, trained and motivated, put them in a lousy system, and the system will win every time.*

In Chapter 12, we go over the specifics of how you can begin a lifetime — yes, a lifetime — of process improvement.

Service standards

Senior executives often ask us how to measure something as seemingly intangible as customer service. The secret is to set specific and measurable standards that specify what behaviors and actions you expect your staff to take with customers in a variety of situations. Your strategy team must decide:

- how standards for service excellence will be developed in your company
- who will develop these standards
- how the standards will be communicated to the staff
- how the standards will be measured and enforced once they're set

For a specific process on how to create and implement standards, see Chapter 13.

Reward and recognition

We've got an old song rattling around in our heads that goes:

You've got to eliminate the negative, accentuate the positive . . .

Countless research studies show that people learn faster and take more initiative when they are given positive reinforcement for doing a job well than when they are given negative feedback for doing something badly. For whatever reason, pouncing on what's wrong always seems easier than recognizing what's right. In short, what gets rewarded is what gets done.

In an effort to improve customer relations in their technical support department, a software company I was working with decided to reward their staff by paying them a bonus based on how many calls they handled per day. At the same time, feedback cards were sent out to customers asking them to rate the technical support person's service. When the results came in, the worst technical support person by far was the one who had received the bonus for the last three months. Clearly, in order to meet the reward criteria, and therefore make the bonus, this person was trying to get the customers off the phone as fast as possible. His call volume was high, but his quality was low. By focusing the reward program on call volume, the company unwittingly encouraged bad service. Soon after, the bonus program was revised to reflect a balance of acceptable call volume *and* positive customer feedback.

Your team must include a strategy for rewarding service excellence if you want it to become part of your company's culture. Rewards can range from a pat on the back to a free vacation depending on the size of your company, the size of the task, and the size of your budget. The point isn't so much the monetary value of the reward as the sincerity and appreciation that goes along with it. For specific ideas on how your team can create an effective reward and recognition program, see Chapter 14.

Please don't throw a "Las Vegas Weekend for Two" or "Employee of the Month Parking Space" at your staff unless they are upholding the values and behaviors of your mission, and you are genuinely appreciative of their commitment. We've seen employees accept a cash reward but still not feel really appreciated, and we've seen a simple *thank you* carry so much appreciation that it would bring a tear to your corporate eye. We feel an anecdote coming on . . . .

On the last day of a week-long coaching session with six, conservative senior-executives, I asked them to pair up and thank the other person for whatever they felt their partner had contributed to them. I also asked them to make eye contact with the other person because doing so helps convey sincerity and interest. They were hesitant but open enough to humor me. As they began to thank each other for their trust, effort, and loyalty, they became teary eyed. Their display of emotion was unexpected, even to them, and during the discussion that followed, they admitted that embarrassment was often what stopped them from recognizing or rewarding people with heartfelt thanks.

It's All or Nothing

Don't fall into the trap of thinking that developing a strategy and taking action in just one of these six essential areas will do the trick — because it won't. We have seen countless companies try to shortcut this process by just *doing training* or putting extra *service blurbs* in the company newsletter. While these are not bad actions to take in themselves, they cannot stand alone. If you are committed to making your company more customer focused, then you are, by default, also committed to changing your company's culture. Doing so requires a willingness to reevaluate, and even redesign, how you do business. No shortcuts are available. If there were, then everyone would be using the same shortcuts, there would be no shortage of good service, and you wouldn't be able to create the service advantage that leaves your competitors eating your dust!

One major airline has developed a system that links all six areas together. Once a quarter, they survey several thousand passengers while they are waiting to retrieve their luggage in baggage claim. The results of the survey are then turned over to task teams whose job it is to look for trends and make service improvements based on the customer feedback. Training courses are then updated to reflect the concerns highlighted in the surveys. The next quarter they start the whole process over again, thus creating a loop between all six essential strategy areas.

Three Critical Questions

Although many companies go through the process of writing strategies for customer service improvement, a surprising amount don't seriously consider the resources (time, money, and effort) that are required to turn a strategy into a reality. Following are the three big questions your team needs to consider as part of finalizing your service improvement plan:

- ✔ How long will this take?
- ✔ Who is going to get all this stuff done?
- ✔ How much is it going to cost?

How long will this take?

Once the plan is formulated, you now have the task of actually implementing the plan. The amount of time it takes to improve customer service within your company depends on the size of your company and how much work you have already done to develop service awareness.

- ✔ A small business (under 250 employees) can probably expect to implement an entire service program (all six areas) within one year and see positive results within the first three months.

- ✔ A middle-size company (250 to 1500 employees) needs closer to two years to implement the entire program but should see noticeable results within the first six months.

- ✔ In a large organization (over 1500 employees), this process takes a minimum of three years to implement, and it will take about one year before any significant results are achieved.

Because becoming more customer focused is a long-term process rather than a short-term, quick fix, we strongly recommend that you let your whole company know that they will not see huge results right away. By giving your staff a realistic timeline of what will happen when, you help them have reasonable expectations and help curb their natural desire to see quick results. In general, you see faster and better results if you focus on the critical few things to get done, rather than the trivial many.

Who is going to get all this stuff done?

By this point, your team may be having nightmares about working twenty plus hours a day to get their regular jobs done as well as taking on all the actions your team is planning. Well, we have good news for you; you don't have to move a cot into your office — not just yet anyway.

Each member of your team is assigned the ultimate responsibility for ensuring that a specific action item is completed. This assignment does not mean that that person is the one who has to carry out the task. On the contrary, he or she is free to delegate selected activities to members of the staff.

How much will it cost?

We have no magic formula to figure out exactly what implementing your company's service improvement will cost. We have met owners of very small businesses who have created entire service improvement programs for $10,000. Then again, we have run across many Fortune 500 companies that have spent millions.

In general, though, a total service improvement strategy — from soup to nuts — will cost you approximately $500 to $750 per employee, sometimes more, sometimes less. Part of your team's challenge is to come up with a budget that is workable for your company *and* is sufficient to get the job done.

There is no free lunch! If your main concern is how to manage this type of strategy on the quick and cheap, then you may want to reconsider how committed you really are to the process. While you can do many things to keep your costs down and under control, this process does require an upfront commitment of time and financial resources.

If you own a small business and find yourself in a cold sweat after reading the previous paragraph, relax. In the following chapters we suggest lots of *lower cost* solutions that you can use to stay within your means and still produce the desired results.

It costs five times more marketing and sales dollars to gain a new customer than it does to retain a current one. Most companies we talk to feel that the money they spent in the short term to improve quality service has actually resulted in long-term savings. If you look close enough, you, too, will probably find that the cost of rework, wasted time, effort, and loss of customer goodwill, as well as actual loss of customers, is far greater than the amount of money you may spend creating a more customer focused company.

Communicate the Strategy

One of the biggest pitfalls we have seen in this process is senior management *forgetting* to communicate the strategy to the rest of the company. By informing your staff about the strategy, you open their eyes to the big picture.

Some suggested methods for communicating your strategy include the following:

- ✔ Hold an all-company meeting.
- ✔ Put a meeting tree in place.
- ✔ Create a corporate video presentation.
- ✔ Use your company newsletter.

Hold an all-company meeting

A fast and easy way to get the message out to your employees is to hold an all-company meeting where the president and/or the senior managers introduce the service strategy. This technique is a great way to get everyone fired up and informed at the same time. This is the preferred method of many small businesses we know since getting everyone together in one place at the same time is usually relatively easy.

This method works great if you already have a company picnic, meeting, or conference scheduled because it provides an excellent opportunity for you to make the event even more special by announcing the service strategy.

Put a meeting tree in place

If you have a fairly large group of employees, you can get the word out quickly by creating the company equivalent of a telephone tree — a *meeting tree*. Your task team begins by meeting with their direct reports, who then meet with their direct reports, who then meet with their direct reports, and so on. Usually within a few days you can cover the whole company.

Be sure to outline the specific content that you want your managers to deliver. Doing so prevents them from interpreting the message to the point where their *creativity* gets too far away from the original point.

Keep meeting tree groups to between five and ten people, have a set agenda that includes time for questions and answers, and keep the meetings to under thirty minutes in length.

Create a corporate video presentation

A corporate video featuring the president of your company (you, perhaps) talking about his or her (your) commitment to customer service can be a very powerful tool to spread the service message. A few important items to keep in mind if you decide to go this route are:

- Hire a professional to shoot and edit the video tape. Nobody likes being subjected to a cheesy, poorly put together video, especially when the tape is talking about the importance of service and quality.

- Make sure that the president of the company has practiced his or her presentation and, if necessary, has received coaching on how to appear lively, sincere, enthusiastic, and interesting on camera. If your president looks like *Dr. Death* on camera, nobody will care about what he or she is saying.

- Keep it short and sweet. Don't try to cover all your company issues in one video. Rather, choose one or two clear messages and stick to them.

Use your company newsletter

If your company already has a widely distributed newsletter in place, you may want to use it to detail the specifics of the service strategy. We recommend you do so *after* you have made a general announcement using one of the previously described methods. Your company newsletter is a good tool for keeping your company updated on an ongoing basis and recording the progress your team is making on implementing the strategy.

Kaizen

Your mind has probably been racing as you read this chapter. If you are like many people, your thoughts have ping-ponged between relief and pride about what your company is doing right and feelings of regret, concern, or guilt about the areas where you fall short.

The Japanese have a word, *kaizen*, that expresses what we think is a good, basic philosophy to keep in mind as you go through this process. Loosely translated it means "small, continuous improvements." If you continue to focus on the little, everyday ways you can improve service, you will find that, over time, your company will be able to face its competitors and its future with confidence.

Remember that the quest for excellent service in your business has to be a way of life. It is a continuing process that is never over and done with.

Chapter 11

You're Never Too Old (or Young) to Learn: Service Training

Ask executives from any company that has achieved consistent improvements in customer service and they will tell you that they could not have done it without putting in place a comprehensive and well-executed training program. A training program not only enhances the service your customers receive but also benefits your company by:

- ✔ increasing teamwork between departments
- ✔ improving the customer service skills of staff
- ✔ helping your managers to understand their role in making service shine

Once you have completed your overall service strategy, training is a natural first step because it reinforces your commitment to service excellence. By bringing training into the picture early, you can comfortably ease your staff into the ideas, concepts, and language of customer service. In creating your training program, you should consider the following:

- ✔ Who should receive training?
- ✔ What types of training do you need?
- ✔ What training methods will work best?
- ✔ How should you prepare your staff for the training program?
- ✔ How will you follow up after the training?

Service is Everyone's Business

A big mistake that we've seen several companies make is training only a small percentage of their staff — usually those who work directly with the customers, such as the customer service department. Doing so is ineffective and dangerous because it promotes the message that customer service is the specific responsibility of a limited group of people. Consider this snippet from a conversation we overheard between a customer and a chemist at a pharmaceutical company:

> *I can't help you, sir, that's not my job. I am a chemist and not involved with service. You should talk to the customer service department.*

Service needs to be a way of life for everyone in your company. As soon as you try to confine it to a single department, it's dead. By providing training to all levels — from your part-time help to the president — you promote the important message that service is everyone's business.

Types of Training

A comprehensive training program includes different types of workshops on a variety of subjects. The types of training you decide to provide depends on the feedback you receive from your staff and customers.

Six core types of training impact the quality of service your company delivers. They are:

- ✔ awareness building
- ✔ customer service skills
- ✔ internal customer service
- ✔ team building
- ✔ problem solving
- ✔ service management

Awareness building (half a day)

This training serves as a basic introduction to customer service and should involve everyone in your company from the top down. This training program is often the first to be conducted because it deals with the general principles of customer service (rather than specific skills), emphasizes the concepts of the internal and external customer, and helps build teamwork between departments.

Customer service skills (one to three days)

This type of training is aimed specifically at staff whose jobs involve frequent contact with customers, either over the telephone or face-to-face. It should be more in-depth than the awareness building program and help front-line staff identify and strengthen the interpersonal and problem solving *skills* they need in order to provide their customers with excellent service.

Your staff will be less likely to open up and talk frankly about important issues if they are sitting in this training session with their manager(s). We recommend that you think about the group dynamic when planning a training session, and be careful not to unwittingly create an uncomfortable situation that may stifle participation.

Technical training

All the customer service skills in the world won't do any good if your staff don't know how to undertake the technical aspects of their jobs. Technical training empowers your staff to do the functional aspects of their jobs, such as:

✔ using the computer

✔ using the phone system

✔ following the correct processes and procedures when helping a customer

We find that many companies have a higher comfort level with *hard* technical training than they do with *soft* interpersonal training. While technical training is important, planning for customer service training must be part of your overall strategy if you want to achieve excellent customer service.

A client of ours spent a few million dollars upgrading their technology. They installed new systems that allowed their customer service reps to locate a customer's goods — anywhere in the world — within nanoseconds. Technologically, they were the leader in their industry, and their customers were impressed with the speedy response time. In spite of this, and much to their bewilderment, they were receiving an excessive number of complaints from customers using their new super-duper system. After conducting several customer focus groups, we found that the cause of the problem had little to do with the new technology and everything to do with the way the customers were being treated. Apparently, the customer service reps had been through technical training on how to work with the new system, but they had received no interpersonal training on good customer service skills.

Internal customer service (one to two days)

Designed for staff who provide services and information to their co-workers in other departments, this type of training focuses on three main issues:

- ✔ helping staff members understand how the *backroom* tasks they perform have an indirect yet critical bearing on the quality of service the paying customer receives
- ✔ identifying who the key internal customers are and clarifying their expectations
- ✔ learning the problem solving and interpersonal skills the staff need to effectively fulfill the expectations of their internal customers

Team building (two to three days)

This type of training helps reinforce the message that customer service is a team sport. Specifically, team building training helps your staff see how they can improve the way they work with each other to provide better service.

For example: Say your customer survey showed a consistent problem with on-time delivery. The root of the problem, you discover, is that the different departments involved in the process don't communicate or relate to one another very well. For whatever reason, they operate in a vacuum, unaware of (and uninterested in) what other departments are doing. You can use team building training to dramatically improve the situation by focusing on the following:

- ✔ how each person's job and department is part of a chain of events, and the chain is only as strong as the weakest link
- ✔ the basic skills necessary for being a team player
- ✔ open and honest feedback and communication between the different departments during and after the training program

You can take three different approaches toward team building training:

- ✔ integrating
- ✔ solving a problem
- ✔ simulating team situations

Integrating

This approach involves integrating the general principles of team building into any existing customer service training.

Solving a problem

Use the training session as a forum for brainstorming and discussing a specific problem. Participants who have a stake in solving a particular problem naturally go through the process of becoming a stronger team.

Simulating team situations

This approach is probably the most effective way to begin team-building training because it highlights and isolates those specific behaviors that foster or hinder teamwork. The training uses a simulated situation. The training group is divided into teams of four or five and then given a prepared scenario (available from training companies) that describes the specific circumstances of their predicament. They are provided with a number of different tasks to perform and the group must come to a consensus on how to complete these. Although the situation is not real, most people become very engrossed in the problem and behave exactly as if they were at work dealing with a real problem. After the exercise, the groups analyze the quality of their answers and how well they listened to and communicated with the other people on their team.

Problem solving (one to three days)

This training provides a foundation for continuous process improvement and should involve everyone in the company from senior management to the front-line staff. The purpose of problem-solving training is to help the attendees understand various models of problem solving, learn specific techniques for analyzing problems, and use a variety of tools for solving problems on the job. For more information about a specific problem-solving process that we recommend, see Chapter 12.

Consider mixing and matching groups of staff in training programs so that different employees from different departments are in the same training class. Employees from different departments and geographic locations then have the opportunity to get to know each other during exercises and breaks. It is wonderful when people who talk to one another over the phone every day, but have never met in person, see each other for the first time at a training class.

Service management (two to five days)

All the managers in your company (including the president and top executives) should attend some type of service management training. This training should focus on the following three areas:

- ✔ improving your managers' awareness of and ability to be a role model for service

- ✔ enhancing your managers' skills and understanding of how to empower and coach staff in providing the best possible service

- ✔ rewarding staff for customer service excellence

We recommend that you use an outside consultant or trainer to lead your service management trainings. An outside specialist is usually perceived as a more credible source of information. He or she has no political ties to your company and is, therefore, freer to challenge the ideas and assumptions of the group without fear of repercussion.

While other types of training such as time management, sales, negotiating skills, and so on aren't basic to customer service, you should consider them a valuable part of enhancing overall excellence within your company and plan to incorporate them into your training curriculum.

Training Methods

Depending on the size of your company and the resources you have available for training, you can take two major paths to implement the types of training you decide to use:

- ✔ classroom training
- ✔ media-based training

Classroom training

Classroom training is conducted in person by a professional trainer. To keep people's attention, the training must be upbeat, highly participative, and include group discussions, team exercises, written exercises, and role playing. The following supplies are recommended when conducting a training:

✔ workbook/materials for each participant

✔ pen or pencil for each participant

✔ note paper for each participant

✔ name tags or name tents for each participant

✔ two flip charts

✔ four black markers and two red markers

✔ podium for the speaker's notes

✔ bar stool or chair for the speaker

✔ water jugs and glasses (optional)

Figure 11-1 provides you with a diagram that you can use as a guideline for setting up your training room.

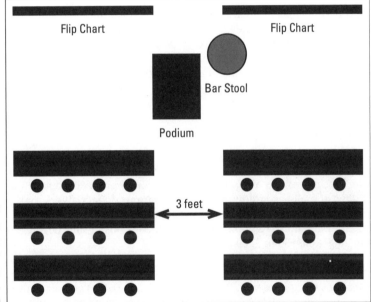

Figure 11-1:
How to set
up your
training
room.

You have two choices for how to conduct classroom training in your company:

✔ in-house programs

✔ public courses

In-house programs

If you want a training program that is customized specifically for your company, your best bet is to develop and conduct your own in-house training program using your human resources or training department. If your company does not have the resources, time, or expertise to offer this type of training, you may want to hire an outside consulting or training firm to do the job for you.

Most established consulting firms work with you to develop and customize a program that fits the specific needs, circumstances, and culture of your company. Once the training is developed, selected members of your staff can go through a train-the-trainer program, conducted by the consulting company, where they will learn both the content of the program and how to effectively present it.

If you go this route, the outside training company will charge you a purchase price for using their training program. In some cases this price will be a flat fee, and in others, the rate will be per participant.

If a train-the-trainer program is not right for you, then you can have the outside firm both develop and deliver the training program. While doing so can become expensive, especially if you have large numbers of staff to train, some companies prefer this route because an outside trainer has an expertise, credibility, and objectivity that can be difficult to find in-house. If you do decide to go with an outside training or consulting company, Chapter 23 offers some advice on the questions to ask customer service consultants before you hire them.

Public courses

If you are a small company and cost is a major consideration, you may want to send your staff to one of the many public customer service seminars that are offered. Universities and public seminar companies send out billions and billions of mailings announcing such programs. In fact, flyers for these seminars probably land on your desk every day and end up in the round file, unread. Public seminars are a good option for smaller businesses because the tuition is a manageable $50 to $100 per person.

Public seminars have two disadvantages. Because they are large (up to 200 attendees compared with the usual 20 in-house), you get very little time to ask your specific questions. Secondly, because they are generic and need to address a diverse audience, the training will not be specifically tailored to your company or industry.

Media-based training

Media-based training does not rely on a trainer's expertise to get the point across. While it is a great way of enhancing classroom training and implementing a follow-up program, we are still not convinced that this type of training works as a main method. The four basic types of media-based training are:

- ✔ video
- ✔ audio
- ✔ books
- ✔ CD-ROMs

Video

We are unimpressed with most of the customer service training videos we have seen. Many of them are overly simplistic, poorly produced, and, the worst crime of all, boring! The result is a tape that doesn't teach, enlighten, or entertain. For this reason, always preview a videotape before you buy it so that you can be sure of what you are getting. Many of the better video programs come with a leader's guide so that you can have a member of your company facilitate the group as they watch the tape.

You have the option of hiring a consulting company to custom design a video training for you. While this is a far more expensive option than buying an off-the-shelf product, the advantage is that you get a highly-customized product that reflects your company's needs and style. A good, customized video-training program can be used for several years and pays for itself over time.

Audio

The scarcity of good, customer service videotapes is made up for by the abundance of very good audio tapes. Many of the tapes on the market are recordings of actual seminars led by business people or consultants who have practical experience in helping companies improve their quality service. Audio tapes are less expensive than videotapes, offer a greater selection of topics, and can easily be listened to on the way to work.

Books

There are some good books available on the topic of customer service, but the selection is limited. The books available fall into two categories:

- ✔ **books written by researchers and academics**

  While these books usually provide a good, solid, theoretical framework on what it means to be customer focused, they are often lacking in real-world, practical, down-to-earth suggestions on what to do and how to do it.

✔ **books full of anecdotal stories and practical tips**

These are written by business people or management consultants who have lots of hands-on experience in customer service. These books are often light on theory but contain lots of useful ideas and examples of how to make your company more customer focused. Both types of books are useful and have their place. If you are looking for additional books on the topic of customer service, we recommend that you peruse your local bookstore and take some time to flip through the various titles available.

CD-ROMs

While the use of this media is not widespread — yet — the day is coming. Several large companies are already utilizing CD-ROM technology to train their staff. CD-ROM programs are usually chock full of information and can contain:

✔ video clips

✔ audio

✔ animated charts and graphics

If the CD-ROM program is well developed, it will be responsive to the learning curve of the individual running the program. For example, if a staff person is moving through a program at a fast rate, the program will automatically take him or her to a more advanced level of content. However, if the staff person at the very next cubicle — running the very same program — is moving at a much slower rate, the program will focus him or her toward the basics.

The clear advantage of this approach is that it allows employees to take training at their own pace, in the comfort of their own work station, and is both cost effective and efficient if you have to train a large number of people in a short period of time — especially if they are in different locations.

At this time, we don't know of any off-the-shelf CD-ROM products that focus on customer service; however new CD-ROM titles are being created every day, so keep your eyes open. Remember that, as with video, you always have the option of hiring an outside company to custom design a CD-ROM program for your company.

Don't let limited resources stop you from training your staff. If you cannot hire an external person and you don't have an inside person to deliver training, use audio tapes, videotapes, and books. Review the tapes or read sections of a book *with* your staff and then discuss how they can apply what they are learning.

Do I Have to Go?

Believe us when we say nothing is worse than standing in front of a roomful of trainees who either think they have been sent to a training program to be "fixed" or, worse yet, have no idea why they are there. Too often managers neglect to prepare their staff for the training they will be attending. Training is a more positive experience and has greater impact when attendees see it as part of the overall service plan — and not just a day spent away from the office. You can prepare your staff for training in two ways.

Send staff a memo regarding the training

Send each person a memo at least two weeks before he or she is scheduled to attend that provides the following information (see Figure 11-2 for an example):

- ✔ the date and time of the program
- ✔ the location of the program, including directions on how to get there, if appropriate
- ✔ the purpose of the program and the main topics to be covered
- ✔ the dress code for the program (business, casual, or black tie!)
- ✔ any preparation required before attending
- ✔ the instructor's name and a brief bio, if appropriate

Some managers make the mistake of sending their staff to training at the last minute with no preparation. After wandering through the hallways, they take a seat in the workshop, apologize for being late, and explain:

> *My manger just told me this morning to show up. I'm not even sure why I'm here.*

Such short notice and obvious lack of preparation undermines the importance of the training program and creates the attitude that the training is an interruption of the staff person's *real job*.

Sample Memo

September 14, 1995

Dear Staff Member:

As an expression of our continued commitment to quality service, Company XYZ is undertaking a comprehensive customer service improvement program beginning in November.

We are pleased to inform you that we will be assisted by ABC Consulting Group, a San Francisco-based consulting firm, who specializes in customer service improvement. Their clients include such well-known companies as Friendly Airlines, Pine Box Productions, and the United States Postal Service.

ABC Consulting Group will be conducting a customer relations course that will help us all provide better customer service. Reducing stress, working with angry customers, and using proper telephone etiquette are among the topics that will be covered.

The workshop you will be attending is scheduled for:

Friday, November 3, 1995
9:00 am to 4:00 pm
Room 2C

Comfortable, casual clothing is recommended.

We are looking forward to working with you in continuing to make Company XYZ an outstanding example of service excellence.

Thank you in advance for your participation.

Bob Cress
President

Figure 11-2:
An example of a memo you may send to staff before training.

Help your staff set training goals

A week or so before your staff go to training, sit down with them and discuss what they want to achieve. Doing so helps them clarify their goals for the training program and provides the basis for a follow-up conversation.

Don't use training as a punishment. Training should never be seen as a vehicle to "fix" a broken employee. This tactic is demeaning to the staff and can create a difficult situation for the trainer. The only effective context for sending an employee to training is a positive one.

Practice Makes Perfect

How many times have you sat through a training program only to have it turn into a distant memory soon afterward? A year later, as you are cleaning out your office, you run across the course workbook that has been sitting on your shelf gathering dust. You think:

> *Oh yeah, I remember when they sent me to that training program . . . what was that about anyway?*

It takes about a month of practice to turn a new skill into a habit. So now that the formal training is over, be sure to go the distance and help your staff put into practice the skills they have learned. By following up and reinforcing the lessons taught in the training program, you reap the greatest rewards for the time, money, and energy you put into training your staff.

Once is not enough. Don't make the mistake of thinking that you can just send your staff to one customer service training class and they will be set for life. Repeated exposure to the ideas and techniques of customer service help make good habits that last a lifetime. Most of our clients do some kind of customer service follow-up training about once a year.

Immediately follow up after training

Meet with any staff member who has just completed a training course within two weeks. During the meetings ask your employees for their feedback on the training. Include the following questions:

- ✔ How did they like the training program?
- ✔ What did they learn?

- Did they achieve their objectives?
- What would they like to see in future training programs?
- How can you support them in practicing what they learned?

Provide on-going coaching

Another way to reinforce what your staff learned in the training is to design a plan for on-going education. People have different ways of learning and what works best for one person may not work well for another.

Find out what types of learning each of your staff prefers. The basic ways people learn are as follows:

- **Hearing about the subject:** going to lectures, listening to audio tapes.
- **Having a direct experience:** role playing, on-the-job practice.
- **Reading about the topic:** books, magazines, manuals.
- **Practical demonstration:** watching an expert or videotape.
- **Talking about the subject:** discussing issues one-on-one or in small groups.

Once you have a grasp on the learning preferences of your individual staff members, co-create a plan with each person for enhancing and reinforcing the concepts and techniques learned in the initial training program.

Thinking that the way *you* learn is the way others learn is a natural tendency. However, this way of thinking is not necessarily true. Make a point of finding out the best way to approach your individual staff members before you conduct any coaching.

Create a training library

Support your staff in self-education by creating a training library. One of our clients did so by emptying a large closet, installing book shelves, and then filling them with audio tapes, video tapes, and books on all kinds of subjects. Some of the usual topics included in a training library are:

- communication
- conflict resolution
- customer service
- dealing with difficult people

✔ giving effective presentations

✔ management skills

✔ managing diversity

✔ negotiation

✔ problem solving

✔ running effective meetings

✔ time management

✔ total quality management

Once you have your inventory in place, the logistics of running the library are easy. Simply set up a sign-in sheet (name, department, title of item, date removed) and put a time limit on how long materials can be checked out (two weeks is standard). The system, once set up, takes very little work to maintain and provides the staff and managers with easy access to a learning resource.

"As a bonus to our customers, we're throwing in a wrist-lock, a neck breaker and a stomp-to-the-groin, free of charge."

Chapter 12

Quality Groups: The Key to Continuous Improvement

*F*lash in the pan service improvement programs are usually the result of short term thinking and ultimately make no real impact on the quality of service your company provides. Excellent customer service never happens overnight. Any company you hold up as a shining example of quality service only got there by paying attention to the details every day, every month, every year.

In many of the companies we have worked with, a good number of the policies and procedures were originally designed for the company's convenience rather than the customer's. Making these processes customer oriented is similar to cleaning out your clothes closet. As you remove the items, one by one, from the closet, you start to discover things that you can't believe you are still holding on to (wide ties, prom dresses, fashion failures, and so on).

Similarly, your company probably has a number of outdated processes, procedures, and policies that are an annoyance to your customers. Many of these may have been hanging around your corporate closet so long that they have become invisible to you. If you suspect they exist and haven't tackled them, it may be because you'd rather not open Pandora's box and take them on.

For your customer service to continually improve and flourish over the long term, you must implement a structure for solving ongoing service problems and making your existing processes and procedures more customer focused. This structure must address two issues:

- ✔ getting your staff involved in the process of change
- ✔ providing a specific method for improving your processes

Quality Groups Kill Two Birds with One Stone

Not a headline in this morning's paper, but the best structure we know for addressing both of the preceding issues. Quality groups provide a step-by-step method for using your staff's talent and knowledge to *permanently* solve service problems. A quality group is made up of a group of staff who are brought together (once a week, for about an hour) to solve a specific service problem; it is disbanded once the problem is solved. The entire process usually takes four to ten weeks, depending on the scope and complexity of the problem.

An auto repair shop decided it wanted to improve its customer service. They discovered, by using a simple, written questionnaire (see Chapter 9) that most of their customers were very happy with the work they performed, but they hated to wait in the small, grimy office until someone in the back garage happened to come in and notice them. The owner set up a small quality group to address the problem. The members of the group came up with a solution that involved painting the office, installing a small coffee maker, and wiring up a buzzer that sounded in the back when the office door was opened. Each day a different person was responsible for replenishing the coffee and a standard was set that required the customer to be attended to within thirty seconds of the buzzer sounding. This simple yet elegant example demonstrates how a small company used a quality group to improve its service.

The Keys to Successful <u>Quality</u> Groups

Those companies that have had the best results with quality groups understand the essential elements necessary to ensure success. They are:

- ✔ a user-friendly process
- ✔ a strong quality-group facilitator
- ✔ support of management
- ✔ start off with the right problem
- ✔ the right mix of staff

A user-friendly process

Quality groups were originally started within manufacturing companies to improve the quality of their products. This environment, not surprisingly, gave birth to a problem solving process that was very heavy on graphs, charts, and statistics.

Many of our clients, being service companies, were not passionate about Pareto charts or histograms (in fact, one staff member thought this term was a surgical procedure), so we went searching for a much simpler and user-friendly process that would better fit the needs of a service business.

We became so disenchanted with how non-user-friendly these processes were that we decided to create our own. What we have outlined for you in the pages to come is a user-friendly twist on the typical quality group process. In our opinion, a quality group process is user-friendly when it has:

- ✔ short and simple steps for identifying, evaluating, and resolving service problems
- ✔ language that is easily understood and not loaded down with tons of jargon
- ✔ problem solving techniques that are based on simple models rather than complex matrices

A strong quality-group facilitator

A quality group is made up of four to eight staff members who are guided through the process by an in-house facilitator. The facilitator should be someone who has strong interpersonal skills and has been trained in the problem solving process your company has decided to use.

Most facilitators are staff members who have attended a special training to learn how to be a group facilitator. Since facilitator duties usually only take about an hour a week, they do not interfere with other job responsibilities.

Training in-house staff to be facilitators gives them an opportunity for professional development and provides you with a group of employees who are experts at problem solving. The facilitator makes the job of the group members easier by:

- ✔ encouraging full participation
- ✔ guiding the team through problem solving methods
- ✔ finding outside resources who can shed light on the problem
- ✔ educating the group members about each step of the process
- ✔ providing a liaison between the quality group and management

If the facilitator has the time and the desire, he or she can work with more than one quality group at a time. For example, if you had two facilitators who were each running two different quality groups, you would have four quality groups working on four different problems. The number of groups a facilitator works with at any one time depends on the size of your company, the availability of the facilitator, and how many pressing service problems you have to solve. In order to prevent burnout, we recommend that a single facilitator work with no more than three different quality groups at one time.

The facilitator does not necessarily have to be familiar with the particular problem the quality group is working on. Sometimes a lack of hands-on involvement can actually help the facilitator stay impartial and objective.

Support of management

When quality groups fail, it is most often because they were not supported by management. We have found the main concerns that managers have about quality groups are:

- ✔ Will I lose control of my department or staff?
- ✔ Will my input on the problem be ignored?
- ✔ What if the quality group comes up with an innovative solution to a problem that I have been trying to solve for years?

In most cases, these fears are unfounded, and, for this reason, we recommend that prior to the first quality group meeting, you meet with every manager whose staff will be participating. Use the meeting to quell management fears by explaining how a quality group works. Topics to cover include the following:

- ✔ An overview of the six-step process, explained later in this chapter.
- ✔ How the manager, although not a member of the group, will be able to address the team from time to time and give his or her input.
- ✔ Ways the manager can support the quality groups, including how the manager will plan for those times when the department is short staffed and he or she cannot afford to let staff attend a scheduled quality group meeting.

The sooner managers are brought into the information loop, the better. Start out on the right foot by inviting the managers to specific quality group meetings so that they can contribute what they know about the problem and, at the same time, start to realize that they have nothing to fear. The first opportunity for inviting a manager to share his or her expertise and knowledge usually comes around the third or fourth meeting when the team is gathering information about the root cause of the problem. Another opportunity to include management is during the team's discussions about a potential solution.

Many managers balk at the idea of involving staff in the process of changing policies or procedures. As one unenlightened vice president put it:

You mean you want me to turn over the asylum to the inmates?

Our experience has consistently been that staff, given guidance and support, will come up with innovative ideas that benefit both the customer and the company.

Start off with the right problem

In most cases, your management team determines which problem a quality group is going to work on. We recommend that you start out the first few quality groups with small problems that are relatively easy to solve. An initial success creates momentum and positive press that you can then use as a springboard for taking on bigger, more complex problems. Try and choose initial problems that are:

- ✔ simple rather than complex
- ✔ local and specific rather than widespread and general
- ✔ free of *heavy* political implications
- ✔ beneficial to both customers and staff

The right mix of staff

The staff members who participate in the quality group must have a hands-on relationship with the problem they are going to solve. When appropriate, including group members from different departments is a good idea. Doing so ensures that the solution the group comes up with addresses how the problem impacts different departments.

Set up your quality group only *after* you have selected the problem. This way you ensure that the members you put on any given team are the right people for the right problem.

The Six-Step Process

Each quality group that you set up in your company will go through the following six-step problem solving process:

- ✔ Step One: Introduce the basics.
- ✔ Step Two: Find the real cause of the problem.
- ✔ Step Three: Brainstorm solutions to the problem.
- ✔ Step Four: Evaluate the possible solutions.
- ✔ Step Five: Develop an implementation plan.
- ✔ Step Six: Present the plan to management.

To make it easy for your company to follow this process, we have created a guide that describes, in detail, what takes place every step of the way. We have also included a special *facilitator's checklist* at the end of each step to provide your facilitator with some valuable tools.

Step One: Introduce the Basics

The first quality group meeting is critical because it introduces the members to an overview of the six steps and gives them the opportunity to ask questions. In addition, the first meeting agenda should:

- ✔ explain the nature of a quality group
- ✔ establish working ground rules
- ✔ confirm dates and locations for future meetings
- ✔ clarify individual responsibilities

Explain the nature of a quality group

One reason your company stays in business is because it successfully and consistently meets deadlines. Most employees understand that decisions at work must be made quickly because time isn't available to do extensive research. Consequently, when it comes to solving service problems, your staff are often forced to come up with a quick fix that satisfies the customer but does not necessarily resolve the root cause of the problem. Doing so would be too complex to deal with casually or quickly.

Everyone knows a problem exists but the culture of *deadline thinking* doesn't give your staff or managers the opportunity, or time, to actually sit down and come up with a thorough and well-thought-out solution that fixes the problem in the long term.

Quality groups are a way of giving your company a short period each week when *deadline thinking* is put on the back burner and *thorough thinking* takes the spotlight. Thorough thinking is different from the everyday work mode because it requires that the group approach problem solving by:

- ✔ sorting out the facts of the situation from the assumptions
- ✔ looking at all the possible solutions — not just the obvious ones

✔ gaining widespread acceptability of the solution rather than imposing it on others

✔ looking at long-term impact as well as short-term gains

Once your staff gets a taste of this way of working, you will find that they take the habits back to work with them and, even when under time pressure, bring a new level of quality to their everyday decisions.

Many companies live by the rule: **There's never enough time to do it right but always enough time to do it over.** Being service focused means taking the time to prevent future problems — not just reacting to current ones.

On more than one occasion the president of a company has said to us: *Quality groups are a good idea but we just can't afford to take the time to do this right now. Our response back is: Can you afford not to take the time?*

Establish ground rules

As a group, you must decide on what specific ground rules — or rules of conduct — you agree to adhere to. On the quality group ground rules worksheet, we have provided you with what most groups consider to be the essential items for running smooth quality groups (see Figure 12-1). Before the first meeting, make copies of the list for each member, and then after a group discussion, delete or add items accordingly.

Confirm dates and locations

Because the meeting day and times are not always fixed and may be different from week to week in order to suit the schedules of group members, make sure that your meeting room is available for all the scheduled dates and double check to see that all members are confirmed for the correct dates and times.

Quality groups typically last between four and ten weeks but may last longer if they are wrestling with a very sticky problem. Once a solution has been found, however, the implementation process is usually fast and efficient because of the planning already done by the team.

Quality Group **Ground Rules Worksheet**

As a group, add any extra ground rules in the spaces at the bottom. Delete those ground rules that you do not agree with.

- Be open and honest.
- Attend every meeting.
- Be punctual.
- Evaluate ideas – not people.
- Stay open – even if you disagree.
- Participate.
- Question.
- Don't complain.
- Listen for the positives, not the negatives.
- Show respect for each individual.
- _____
- _____
- _____
- _____

Figure 12-1: The quality group ground rules worksheet.

Clarify individual responsibilities

Nothing is more annoying than having a meeting slowed down because one or more group members did not do what they were supposed to do. This problem frustrates the other members of the group and hurts the credibility of the person who did not deliver. Each group member is responsible for showing up on time and bringing with him/her the results of any assignment he/she agreed to take on.

Facilitator's checklist

If you are the facilitator of a quality group, this section is especially for you. It contains tips, techniques, and ideas about how to make your quality group meetings a roaring success. Your level of enthusiasm and excitement at this first meeting is especially critical to setting the stage for a great quality group and creating rapport with the team members.

Keep the following things in mind for this session.

Make everyone feel welcome

Once everyone is seated, go around the group and have each person introduce him or herself. If everyone already knows each other, you may want to ask each of them to explain why he or she is in the quality group and what he or she would like to personally gain by participating.

Write the problem on the flip chart

Ask if anyone in the group has any questions about the problem (what it means, is it stated clearly, and so on).

Talk about the importance of teamwork in the quality group

Explain that good teamwork in the quality group is achieved by combining effective interpersonal skills (such as listening, supporting each other, and offering constructive ideas) and creative problem solving (brainstorming, looking for realistic solutions, and not making assumptions).

Answer any questions that members have

Some common questions may include: Are the meetings approved by upper management? Will we be meeting in the same place each week? Will you always be this group's facilitator?

If you do not know the answer to a question, don't make something up

Nobody expects you to have all the answers, and you will develop trust by telling it the way it is. Please don't try to snow the group with your infinite wisdom!

Be sure that the next meeting is set up and ready to go

Since each group member's attendance is key to the success of the quality group, verify that everyone knows the date, time, and location of the next meeting and that all members are able to attend. In addition, check to see that you have a room reserved for the next meeting and all necessary supplies including:

- ✔ a flip chart with markers and masking tape or thumb tacks
- ✔ any blank forms that will be needed
- ✔ a blank minutes sheet for the notetaker

Use the action plan sheet

Any agreed upon actions should be written down on the action plan worksheet and brought to the next meeting (see Figure 12-2).

Arrange the note taker for the next meeting

Before the end of the first meeting, decide who will be the note taker for the next session. Be sure to have that person make a copy of the minutes sheet and bring it along to the next session (see Figure 12-3). Because the note taker will be focusing on recording what is said, he will probably participate less in the discussion than the other members. For this reason, it is important that every member eventually takes his or her turn at this job.

Step Two: Find the Real Cause of the Problem

Unlike the first step, this step usually takes more than one meeting because finding the real cause of any problem involves two things:

- ✔ listing all the possible causes
- ✔ evaluating the various causes

TASK/PROJECT	ASSIGNED TO	DUE DATE	STATUS/REMARKS

Action Plan **Worksheet**

Quality group name: _____ Date: _____ Page: ____ of ____

Figure 12-2:
The action plan worksheet.

Quality Group Name:	Quality Group **Minutes Worksheet**	Quality Group Facilitator:

Number of quality group members in this meeting: _____

Quality group members **not** present:

_____
_____
_____

Guests present:

_____
_____
_____

Activities, actions, and so on:

_____
_____
_____
_____
_____
_____
_____
_____
_____
_____
_____
_____

Notetaker: _____

Figure 12-3:
The quality group minutes worksheet.

Listing all the possible causes of the problem

Determining a problem's causes is a brainstorming activity (see the sidebar "The rules of brainstorming"). During brainstorming, each member of the group says what he or she thinks the possible causes of the problem are. The facilitator lists the causes on a flip chart. When each group member has spoken, and all possible causes have been listed, the group is ready to discuss and evaluate them.

The rules of brainstorming

Brainstorming is a technique designed to get as many different ideas as possible expressed about a specific subject. The focus is not on the *quality* of ideas but on the *quantity*. Ideas are thrown on the table and whatever is said is accepted — regardless of whether other people agree or disagree or the ideas expressed seem silly. In fact, criticism or evaluation is the enemy of brainstorming because it can stop people from thinking creatively and speaking freely.

By giving people free reign to express their ideas, brainstorming taps into less traditional and more innovative ideas. Guidelines for brainstorming include the following:

- Give only one thought at a time.
- Some groups do better to take turns in sequence, others prefer to be more random.
- Don't criticize ideas.
- Don't discuss ideas — except for clarification.
- Build on the ideas of others in your group.
- Record ideas on a flip chart and tape up full pages so that they are visible to everyone in the group.

Evaluating the various causes

Now that all the various causes are laid out on the flip charts, the group can begin to discuss and evaluate them. First, the group should eliminate those causes that they see as having a minor impact on the problem. Once this task has been done, the group must come to a *consensus* decision (see the sidebar "Consensus decision making") on the causes they feel are most significant to the problem. At this point, doing some further investigation and gathering more information on the supposed causes is often necessary. Since this investigation usually happens between meetings, you will likely have several different action items to be carried out by several different people. Use the action plan worksheet shown in Figure 12-2 to keep track of who will do what by when.

Often, when team members are very familiar with a problem, or the problem has been around for a long time, a tendency exists to quickly come up with a solution without stopping to really understand why the problem exists. This inclination is why looking beyond the symptoms of the problem to the root causes is important.

Consensus decision making

In the normal course of work, groups use many different methods to make decisions, including:

- ✔ voting

- ✔ assigning a leader who makes the ultimate decision

- ✔ doing nothing and letting the circumstances decide

- ✔ letting the customer make the decision

In a quality group, however, many of the discussions are aimed at helping the team come to a consensus decision. This type of decision is one that is supported by *all* the members of the team. That is not to say that all group members will be head over heels with the decision, but they will be able to *genuinely* support it. For example:

A group member who has participated actively in the discussion may at some point say, "This option would not be my first choice, and it wasn't what I originally thought we would do, but I can live with the decision." Chances are that this team member will feel that his or her point of view has been heard, and appreciated, and will continue to participate wholeheartedly in future meetings.

On the other hand, consensus decision making is *not* forcing group members to acquiesce by ignoring their opinions or intimidating them. For example, if a group member feels that his concerns have not been listened to, he may say, in frustration, "Okay, go ahead if that's what you've decided to do. I won't get in your way." The tone in his voice and his body language will obviously show that he doesn't really support the decision and is just going along because he feels too frustrated to do anything else. When this situation occurs, chances are that he will begin to participate less and then bring up this unresolved issue in later meetings — much to everyone else's frustration. Without consensus decision making, the quality group will have a hard time moving on to the next steps.

Facilitator's checklist

Since this is the first time your group will be using the brainstorming and consensus decision-making techniques, be sure that you manage the process so that everyone feels that he or she is making a contribution to the group.

Following are some tips to make this step smooth as silk.

Write all brainstorm ideas down on a flip chart

Once you have filled up a page, tear it off and stick it to the wall with masking tape or thumb tacks so that everyone in the room can easily see it. Having all ideas clearly visible to every member helps stimulate creativity.

Ask your group the following questions to help them to cover all the bases

- ✔ What percentage of the problem would be eliminated if this cause was fixed?

- ✔ Is this cause a consistent or intermittent cause of the problem?

- ✔ Are we overlooking a cause that is leading to this cause?

- ✔ Are we making any assumptions about this cause?

- ✔ Do we need any extra information about this cause?

Avoid filling up the whole time period if you reach an ideal stopping point

If you find that you are 15 minutes away from the meeting's scheduled ending time and think that the next discussion will take longer than 15 minutes to complete, feel free to stop at this point. Begin with the tabled topic at the next meeting.

Have the team pick a name for their quality group

Now that your group has had a chance to work together, have them come up with a team name. Doing so helps give them an identity and is a useful tool for publicizing the group's achievement.

Invite potential problem people to attend

The rest of the process will go much easier and smoother if you begin working right away with any difficult personalities within your company who may be roadblocks to change. When appropriate, you may want to invite some of these people into a group meeting as a resource to present information and ideas on the problem. The sooner your team develops a positive partnership with these difficult personalities the better.

Set your team up to do interviews as needed

Throughout this process, group members will be interviewing other people who work within the company to obtain specific information that relates to the problem. An interview will be more successful if you do the following:

- ✔ Choose a time when your interviewee won't be rushed.

- ✔ Let him or her know what you want to talk about and how long it will take.

- ✔ Get permission from the interviewee's manager if necessary.

- ✔ Develop a list of specific questions to ask during the interview.

- ✔ Focus on what the interviewee is saying rather than expressing your own opinions.

✔ Make notes on what is said so you can remember it later.

✔ At the end of the interview, thank the interviewee for his or her time.

Step Three: Brainstorm Solutions to the Problem

Now that your team has identified the major causes of the problem, they are ready to begin brainstorming possible solutions.

Get ready to brainstorm

Because you have already done the ground work to identify the real causes of the problem, the group will take less time and come up with fewer possibilities (probably four or five) during this session.

Facilitator's checklist

At this point, your team is in the middle of the quality group process. The potential danger here is that team members will become embroiled in their different points of view about the *right* way to solve the problem.

Following are some things that you can do as a facilitator to make this step productive.

Be aware of any change in a group member's behavior

Pay attention to any member who is usually very active in the group and suddenly begins to behave in an uncharacteristically quiet manner. This behavior may mean that he/she feels as if his/her ideas or opinions are not being listened to.

Be sensitive to the fact that some group members may be overwhelmed

In this part of the process, you are dealing with large amounts of information and some members may begin to feel buried in details and want to either throw in the towel or go along with the team members who are the most persistent and forceful. Show your sensitivity to this situation by explaining that feeling overwhelmed is not uncommon; the group will soon be out of the woods.

Use a variety of techniques to encourage full group participation

Part of your job as facilitator is to ensure that everyone participates. You can use several techniques to accomplish this goal such as:

Ask group questions

These questions allow everyone to participate and are a good way of beginning a brainstorming session. In general, open-ended questions (questions that begin with *what, where, when,* and *why*) work best for brainstorming. For example, you might ask the whole group, "What do you think are some of the main causes of this problem?"

Ask an individual a question

These questions help involve those group members who are not yet participating because they may be more quiet or a little bit shy. For example, you might say "Jose, how do you feel about this option?"

Gather specific information

If a member is presenting information that is too general, use closed-ended questions (questions that begin with *did, does, do,* and *can*) to get more specific information from them. For example, "Can you be more specific?" or "Do you have an example?"

Acknowledge what group members say

It is important that the group member speaking knows that you understand and are interested in what he/she is saying and know that his/her comments are important. For example, nod your head, lean forward, and say, "I see," "Okay," "Yes," or "Uh-huh" to encourage the person to continue.

Practice active listening

This technique is also called *paraphrasing.* You repeat back the main points of what a group member has said to you. For example, if a team member feels the only solution to the problem is buying a new computer system, you would say back to him, "Let me see if I understand. You don't think updating the old computer system will fix the problem. You feel we need to invest in a new one. Is that correct?" This technique clarifies what the person has said and lets him know that you have heard and understood him.

Remain silent

Often, you will not want to speak or initiate conversation. Your not speaking allows the team to think about the topic on the table. This time to think is especially important when you start a brainstorming session because people usually need a minute or two to gather their thoughts.

Sustain Participation

If you find a lull in the conversation, asking the question, "What else?" helps stimulate the group to take a deeper look at the issue before them. It keeps the discussion going when you know that there is more to be said.

Conclude

When the group has nothing more to say and you feel that all the feedback has been given, wrap up the discussion by using the phrase, "Anything else?" Doing so lets group members know that this is the last call for feedback on this part of the discussion.

Step Four: Evaluate the Possible Solutions

Some of the solutions the team comes up with will be better than others and must be evaluated for how feasible they will be to implement. This step helps you eliminate those solutions which look good on paper but won't work in reality. The solution evaluation worksheet (see Figure 12-4) will help the group evaluate each possible solution against important criteria. Review the form and add anything which your group feels is critical.

Find the most viable solution

As each box in the form is filled in, the group should stop and discuss any pertinent issues. If it is determined that more information is needed, be sure that enough time is allowed between meetings to gather the information. When each solution has been fully evaluated, the ratings are totaled and the solution with the highest score is the winner — and usually the all around best solution.

Facilitator's checklist

At last your group is ready to talk about solutions. In order to avoid getting slowed down by personality conflicts and different points of view, keep the group moving toward consensus decision making and use the following strategies:

Respect differences of opinion in the group

You can count on different degrees of agreement and enthusiasm from the group members as you go through this step. For example, those members that are detail oriented may want to dwell on certain issues until they are completely satisfied that every facet has been examined. Others who see a bigger

Solution Evaluation Worksheet							
POTENTIAL SOLUTION	Can team implement?	Short-term impact	Long-term impact	Relatively low cost	Resources readily available	Management commitment level	TOTAL

Rate each of the above criteria on a scale of 1 through 5.
1 = low or unlikely
5 = high or likely

Figure 12-4:
The solution evaluation worksheet.

picture won't want to dwell on details that they find "boring and insignificant." These two different perspectives can create a synergy where the whole is greater than the sum of its parts. Remember that your job as the facilitator is to respect each person's point of view, ask questions that reveal assumptions, and help your group move forward.

Recognize each team member's unique contribution

The people in your quality group each bring unique strengths and talents to the table. Some members may have a natural inclination toward working with numbers, others are better at interviewing, and still others may excel at creating charts, graphs, and diagrams. The success of your team depends largely upon each member appreciating what the others bring to the party.

Don't rush this step

Your quality group will probably be very enthusiastic about this part of the process. Don't let their enthusiasm stop them from being thorough. You don't want to get caught with your pants down around your ankles in the management presentation.

Step Five: Develop an Implementation Plan

The quality group is finally ready to organize its plan for implementing the chosen solution.

Fill out the checklists

Between meetings, each group member should individually fill out the *predetermined* as well as the *blank* implementation checklist worksheets as shown in Figures 12-5 and 12-6. Once this assignment is complete, the group meets to discuss the results, resolve any issues that arise from disagreement, and begins to develop a master plan for implementing the solution.

Facilitator's checklist

You are into the home stretch of the process. At this point, you want to make sure that the momentum the group has gained keeps going.

Keep the following tips in mind.

Use the blank checklist form to customize your action plan

In addition to the eighteen general action items listed in Figure 12-5, your group may want to use the blank checklist (Figure 12-6) to add their own list of action items that are specific to your quality group.

Use the implementation checklists for review

By the time your group gets to this step, many of the items on the checklists will have been discussed, documented, or even completed. In this case, you can use the checklists as a review of the items already accomplished and to highlight those items that still need work.

Resist the group's urge to move too quickly

Because the end is now in sight, the group may feel like they want to hurry up and get to the finish line. While this urge is natural, you want to avoid overlooking any issues that could potentially damage the viability of the solution.

Run the plan by the necessary people

Because some individuals and departments will be affected by the changes, getting their feedback on the proposed plan is important. Assign group members the responsibility of talking to these people so that their input is included in the final plan.

Write the plan

Choose a member of the group who will be responsible for writing up the plan. Make sure the plan is thorough, neat, and clear because it will be the foundation of the next and most exciting part of the process — the management presentation.

Step Six: Present the Plan to Management

Effectively presenting the findings and recommendations of the quality group is, in some ways, the moment of truth. It is where all the hard work that has been done over the past weeks comes to fruition.

Successful execution of this step involves three things:

- ✔ preparation
- ✔ rehearsal
- ✔ showtime!

Implementation Checklist Worksheet

ACTION STEP	COMPLETED	PARTIALLY COMPLETED	NOT COMPLETED	WHAT FURTHER ACTION IS NEEDED?
1. Identify which departments will be **directly** affected by the proposed solution.				
2. Identify which departments will be **indirectly** affected by the proposed solution.				
3. Get feedback and input from those affected by the solution.				
4. Review the solution from the perspective of those affected.				
5. Will the solution mean changes in methods or workloads? If so, make a plan for overcoming possible resistance.				
6. Anticipate any further sources of resistance and make plans to overcome it.				
7. Plan actions to overcome any negative consequences of solutions.				
8. If solution involves changes in systems, procedures, and so on, plan education/training.				
9. Will solution change the way results are measured or reported?				
10. Ensure that the management presentation clearly spells out your actions for change as well as the results of your analysis.				

Figure 12-5: The implementation checklist worksheet.

| (continued) | | | | Implementation Checklist **Worksheet** |

ACTION STEP	COMPLETED	PARTIALLY COMPLETED	NOT COMPLETED	WHAT FURTHER ACTION IS NEEDED?
11. If the solution means a decrease in production during implementation, inform the appropriate supervisors/managers and get approval.				
12. List all the possible positive and negative consequences of the proposed solution.				
13. Ensure that all physical conditions have been taken into account in the implementation plan (for example, that there is room for ten people to work in one office).				
14. List the resources necessary to implement the solution.				
15. Ensure that managers understand changes in procedures, and so on, before starting implementation.				
16. Ensure that the implementation plan has specific milestones for completion.				
17. Set up critical dates on which you will discuss the progress of implementation with key managers.				
18. Make sure that the proposed changes involved in the solution do not conflict with other major changes occurring in the work area.				

Figure 12-5:
The implementation checklist worksheet continued.

Implementation Checklist **Worksheet**

ACTION STEP	COMPLETED	PARTIALLY COMPLETED	NOT COMPLETED	WHAT FURTHER ACTION IS NEEDED?

Figure 12-6:
The implemen-
tation
checklist
worksheet.

Preparation

The more well-organized and prepared the quality group is, the more confident they will be when the presentation rolls around. Prepare for the meeting by doing the following:

- Decide who will make the presentation.
- Determine what materials and equipment are needed.
- Invite the appropriate managers to attend.
- Prepare the structure of the presentation.

Decide who will make the presentation

Before the quality group begins planning the structure of the presentation, they should decide who will make the presentation. You may want to consider some of the following ideas:

- Have different quality group members present different parts of the presentation, depending on their expertise or depth of involvement in a particular area.

- Have two members of the group give a brief talk on the benefits that they personally received from being involved in the quality group.

- Have all the team members attend the presentation. To miss it would be to miss the grand finale.

- If all the team members cannot attend, they should be directly involved with some aspect of preparing the presentation.

Determine what materials and equipment are needed

Does the team have all of the graphs, charts, overheads, handouts, and so on that they need to make the presentation? Is any special audiovisual equipment needed such as an overhead projector, VCR, computer, television, and so on? Make sure that you have all of the research, evidence, and analysis needed to back up the team's proposals.

Invite the appropriate managers to attend

The key audience members are those managers directly involved in approving the quality group's recommended solution. Send out a memo letting the managers know the location, date, and time of the presentation and reconfirm attendance the day before.

Prepare the structure of the presentation

The presentation should take no longer than an hour. The group should prepare the presentation (including who will present what) using the following guidelines:

- ✔ introduction of the quality group and the problem worked on
- ✔ how long the quality group took to come to resolution on the problem
- ✔ description of the key causes leading to the problem
- ✔ general direction taken and methods used for arriving at the solution
- ✔ explanation of the proposed solution and its expected impact
- ✔ description of how the effectiveness of the solution will be measured
- ✔ thank the people who contributed information and assistance but were not on the team

Rehearsal

Preparation and practice are the secrets to making the management presentation a success. In order for members to feel comfortable and confident about the information they are presenting, they should do the following:

- ✔ Rehearse the complete presentation at least twice, using all visual aids (charts, graphs, diagrams, and so on) that will be used during the official presentation.
- ✔ Keep track of rehearsal times so that the presentation takes no longer than planned. If it does, then look for ways to shorten it without destroying the integrity of the presentation.
- ✔ Do at least one of the rehearsals in front of a small, *pretend* audience, such as a group of supportive co-workers. When finished, ask for their constructive feedback.
- ✔ Videotape the rehearsal and review the tapes to get further pointers on where the presentation can be polished and tightened.

Showtime!

The curtain is up! The big moment has arrived. The team members are both excited and nervous at the same time. If the preparation and rehearsals have been thorough, then the presentation should go relatively easy. The challenge before the team now is to deliver the information in a way that keeps the audience interested and engaged. The following presentation style tips can make a big difference in the way the management team responds to the presentation:

✔ **Stand with your weight evenly distributed on both feet.**

Shifting from foot to foot is taken as a sign of nervousness and lack of confidence in what you are saying.

✔ **Stand in the middle of the front of the room.**

Don't hide out by the flip charts or hug the blackboard for safety. Only go to the flip chart when writing or referring to information on it.

✔ **Move your upper body to different sections of the group.**

Avoid locking your body and head in one position. You don't want to look like a deer caught in the headlights of a car. Instead, turn your body toward different sections of the room from time to time.

✔ **During a long part of the presentation where you are talking a lot, move about.**

Taking deliberate and relaxed steps shows that you are confident about what you are saying. Do not nervously rock back and forth.

✔ **Make eye contact and look at individual's faces.**

Avoid scanning the room and grazing over the heads of your audience. Making direct eye contact with individuals helps create rapport.

✔ **Use your arms and hands naturally.**

Use hand and arm gestures that are deliberate and not distracting. Avoid nervously fidgeting with your hair, face, or objects in your (or anyone else's) pocket. Don't become a stick figure and lock your arms at your sides for the entire presentation. Studying a videotape of a practice run-through will help you to identify any unnatural gestures.

✔ **Speak loud enough for everyone to hear.**

Don't speak so softly that the audience needs to strain to hear you. Remember that the more people in the room, the more the sound will be absorbed. On the other hand, don't shout at your audience either.

✔ **Welcome questions.**

It is easy to get thrown off track or intimidated when one of the management team asks a question or challenges what you are saying. The best way to handle this situation is to be receptive to questions (not defensive) and to answer them in a straightforward manner, stating the facts and explaining the process the team went through to come up with the solution. Always ask the person if you answered the question, and thank him or her for asking it.

Chapter 13

What You Can Measure, You Can Manage: Service Standards

Service standards serve two purposes. First, they are a powerful way of shaping the image that your customers have of you. Secondly, they are a great management tool for measuring how well each person in your company meets the levels of service to which you aspire. In our view, too few companies have meaningful standards because they do not know how to translate a general service quality into a specific service standard.

A company we once worked with balked at the idea of having everyone in the company answer the phone with the same greeting. "Won't this make us sound like robots to our customers?" the staff moaned. We assured them that customers see standards as evidence of service consistency and reliability, so they needn't worry about sounding artificial to customers. A few months later, we conducted a survey for the same company, and many customers had positive comments on the new phone standards and praised the company for its efforts.

You Can't Measure Friendly

General service qualities can be defined by adjectives that describe the basic ways you want your staff (and managers) to treat your customers including:

✔ friendly	✔ pleasant
✔ responsive	✔ helpful
✔ courteous	✔ caring
✔ efficient	✔ prompt

Companies often write policies proclaiming how staff should exhibit these qualities. For example:

> When greeting customers, act in a friendly way.
>
> Be prompt in responding to customers' requests.
>
> When dealing with upset customers, show them that you care.

While these are all worthy goals, they mean different things to different people. If you ask ten staff members to define *being friendly to a customer,* you will receive ten different answers. General service qualities, such as *friendly*, are not specific or measurable and are, therefore, open to individual interpretation.

Service qualities are important because they provide your staff with general guidelines to follow in unpredictable situations where you have set no specific service standards. However, if these qualities are going to be consistently put into practice, they must be made measurable.

You Can Measure Smiles

Service standards go one step further by turning general service qualities into specific, measurable actions that you expect your staff to take in given situations. In order for your staff to understand what you mean by friendly service, you must break the definition down into the components that make up friendly, such as:

❏ **Smile at customers as they approach.**

❏ **Make direct eye contact while explaining the situation.**

❏ **Greet customers with "Good morning" or "Good afternoon."**

❏ **Use the customer's name at least twice during the conversation.**

By taking these observable actions, your staff convey *friendliness* to your customers. Table 13-1 lists some examples of how general service qualities can be turned into specific service standards. The measurable aspect of each standard is in **bold type.**

Table 13-1:	From general service qualities to specific service standards
Service Quality	*Service Standard*
Answer the phone promptly	Answer the phone within **three rings.**
Return customer calls in a timely fashion	Return all customer calls within **24 hours.**
Be attentive to the customer	Make eye contact with the customer within **5 seconds** of their approaching you.
Be empathetic with an upset customer	**Always apologize** if a customer is upset.
Take personal responsibility for helping the customer	**Always** give the customer **your name, phone number and extension.**
Dress appropriately for work	Wear your uniform **at all times** including the cap and tie.

Criteria for Effective Service Standards

Seven criteria make a service standard effective. We recommend that you review your current standards against this list and revamp those that need it:

- ✔ specific
- ✔ concise
- ✔ measurable
- ✔ based on customer requirements
- ✔ written into job descriptions and performance reviews
- ✔ jointly created with staff
- ✔ fairly enforced

Specific

Standards tell service people precisely and exactly what is expected of them. They do not have to guess about your expectations or make anything up.

Concise

Standards do not explain the philosophy behind the action. Instead, they go right to the point and spell out who should do what by when.

Measurable

Because the actions in a standard are all *specific* criteria, they are observable and objective, which makes them easy to quantify.

Based on customer requirements

Standards should be based on customer requirements and not just your industry's standards. Fulfilling your customers' expectations gives you an advantage over your competitors.

Written into job descriptions and performance reviews

If you want employees to adhere to the standards, then write them down and make them part of each employee's job description and performance review. Using standards as a management tool gives them more credibility.

Jointly created with staff

The best standards are created by management and staff together based on their mutual understanding of customer needs. You may want to consider using Quality Groups (see Chapter 12) as a vehicle for having staff come up with service standards.

Fairly enforced

Standards that are enforced with some people and not with others quickly erode. Company-wide standards require that everybody, including the top brass, conform to them. Department-specific standards apply to everyone within that department, including the manager.

The Invisible Score Card

How are customers judging the service they receive from you? Customers, it seems, have an invisible *mental* score card on which they are continually judging your service. Based on our research, your company is being evaluated on three basic areas:

- ✔ product quality
- ✔ ease of procedures
- ✔ personal contact quality

The Malcolm Baldridge National Quality Award

The Malcolm Baldridge National Quality Award was created by an act of Congress in 1987. According to the application guidelines, the award is designed to promote the following:

- ✔ awareness of quality as an increasingly important element in competitiveness

- ✔ understanding of the requirements for quality excellence

- ✔ sharing of information on successful quality strategies

Each year hundreds of large and small businesses alike complete an application in the hopes of winning one of the most prestigious awards a business can receive. Past winners have included such companies as Xerox, Motorola, Federal Express, and Cadillac.

The award is based on seven categories of criteria with "customer satisfaction" leading the pack. Less than 30 percent of the companies that apply are service businesses. For those service companies who do apply, standards is one area where they receive the lowest ratings because they are too general, not measurable, and not based on customer requirements. Service businesses, in general, seem to focus on communicating general service qualities to their staff and not specific service standards.

If you are interested in reviewing the criteria for the Baldridge Award, contact: The National Institute of Standards and Technology, Route 270 and Quince Orchard Road, Administration Bldg., Room A 537, Gaithersburg, MD 20899.

Because these qualities are fundamental to your customers' experience of doing business with you, we strongly recommend that you develop service standards in all three areas.

Product quality

This is the physical quality of the product you produce. In a service business, the product is only one aspect of the customer's overall experience. When eating out, for example, the product is the food you are served. You evaluate the restaurant based on the way the food is cooked, how it tastes, and the way it's presented. Examples of product quality standards in a restaurant may include:

- ✔ all vegetables to be purchased and served fresh daily
- ✔ two ounces of bay shrimp per house salad
- ✔ all entree dishes to have a fresh fruit garnish

You can't always count on companies having basic product standards in place. I recently bought four new tires for my car. After having them fitted and balanced, I drove away upset at the bumpy ride I was having. I took the car back in and they rechecked it. They couldn't find a problem and said the tires were balanced perfectly. They started to give me a negative filter by eyeing me with suspicion (for more about negative filters, see Chapter 15), so I had them take a test drive to see for themselves. The mechanic returned, climbed out of my car and said, "I know what the problem is. The tires aren't round. They're almost round." Call me picky but *almost round* is one standard for tires that I can't yet embrace. I left the station with all new tires from a different manufacturer — one who obviously had better product quality control standards in place.

Ease of procedures

These are the standards that make it easy, fast, and efficient for the customer to do business with you. In a restaurant, excellent food is only part of the picture. Customers also expect not to have to wait too long for their meal or their check. Some typical procedural standards in a restaurant may include:

- ✔ Bring all food to the table within three minutes of it being put up.
- ✔ Set up a baby seat before escorting a party with a small child to their table.
- ✔ Pick up check within two minutes of money being put down by customer.

Personal contact quality

Standards for this area include the attitudes, actions, and behaviors you expect your staff to show your customers. Your restaurant experience — no matter how mouthwateringly delicious the food — can be ruined by a rude server. Some personal contact standards that would help make this experience positive include:

- greeting customers with a smile and saying, "Good evening. Welcome to The Feedbag."

- asking if customers have any questions about the menu before taking their order.

- saying, "Thank you for dining with us tonight. We look forward to seeing you again" as you hand the customer the check.

A Four-Step Technique for Developing Service Standards

The key to developing service standards is organizing the process into bite-sized pieces. There are four steps for doing this:

- Define your service sequences.

- Map out the steps.

- Determine your experience enhancers.

- Convert your experience enhancers into standards.

Start by viewing your business as a series of separate but connected interactions. We call these service sequences.

Define your service sequences

A service sequence is to your business what chapters are to a book. They are a way of conveniently subdividing the aspects of your service so that you can discover the specific customer encounters that need standards. For example, if you were in the hotel business your basic service sequences might go something like this:

❑ Reservations
❑ Check in
❑ Use the room
❑ Check out

View your service sequences from your customers' perspective. If they looked at your business as separate chunks, what would they see? Not all of the services you provide will follow precisely one after the other. The important thing is to subdivide your business into the different aspects of the service you provide.

Map out the steps

Once you break your business up into its various chapters, choose one area that needs improvement (as indicated by customer feedback). Next, map out the major chronological steps that make up that particular customer encounter (like the paragraphs within a chapter). For example, the check-in sequence for a hotel includes the following steps:

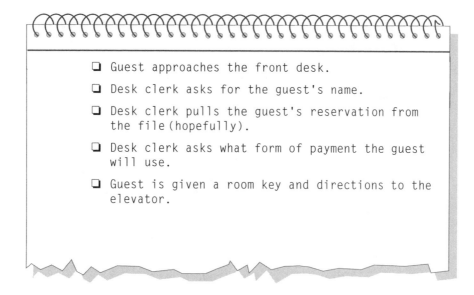

❏ Guest approaches the front desk.

❏ Desk clerk asks for the guest's name.

❏ Desk clerk pulls the guest's reservation from the file (hopefully).

❏ Desk clerk asks what form of payment the guest will use.

❏ Guest is given a room key and directions to the elevator.

In this encounter, no value has been added to the basic interaction. It is simply an accurate, step-by-step process that probably reflects how every hotel in the world checks in a guest. To add value to the guest's experience of staying at this particular hotel, you need to define the key experience enhancers.

As in life, basic service sequences do not always go as planned. Our hotel guest may have made a reservation, but the desk clerk may not be able to find it in the system. In such a situation, the clerk will deviate from the normal sequence of events and go off onto a new branch of the service sequence. Regardless of how many twists and turns there may be, the basic process for developing standards is the same.

Determine your experience enhancers

For each individual step, ask yourself:

> *What general service qualities will enhance the customer's experience of doing business with my company during this step?*

The first step in the sequence, "Guest approaches the front desk," is critical because your actions here make an immediate first impression on the guest. Two of the most important general service qualities at this point are being *friendly* and *attentive* to the guest.

Carry out this same procedure for each step until you have determined the key experience-enhancing qualities for each step.

Convert your experience enhancers into standards

Finally, rewrite the step-by-step interaction by converting your general service qualities into the three types of service standards: personal, product, and procedural. In the hotel example, the rewrite would look something like the following:

Checking in a Guest

❑ When more than three people are waiting in line, call the desk supervisor to come out and assist.

> *This process standard reflects promptness.*

❑ Smile at the customer as he or she approaches the front desk, make direct eye contact, and say "Good morning," "Good afternoon," or "Good evening."

> *This personal standard conveys friendliness.*

❑ Use the guest's name as soon as you know it.

> *This personal standard conveys recognition and attentiveness.*

❑ Ask the guest if he or she would like a wake up call in the morning.

> *This process standard shows initiative.*

❑ Call the guest within fifteen minutes of checking in to make sure that everything in the room is satisfactory.

> *This product standard ensures the quality of the guest's room.*

As your business grows and changes, remember to periodically update your standards. Don't get stuck in defining one set of standards and keeping them for life. You should review your standards at least once a year and update them as necessary to reflect changes in your market and your business.

Chapter 14

Beyond Employee of the Month: Reward And Recognition

. . . .

In This Chapter

▶ How to praise your staff

▶ Recognition on a budget

▶ The makings of a good reward program

▶ Five great rewards for staff

. . . .

*A*ll people have a natural need to feel good about the job they do. By regularly rewarding and recognizing your staff when they do something right, rather than only noticing and commenting when they do something wrong, you help motivate them to keep up the good work. You can let your staff know that they have done a good job in two ways:

✔ **Informal Recognition**

This is the spontaneous, everyday type of recognition that lets your staff know you appreciate the job they are doing, and it takes very little time, money, or planning to execute.

✔ **Formal Reward Program**

This is a preplanned, company-wide program for rewarding individuals, departments, and teams who achieve outstanding results in customer service. In general, they take time, money, and a good deal of planning to implement.

Why should I recognize or reward my staff for doing something they already get paid for?

This attitude is one of the big stumbling blocks that managers have when it comes to informally recognizing their staff. Some managers believe that people shouldn't need a lot of strokes or *attaboys* because they receive financial compensation for doing their jobs well. This is not true. Experience shows that people thrive when they receive personal recognition for the work they do.

While a paycheck is important, it will never replace the need for genuine appreciation for the efforts your staff put in. While everyone is expected to do their job well, recognition encourages and motivates staff to exceed what is expected of them.

Informal Recognition

Studies have shown that regularly giving informal recognition to an employee is a stronger motivator than providing him or her with formal rewards. Simple praise is remembered long after the event because it tells your employees that you noticed their efforts and took the time and trouble to personally thank them.

If your heart is in the right place and you follow these recommendations, we promise that your praise will be warmly appreciated by others.

Basic praise primer

Although informal recognition is effective, inexpensive, and convenient, many managers don't give their staff as many pats on the back as they could. Consequently, when they do praise their staff, the manager's inexperience (and often awkwardness) can be interpreted as a lack of genuine appreciation.

To set matters straight, here are a few basic skills that will complement your compliments:

- Don't do it in the hallway.
- Go to them.
- Maintain eye contact.
- Don't delay.

Don't do it in the hallway

Always make sure that you have the other person's full attention before you praise him or her. Don't try to give your staff a compliment when they (or you) are scurrying down the corridor, rushing to a meeting, or trying to meet a deadline. Instead, set up a time and place that is convenient for them. If you are acknowledging a team of people for their efforts, set up a time when you can meet with them all in one place and praise them as a group.

Go to them

Talk to your staff on their own turf or some place where they will feel comfortable and relaxed, such as their desks or the lunch room. Don't ask staff to come to your office because they may mistakenly think that something is wrong.

Maintain eye contact

Because people can perceive lack of eye contact to mean insincerity or lying, looking at your employees when you recognize them is critical. On the other hand, your employees are quite likely to look away from you because they probably haven't had a lot of practice at accepting honest, straightforward praise.

Remember, you don't want to be standing up and looking down on your staff when you praise them. Stay level with them by taking a seat next to them.

Don't delay

In order to have the biggest impact, you should recognize your staff as quickly as possible after the achievement has occurred. Don't wait until the Christmas party to praise the heroes of last spring. The further away you get from the event, the less impact the acknowledgment has.

The most heartfelt praise will miss it's mark if your tone of voice does not convey genuine enthusiasm. Your level of excitement, as well as your words, tells your staff how you really feel.

Always reward the behavior that you want repeated. When staff receive positive feedback, they look for ways to repeat the behavior. Sincere praise is the best way to ensure that good service habits stick.

Recognition thought starters

While you may like nothing better than to show your appreciation to service heroes by sending them to Hawaii, many other things can be done that don't cost an arm and a leg. Often the simplest, most spontaneous ideas yield the best results and the most fun. You can use the following checklists to find a form of recognition that will fit the employee, your budget, and the occasion. The checklists are divided into three price categories.

Ideas that cost less than $25

❏ **Send a thank you note.**

You can personally hand the note to your staff person, leave it for him to find on his desk, or tape it to the door of his office. Be sure to let the employee know the specific actions for which you are thanking him.

❏ **Have a senior executive personally thank the employee.**

This form of praise is always special because your staff know that an executive's time is a precious commodity. If possible, have the employee and executive meet face-to-face. If this arrangement can't be worked out, then a telephone call will do. In addition, make sure the executive is well briefed on what the service person did and why his or her action deserves this special recognition. Be sure to ask the senior executive who is in charge of that department to recognize the employee.

❏ **Send a letter of praise from a senior executive.**

This alternative to a personal visit or a phone call has an added advantage because the letter can be placed in the employee's personnel file. This differs slightly from a thank you note because it comes from a senior executive, not the immediate supervisor or manager.

❏ **Create a hall of fame for service heroes.**

Use a lunchroom wall or some other area that is seen by everyone and put up postcard-size photos (Polaroids are convenient and work just fine) of your service heroes. We recommend that you update the photographs with new service heroes every one or two months. Beneath each picture, put a short caption about what the person did to earn a place on the wall.

❏ **Put up customers' letters of praise.**

Similar to the hall of fame, pick a common area that is traveled by everyone and put up framed letters of praise that customers send to staff.

❏ **Highlight service heroes in the company newsletter.**

Regularly dedicate a part of your company newsletter to recognizing service heroes. Include a brief description of their achievement in the article.

Create an award for those people not usually in the limelight. This award can be any form of recognition that you choose, but it should have a specific name and be given to those people whose work is usually out of sight or low profile. Call it something like the *Backroom Award,* make a big deal about it, and present it on a regular basis (once a month or quarter).

A few years ago we had a big earthquake in San Francisco and one of our downtown clients sustained a lot of damage to their offices. Most of the ceiling tiles in the customer service department had crashed down on the staff's desks. Thankfully no one was hurt, but the place was a mess. The manager, wanting to lift his staff's morale, took one of the ceiling tiles, spray painted it gold, and inscribed it with the words *The Mover and Shaker Award*. Each week he put the award on the desk of the best performing customer service representative. This manager proved that it isn't the award that counts as much as the spirit in which it is given.

Ideas that cost less than $50

❏ **Lunchtime pizza party.**

Send out for pizzas and soft drinks and have them waiting in the lunch-room for your team or department (do this on a Friday and end the week on a high note). Be sure to make a brief speech about how the food is just your way of saying thank you to everyone for a week of great results.

❏ **Take employees to lunch.**

If you have an employee or a few employees who really went the distance for a customer, thank them by inviting them to join you at a restaurant for lunch. (The cost is kept down by making the meal a lunch rather than a dinner.) Be sure that you leave yourself enough time to recognize all the participants for their contributions without being rushed.

❏ **Surprise employees with balloons.**

For the biggest impact, deliver the balloons to the employees' desk while they are away from their work area. This way, they will have a pleasant surprise when they return. Be sure to attach a personal thank you note to the balloons recognizing each person's achievement.

❏ **Send flowers.**

A simple bouquet of fresh cut flowers always brightens a person's day. If they are delivered, the cost will be a little bit higher, but the recognition will be even more special.

❏ **Buy a plant.**

Since cut flowers have a limited life, try recognizing a staff person for something special by giving him or her a potted plant, such as an orchid, which stays in bloom for several weeks.

❏ **Give away tickets to a sporting event.**

We know many companies who get discount tickets for their local sports teams. Have tickets available for different sports and always give them in pairs so that the staff member can take a friend or family member along, too.

❏ **Let the employee come to work an hour late (with pay).**

This thank you always seems to work well. The time can be increased to fit the deed. We recommend a maximum of two hours because more than that may require extra planning to cover the person's job. An alternative to this idea is to let the employee leave work an hour early.

❏ **Buy a magazine subscription.**

Most monthly magazines cost less than $30 a year for a subscription. Select a magazine that reflects the employees' interests or let them select their own. Magazines take a while to be delivered after the order has been placed, so figure this lag time into your timing. The award can be presented by giving the employees a letter that tells them about the magazine. Every month when they receive their magazine, they will be reminded of their achievement.

❏ **Give a gift certificate.**

Today, gift certificates can be found for almost any product or service. In particular, gift certificates to bookstores, record stores, restaurants, and movie theaters are always popular.

Ideas that cost less than $100

❏ **Treat an employee to dinner for two.**

Select a good restaurant and arrange for a gift certificate. Determine a dollar limit ahead of time that covers dinner, dessert, and beverages for two.

❏ **Give the employee a day off.**

When one of your staff does something really special, consider giving her an extra day off with pay. Friday is a good day to choose in most businesses because it is often the least busy day of the week, so the interruption at work is minimized, and the employee gets a three-day weekend.

❏ **Send the employee to an outside training program.**

Show your appreciation for your staff by investing in their education. Let them choose a training course that supports their personal or professional interests and have the company pay. This course could be anything from a cooking class to a time management workshop.

Formal Rewards

Although they don't have the same *everyday* impact as informal recognition, formal awards are, nonetheless, an important part of your strategy for service improvement. Yearly or semi-annually award presentations should be highly publicized and send a clear message about what values and behaviors your company holds in high esteem. Managers and supervisors also benefit from a formal reward program because it lends credibility to the values and behaviors that they have been informally recognizing.

Formal reward programs take time and planning because your strategy team must come up with a simple and practical way to measure who wins. Attention must be given to every department and group so that those people who have little or no customer contact have as much chance of winning as those with front-line service jobs.

Four methods will help make your formal reward program a success:

- ✔ Keep the rewards interesting.
- ✔ Vary the rewards to suit the person.
- ✔ Make the size appropriate to the achievement.
- ✔ Make it fun.

Putting a formal reward program in place works best after your staff has had a chance to understand and put into practice the service standards expected of them (see Chapter 13).

Keep the rewards interesting

Formal reward programs that stay the same year after year eventually stop being special. Winners begin to feel that their rewards are just routine, and other employees lose interest in winning. To keep your reward program dynamic and alive, update it from year to year by altering the ceremony, the prizes, and the criteria for winning.

Vary the rewards to suit the person

When dealing with formal reward programs, taking the one-size-fits-all approach is a big mistake. Having a variety of awards available ensures the prizes you offer have meaning to the individuals who receive them. So if you have a winner who hates sports but loves music, give him tickets to the symphony, not the ball game. Prizes are most often given at a special event, such as an all-company meeting, picnic, or, if appropriate, a company dinner. Awards can range from personalized mementos to family vacations depending on the size of your company, your budget, and the achievement. Following are five awards that you might consider for a formal reward program.

A fancy dinner

This is a wonderful way to celebrate a winning team's achievement. The team becomes your guest at a good restaurant and you host the evening. During the dinner, you can highlight their accomplishments and invite other team members to speak. If your group is larger than six people, hearing each other in a crowded restaurant can become difficult, so consider going to a restaurant that has a private room. The dinner should be highly publicized by memo, bulletin board, or newsletter so that other staff members are aware of the achievement.

Customized gifts

These are available from catalogs or companies who specialize in incentive and motivational products. Some of the items that are easily personalized and readily available include:

- pen and pencil sets
- notepads
- T-shirts
- paperweights
- award pins

Some of these incentive companies have catalogs that allow the winner to choose his or her own prize ranging from clocks to chainsaws.

Customized trophies

These are plaques, silver cups, desk awards, and so on that are engraved with the employee's name, the date, and a brief description of the achievement.

Travel

Travel award trips range from a weekend getaway at a nearby bed and breakfast to a week-long vacation at a resort. The award always includes travel and lodging expenses for two and sometimes an allowance for meals and incidentals. If the vacation is a week long, remember to arrange for the winner's work to be handled in his absence. Otherwise, his vacation memories will quickly sour on the first day back on the job.

Cash

Two schools of thought exist about giving cash awards to staff. Some companies don't give monetary awards because they feel that the money will be used to pay bills and provide no lasting memory. Other companies feel that their employees appreciate extra money more than anything else and cash awards are the best motivators. One suggestion is to develop an award program that incorporates both cash and prizes.

Make the size appropriate to the achievement

Be careful not to cheapen the value of an award by making it less significant than the achievement calls for. For example, don't give a personalized pencil cup to the service hero whose initiative saved your largest account.

The most successful and well-designed formal reward programs are simple to administer. They give everyone in every position a chance to win, and have simple, easy-to-understand rules and goals that everyone considers attainable.

Make it fun

Finally, we urge you to make your rewards and recognition fun! We have discovered over the years that an environment of good humor helps everyone learn more, work harder, and show added interest in whatever task is at hand.

1001 ways to reward employees

If you are looking for a good reference book on reward and recognition, we suggest *1001 Ways To Reward Employees,* by Bob Nelson (Workman Publishing, 1994). This book provides a lot of specific information on how to set up and administer a reward program, including a ton of specific examples from companies that have done just this. One bonus is that the book has an appendix listing over 150 companies that provide incentive rewards and consulting on setting up a reward program.

Part IV
Dealing with Difficult People

The 5th Wave   By Rich Tennant

OH GREAT—AS SOON AS MY SHIFT STARTS, THE HUNS SHOW UP!

WEAPONS'N MORE
CUSTOMER SERVICE

BAZ
AL

In this part...

Think of someone — a customer or co-worker — whom you dread dealing with. Imagine the phone ringing at work. You pick it up, and it's him or her!

How do you feel? Are your palms starting to sweat? Is your throat getting tight? Are you reaching for the aspirin bottle? If so, read on. In this part, you learn how to reduce the effects of stress when dealing with conflict situations and how to calm down angry and upset customers (and co-workers!).

This part of the book also contains a process that we have taught to over 50,000 people in companies and jobs like yours for turning difficult situations into win-win opportunities.

Chapter 15

How to Win Over a Difficult Customer

Service providers who don't learn how to work well with difficult people lose their hair, their marbles, and their customers. The nature of your job requires that you sometimes work with customers who may drive you up a wall. Regardless of whether your customers are rude, frustrated, confused, or irate, most minor clashes don't have to turn into guerrilla warfare. This chapter teaches you a basic six-step process that will help you through trying times with difficult customers. The six steps are as follows:

- ✔ Let the customer vent.
- ✔ Avoid getting trapped in a negative filter.
- ✔ Express empathy to the customer.
- ✔ Begin active problem solving.
- ✔ Mutually agree on the solution.
- ✔ Follow up.

Step One: Let the Customer Vent

When your customers are upset they want two things: First, they want to express their feelings, and *then* they want their problem solved. The customers' need to let off steam can be so strong that they will vent to the first person in the company they get their hands on. Some service providers view the customers' venting as a waste of time because they want to move on and solve the problem. However, trying to resolve the situation without first listening to the customers' feelings never works. Only after your customers have vented can they begin to hear what you have to say.

Zip your lip

Nothing heats up customers with a problem faster than being told to calm down while they are venting. If you try to stop customers from expressing their feelings, you will push them from annoyed to irate in a matter of moments. The best plan is to stay quiet and not make matters worse by interrupting the customer. In particular, here is a list of words and phrases you want to avoid:

- ✔ You don't seem to understand . . .
- ✔ You must be confused . . .
- ✔ You have to . . .
- ✔ We won't . . . We never . . . We can't . . .
- ✔ You're wrong . . .
- ✔ It's not our policy . . .

While you don't want to interrupt customers when they are venting, you do want to let the customers know that you are listening to them. You should do three things while they vent away:

- ✔ Nod your head frequently.
- ✔ Say *uhh-huh* from time to time.
- ✔ Maintain eye contact.

Don't take it personally

When customers vent, they may be expressing frustration, annoyance, disappointment, or anger. Of all of these emotions, anger is the one you are the most likely to take personally because anger is such an *in-your-face emotion*. Raised voices, bulging blood vessels, rude comments about your mother, and wagging fists can make you want to run and hide or retaliate in kind.

Anger is an emotion that is always looking for someone or something to blame. If you stub your toe on the couch, you get angry at the couch. If a mosquito bites you, you get angry at the mosquito. If you lock your keys in your car, you get angry at yourself and then give the tire a good kick to vent your frustration. So even though the customer's anger may appear to be directed at you, remember that you are simply the person they are venting to and don't take it personally.

Step Two: Avoid Getting Trapped in a Negative Filter

The friction between you and a difficult customer is often worsened by how you interpret his or her behaviors. Take a moment and think of some of the names that you call your difficult customers — not to their face, but privately, under your breath. You may even want to jot a few of your favorites down in disappearing ink.

A negative filter is born

Following is an example of how a negative filter is created in a conversation between a bank teller and a customer.

Customer	—	Good morning. I want to deposit this check.
Teller	—	The back isn't signed!
Customer	—	Sorry about that, do you have a pen?

Negative filter name calling

Here are some of the most popular names we hear for difficult customers in our seminars:

- jerk
- bozo
- rude
- stupid
- creep
- liar

- pushy
- clueless
- moron
- turkey
- loser
- x#%**&*!!

As soon as you pin one of these labels on a customer, it becomes a negative filter that dramatically changes how you see, speak, and listen to the other person.

Teller	—	(sighing) Yes, here.
Customer	—	By the way, I ran out of deposit slips and don't know my account number. Will you please look it up for me?

At this point in the conversation, the teller suddenly finds himself thinking: "This person is stupid!" The instant the teller has this thought, an invisible, negative filter comes down between him and the customer. From now on, the manner in which he relates to the customer will be distorted by the negative filter. The teller's choice of words and his tone of voice will reflect his silent opinion of the customer. The rest of the conversation would probably go something like this:

Teller	—	Most people can remember their account number.
Customer	—	(feeling scolded) I know and I'm sorry, but as I said, I don't have a deposit slip, and I didn't write down my account number.
Teller	—	(annoyed and sighing again) You will have to wait while I go and look it up . . . maybe you should write it down and keep it in your wallet.

The service provider is speaking to the customer as if she is stupid. Being a professional he knows better than to come right out and say, "Hey, lady, you're not too bright, are you?," but the negative filter still comes through, loud and clear.

KAREN ANECDOTE

Negative filters are contagious

I was teaching customer service to the staff of a large hospital when I found that nurses on different shifts were unintentionally giving their negative filters to each other. The night nurses would write down a few comments about their patients' behaviors on the bottom of their charts. Sometimes the comments were positive, sometimes negative. For example: "Mr. Smith has been in a very bad mood tonight ." When the day nurse came on duty, she would pick up the chart and, boom, just like that, she had an instant negative filter about Mr. Smith. The day nurse, in turn, then noted her negative comments about Mr. Smith, reinforcing the night nurse's point of view, and so on. Within a day or two, word would get around that Mr. Smith in room #206 was a pain in the elbow and all the nurses on the floor, day or night, knew to be on guard when dealing with him. If left unchecked, negative filters can get out of control and spread like wildfire, creating a situation where positive communication with a customer is extremely difficult, if not impossible.

During a recent flight home, I was chatting with the gentleman sitting next to me when he accidentally spilled his coffee. He called over the flight attendant to help mop up the spill. Once the spill was cleaned, she asked him if he would like another cup of coffee. He said he would. She brought it a few minutes later and, again, the poor man accidentally knocked it over! He was embarrassed and apologetic. When the flight attendant came over and saw what had happened, her attitude immediately changed. She transformed into a mother and my seat mate took on the sheepish and guilty qualities of a scolded three-year-old. I realized that in her mind it was forgivable to spill one cup of coffee, but spilling two cups meant that he was a klutz. For the rest of the trip, and especially when she served dinner, the flight attendant viewed my traveling companion through her *klutz filter*. This, of course, made my traveling companion feel embarrassed and self-conscious the rest of the flight.

I'd rather switch than fight

Inevitably, you'll have negative filters about some of your customers, some of the time. The idea is to avoid getting stuck in these negative filters. Understanding the harmful effects of a negative filter will not necessarily make them go away, but you do have a choice about whether you are going to focus on them or not. The way out of a negative filter is switching to a service filter. You do so by asking yourself the question:

> ## "What does this customer need and how can I provide it?"

This question provides you with an alternative filter because as soon as you ask it, your focus changes. The negative filter instantly slides into the background, and the service filter slides into the foreground. The switching technique works in much the same way as a flashlight in a dark room: By changing where you aim your attention, you illuminate the issues that need to be addressed — rather than your personal feelings about the customer's behavior.

Step Three: Express Empathy to the Customer

If you give customers a chance to vent, they will eventually run out of steam; then you can begin to participate more actively in the conversation. Giving a brief and sincere expression of empathy works wonders to calm a difficult customer. Empathy means appreciating and understanding someone else's feelings while not necessarily agreeing with them. By letting customers know that you understand why they are upset, you build a bridge of rapport between you and them.

Empathy is not sympathy. Sympathy is when you over-identify with the other person's situation. For example, if an angry customer comes up to you and says, "Your company really doesn't care about service!" a sympathetic response would be, "You're right, we care more about the almighty dollar than anything else!"

Empathic phrases

Empathic phrases are a simple and easy way of conveying that you understand your customer's situation. The types of phrases that best express empathy to a customer include the following:

- ✔ I can see why you feel that way.
- ✔ I see what you mean.
- ✔ That must be very upsetting.
- ✔ I understand how frustrating this must be.
- ✔ I'm sorry about this.

Empathy means always having to say you're sorry

Some service providers feel uncomfortable apologizing to the customer because they see it as an admission of guilt. Saying *I'm sorry* to a customer does not imply that you or your company did anything wrong; it simply conveys that you are genuinely sorry that the customer has had a bad experience.

The tone of your voice goes a long way in helping you convey empathy. If you say all the right words but deliver them with a coldness in your voice, the words will have an insincere ring to them. By using a genuinely warm and caring tone, you enhance the meaning and effectiveness of empathic phrases.

Step Four: Begin Active Problem Solving

Until now, you have been on the receiving end of the conversation with your customer. You can begin active problem solving by asking questions that help clarify the cause of the customer's problem.

As you ask the customer questions, be sure to listen to everything she says, and don't jump to conclusions. Because you may have been through similar situations before, you can easily think that you already know the answer and miss details that are specific to this customer's situation.

Gather any additional information you need

Customers sometimes leave out critical information because they think it is unimportant or they just forget to tell you. When you need specific information from a customer (especially when he is off in another direction), use the *Bridging Technique*. This technique builds a bridge between what the customer is saying and where you want the conversation to go. As you notice the conversation veering off track, wait for the customer to take a breath. (It may be a quick breath, but they all breathe eventually.) This is your cue to jump in with an empathic phrase followed by a question that steers the conversation back on course. For example, the customer may say:

> *I never asked for a subscription to your publication. I don't even like your publication. How did you get my name? Did you buy it from a mailing list company? I get so much junk mail I've had to get a bigger mailbox . . .(breath) . . . .*

At this point, you quickly and politely say:

> *Mrs. Jones, I understand your annoyance at receiving a subscription that you didn't want — may I have your address so that I can correct the situation for you?*

Chances are that the customer will immediately come back to the point and provide you with the information you need.

Double check all the facts

Upset customers rarely present the facts of their story in a neat little package. You may have to do some detective work to make sure that you understand everything they are telling you. Use the *Mirroring Technique* to summarize your understanding of what the customer says, and then reflect it back to them. For example, imagine your customer says:

*Last Tuesday I received a fax saying the order had been canceled, then I got
a phone call from your warehouse saying to ignore that fax. Today I still
don't have the shipment, and nobody seems to know where it is!*

To make sure that you understand the situation, you might mirror it back by
saying:

*What you are saying is that the order that should have been delivered last
week still hasn't arrived, and you haven't been able to find anyone who can
help you. Is that correct?*

The customer then has the chance to verify or correct your understanding of
the situation.

Step Five: Mutually Agree on the Solution

Once you gather all the facts, you need to work with your customer to come up
with an acceptable solution to the problem. If you haven't already discovered
what will make him happy, ask. You may, at this point, find it necessary to take a
brief time-out from the customer so that you can do the behind-the-scenes work
necessary to solve the problem. In this case, be sure that the customer knows
exactly why you are asking him to wait and how long it will take for you to get
back to him. Finally, when you both agree on how to resolve the problem,
explain the steps that you will take to implement the solution.

Don't promise what you can't deliver. Be honest and realistic when telling the
customer what you will do. We always recommend that you *under promise and
over deliver*. Doing so sets an expectation in the customer's mind that you will
have a good chance of meeting and, hopefully, exceeding. For example, if you
are sending a replacement product to the customer and you know that the
shipping process usually takes three days, you might tell her to expect the
package within a week. With this action, you build in a little time for unforeseen
delays and the customer is pleasantly surprised when the package arrives
earlier than she expected.

Step Six: Follow Up

You can score big points on the service scoreboard by following up with your
customers — by phone, e-mail, or letter — to check that the solution worked. If
you contact the customer and find out that he or she is not satisfied with the
solution, put out the *the buck stops here* sign and continue to look for another,
more workable solution.

Effective follow up also includes fixing the procedures that are causing the problem to begin with. By spending time solving internal service delivery problems, you prevent them from occurring in the future. (For more information on how to do this, see Chapter 12).

Symptoms That the Heat Has Got You Beat

Catching yourself losing control when you are dealing with a difficult customer isn't always easy. However, certain red flags do pop up that tell you it's time to begin the six-step process outlined in this chapter:

- ✔ tight neck and shoulders
- ✔ cringing at the sound of the customer's voice
- ✔ dreading the ringing of the telephone
- ✔ headaches
- ✔ anger
- ✔ being short or curt
- ✔ raising your voice unnecessarily
- ✔ strained tone of voice
- ✔ breaking out in hives
- ✔ grinding your teeth

 Practice becoming aware of these symptoms, and when you notice them, use the cheat sheet we outlined in this chapter to help you beat the heat. You will find that practice makes perfect, and the more you use the six steps, the better you will become at winning over difficult customers.

Chapter 16

Wrinkled Foreheads and Clenched Fists: Stress Management

*W*e read a *New York Times* article a while ago that highlighted the ten most stressful professions. Among the top ten listed were policeman, fireman, air traffic controller, and customer service representative! Having a job that requires dealing with angry, irate, or frustrated customers can make your blood boil (literally). Even if you are not a customer service representative, some degree of stress is inevitable no matter what job you do (with the possible exception of sloth groomer at the zoo). Believing that you will find a stress-free job is wishful thinking. Imagine going into your place of work and hearing your manager say:

> *As soon as you sense the customer is getting angry, just put the phone down.*

> *You've got all your work done — why don't you go home early and relax?*

> *I know it's Thursday and our deadline is Friday . . . but don't worry, I can always hire a few extra hands to help us get it done on time.*

> *I'm giving you a 20 percent raise because you're doing more than your job description calls for.*

Give it up, it won't happen, not in our lifetime anyway. So the answer isn't waiting for the circumstances of your job to change, it's learning how to manage your stress before it manages you.

Assess Your Stress

The degree of stress that you experience at work is not only a result of having to deal with difficult people, but is also affected by other factors such as:

- your physical work environment
- how organized you are
- your level of satisfaction with your job
- how well you get along with your boss and co-workers
- your balance between work and personal time
- how you manage your time

Stress test

This quick 20-question stress test will help you assess your current level of stress at work. Answer each question by checking the yes or no box.

1. Do you find dealing with angry or disgruntled customers upsetting? ❏ Yes ❏ No

2. Do you feel that your boss does not listen to suggestions you make? ❏ Yes ❏ No

3. Do you often eat lunch at your desk while doing work? ❏ Yes ❏ No

4. Do you find that constant interruptions make it hard to focus? ❏ Yes ❏ No

5. Does your job involve meeting constant deadlines? ❏ Yes ❏ No

6. Do you get impatient easily with customers and co-workers? ❏ Yes ❏ No

7. Are you regularly late for important activities or appointments? ❏ Yes ❏ No

8. Do you find communicating with your boss difficult? ❏ Yes ❏ No

9. Is delegating work when you get busy difficult or impossible? ❏ Yes ❏ No

10. Do you regularly take less than thirty minutes for your lunch? ❏ Yes ❏ No

11. Is your work environment stuffy, cramped, or noisy? ❏ Yes ❏ No

12. Do you drink more than three cups of coffee a day? ❏ Yes ❏ No

13. Do you have less than two days off a week? ❏ Yes ❏ No

14. Do you regularly work extra time during evenings or weekends? ❏ Yes ❏ No

15. Do you feel that you carry the brunt of responsibility in your job? ❏ Yes ❏ No

16. Do you regularly run out of time on important projects? ❏ Yes ❏ No

17. Do you juggle several items at once during your workday? ❏ Yes ❏ No

18. Do you feel stuck in your job? ❏ Yes ❏ No

19. Do you work straight through the day without breaks? ❏ Yes ❏ No

20. Do you feel that you spend too much time at work? ❏ Yes ❏ No

Scoring the stress test

Go through the list of questions and assign one point for each yes answer you checked. Total up the number of points and review your score below:

0-5 Points: Low Stress Level

Your stress level at work is currently low and you are either retired, medicated, or well practiced in the skills of stress management. If you scored at this level, please write us with any tips you have at 180 Harbor Drive #212, Sausalito, CA 94965 or send us an e-mail at *sterconinc@aol.com*. We are always looking for good ideas.

6-12 Points: Average Stress Level

Your stress level at work is about average but may still be higher than you want. Review the techniques for stress management explained later in this chapter. Pick one or two areas to work on, and practice the techniques until your stress level drops.

Positive changes cause stress

Today, more than ever before, we are bombarded by information about stress and its damaging effects on our lives. Most of what we hear relates to negative situations, such as too much time spent at work, not having enough money, arguing with a loved one, and so on. But stress can also be caused by positive life changes such as:

- going on vacation
- getting married

- traveling abroad
- having a new family member
- getting a promotion
- earning more money
- buying a new home

Learning to cope with positive life changes that can cause stress is just as important as learning how to deal with negative circumstances.

13-20 Points: High Stress level

Your stress level at work is at the point where your health may be affected, and you should make some immediate changes. Scheduling more time for yourself and the things that you enjoy doing is important. See the section "How to Reduce Stress for a Lifetime" later in this chapter, and start using the techniques suggested.

As a manager, you can help reduce your staff's stress by recognizing what research has shown are the three main causes of employees' stress on the job: not knowing what is expected of them, not getting any feedback on their performance, and not knowing if anyone cares about what they are doing in their job. Taking some basic actions to alleviate these concerns goes a long way in reducing stress for your employees.

The Chemistry of Stress

Stress is your body's natural reaction to any demand (physical or psychological) that is put upon it. For example, imagine that you arrive at work a little late one morning and find a note on your desk that reads . . .

Come to my office right away!

written by your boss. How would you feel? What thoughts would start running through your mind? Anxious to find out what she wants, you hurry to her office, but she's out until tomorrow. Now how do you feel? What are you thinking as you drive home that evening?

The next morning you rush up to your boss's office and calmly ask her what she wanted to see you about. Beaming with pride, she says:

> *I just heard back from our client, and they were delighted with the work you put in on their report. Well done!*

When we run this scenario by people in our workshops, they usually start squirming as they visualize the amount of stress their negative thoughts would be producing. The anticipation and worry that the situation generated are all imagined, but the stress is very real and can ruin your whole day, not to mention keep you from getting a good night's rest.

Understanding how your mind works to create chemical stress in your body is an important part of both preventing stress before it occurs and curing stress once you've got it.

The "fight or flight" mechanism

When physical or psychological demands become extreme, your brain alerts the hypothalamus gland (located at the base of your brain) that triggers a complex chain of events known as the *fight or flight* mechanism. This mechanism puts your body on red alert to gather the strength it needs to meet a challenging situation. Some of the ways your body prepares itself to meet a challenge are as follows:

- ✔ The heart pumps faster to get more blood to the muscles.
- ✔ Breathing speeds up to get more oxygen into the blood stream.
- ✔ Muscles tense up in preparation for action.
- ✔ Perspiration increases to reduce body temperature.

Different mammoth — same response

The fight or flight mechanism has been around for thousands of years. Our cave dwelling ancestors had two basic responses when dealing with a hairy mammoth that was looking for a human snack: stay and fight or run like the devil. This fight or flight response prepared the caveperson, within seconds, to have the extra strength needed to carry out either of these options.

The hairy mammoths of yesterday have been replaced by the difficult customers and deadlines of today, yet our hypothalamus gland continues to ignite our body's reactions in the same old way. Unlike our ancestors, however, we don't usually have the option of fighting or running away when confronted with an angry customer (although we're sure you've wanted to do both). The result is that your body gets all revved up with nowhere to go. The chemicals released into your system for extra strength don't get dissipated and can keep you stressed out all day long.

Your hypothalamus isn't paid to think

Recent research has revealed that the hypothalamus gland will trigger the fight or flight response in situations that are viewed as threatening even when, in actuality, they are not. The hypothalamus gland reacts to the signals your brain sends it without distinguishing between what is real and what is imagined. *In other words, your negative thoughts are powerful enough to turn on the stress machinery in your body.*

The last time I was on vacation in Hawaii, I remember lying on the beach looking up at palm trees and hearing, **"No, Jack! They can't do that! They have a contract with us! That is unacceptable. We're in this deal to make money — not friends!"** Aroused from my sun-drenched stupor, I looked around to see a man, in shorts and sunglasses, pacing up and down the beach yelling into a cellular phone. His head looked as if it was about to explode. He was oblivious to the golden beach, the blue water, and the red Hibiscus flowers that were in full bloom and totally stressed out by his internal irritation. I suddenly realized that if he could create tension in the middle of such calm circumstances, then it stood to reason that he could also create calm in the midst of tense circumstances.

How to Reduce Stress at Work

Literally dozens of techniques are available for reducing stress in the work place. While we can't cover all of them in detail, here are the ones that we use the most:

- ✔ change from stress talk to smart talk
- ✔ don't worry, be concerned
- ✔ manage your time more effectively
- ✔ improve your physical work environment

Change from stress talk to smart talk

How you talk to yourself about your circumstances can either prevent or activate your cave dweller, stress-creating response. For example, imagine that you have just been on the phone with a difficult customer who insisted that he get a refund on a product that he purchased from you six months ago. You sincerely apologize and explain why you can't offer a refund. The customer gets upset, interrupts you, and asks to be transferred to your supervisor. After talking with the customer, your supervisor comes up and tells you that he bent the rules and okayed a refund.

You now have to decide how you are going to talk to yourself about this situation. Are you going to use stress talk or smart talk?

Stress talk

If you put too much of a negative spin on the events, you will create stress talk and end up with your shoulders around your ears. Your stress talk in the above situation might go something like this:

> *I can't believe it! He always undermines my authority! He just doesn't have the guts to say "no" to difficult customers! He should support whatever decision I make. This always happens to me! I can't win with him! There's no point in talking to him about it because he never listens and it wouldn't make any difference anyway....*

Some of the common themes found in stress talk are as follows:

- **Exaggerating** — Using definitive words like always, never, and won't usually blows things out of proportion and exaggerates the incident. Things you say may feel true but probably aren't:

  ...He never listens...

- **Negative labels** — Taking a single action or behavior the person has done and putting a general negative label on it:

  ...He just doesn't have the guts to say "no" to difficult customers...

- **Negative outcomes** — Expecting the situation you are in to have a negative outcome and behaving as if the negative outcome is a forgone conclusion:

  ...There's no point in talking to him...

- **All or nothing** — Looking at a situation as black or white, all or nothing:

  ...He should support any decision I make...

- **Eliminating the positive** — Ignoring all the positive aspects of the situation and focusing exclusively on the negative ones:

  ...It wouldn't make any difference...

Smart talk

Smart talk is constructive self-talk that helps you create less stress, live long, and prosper. Your smart talk in the above situation might go something like this:

> *I'm really upset, but I know my manager was just trying to keep the customer happy. It must have been an awkward position for him to be in. It would have been difficult for me, too. I know that if I talk to him, we can work out a better way to handle this in the future. Since this doesn't happen all the time, there is no point in getting upset about it.*

Some of the common themes found in smart talk are as follows:

✔ **Assuming good intentions** — Taking the point of view that whatever action the person took, be it good or bad, he did it with good intentions in mind:

> *...I know my manager was just trying to keep the customer happy...*

✔ **Positive outcomes** — Expecting the situation you are in to have a positive outcome and behaving as if the positive outcome is a forgone conclusion:

> *...We can work out a better way to handle this in the future...*

✔ **Focusing on the positive** — Seeing the positive aspects of the situation and including those in your self talk:

> *...This doesn't happen all the time...*

✔ **Seeing shades of gray** — Being able to look objectively at the situation from both points of view and see how each person is right in his or her own way:

> *...It must have been an awkward position for him to be in...*

✔ **Empathize** — Being able to empathize with the circumstances the other person is in, even if you don't agree with the outcome:

> *...It would have been difficult for me, too...*

Don't worry, be concerned

The second technique for preventing stress is to learn how to convert worries into concerns. Many people spend a lot of time worrying about things that never happen. Here are some facts about the things people worry about:

✔ 40 percent will never happen.

✔ 58 percent will turn out better than you think.

✔ 2 percent are actually worth worrying about. (Now you can worry about which two percent you should really be worrying about!)

A worry is something that you *cannot* do anything about; no action you take can resolve it. For example, suppose you are worried that it will rain on your day off. Obviously you can do nothing to control the weather, so what's the point of worrying? What difference will worry make other than to make you feel tense and upset?

Concerns, on the other hand, are things that you *can* do something about; you can take some action, no matter how small, to help resolve the situation. For example, if you are concerned that you will be late to a meeting, you can call and let the other participants know that you are running a few minutes behind.

If you are worried about something that you can do nothing about, let it go. If you are worried about something that you can do something about, learn to turn the worry into a concern by taking some action.

Manage your time more effectively

Not understanding and utilizing the basic principles of time management can run you ragged. In working with thousands of people, we have found that the time-management tips that have the biggest impact on lowering your stress include:

✔ practicing long-term planning

✔ using a time-management system

Practicing long-term planning

If you build a house, you don't lay the foundation before you have a blueprint drawn up. You want to be sure that by the time you put the walls up, they all meet in the right place. Your projects at work are the same. A little long-term planning now saves you a lot of grief later. In our workshops, we often ask people to write down their objectives for one month, one year, and five years from now. Invariably, the participants come up with plenty of one month goals but usually have very few one year and even fewer five year goals. For many of us, thinking past today's agenda to tomorrow's vision is difficult, yet most of the things that bring satisfaction and success at work — and in life — require long-term planning.

Most people do not get to the end of their lives and say:

> *I didn't spend enough time at work!*

Be sure that you make time for yourself, family, and friends. Having long term goals for your leisure time is just as important as having them for your career.

Using a time-management system

Busy people always seem to be scurrying from appointment to appointment clutching their time-management books for dear life. If you don't have an organizer, you can find a good selection at your local stationary store. Whichever type you choose, we recommend that you buy a book with refillable, dated daily pages. Once you have your system, you can get the most out of it by doing the following:

1. **Write down all your appointments.**

   A good way to avoid being late or missing appointments is to write them down. Don't juggle all this information in your head or keep your dates and times on scraps of paper (like old napkins and burrito wrappers), just regularly check your book.

2. **Keep a daily To Do list.**

   At the beginning of each day, or the night before, whichever you prefer, write down the tasks that you plan to do. As you complete each task, check it off. If the task doesn't get done, transfer it to another day when you plan to do it, and so on. As you plan your day, keep in mind that much of your time at work may be taken up with interruptions. If you work an eight-hour day and two hours are taken up with interruptions, you have six hours in which to complete your To Do list. By being honest about how much time you actually have, the interruptions become less upsetting.

3. **Prioritize your daily To Do list.**

   Because some of the items on your daily To Do list will be more important than others, you should prioritize them using a basic A, B, or C prioritizing system. Items that you mark with an A are the most important and critical to get done. Those items you mark with a B are important but not as critical. What's left over are the C items that are routine, mundane, and usually not critical. Be careful not to fall into the trap of spending most of your day doing C activities because they are easy to do.

For the longest time, one of my clients refused to use a time-management system. "I keep everything I need right here," he would say as he tapped his head. As his business grew, he started forgetting appointments and felt overwhelmed by all the things he had to do. Finally, he broke down and bought a time-management system. Months later, returning from a business trip in Europe, his luggage was lost by the airline. He was frantic because his system was in one of the lost suitcases. "My whole life is in that book," he told me, "I can't wait to get it back." When his luggage finally arrived, the first thing he did was rip through it to find that little book. Only after you use a system like this for any length of time do you really come to appreciate how much time and energy it saves you.

Time-management resources

A trip to your local office supply store is a good place to start if you are looking for a time-management system. Some of these systems are not carried in stores and can only be obtained through mail order. While many systems are available, some of the most popular are:

✔ The Franklin System (800-644-1776) — mail order and Franklin Quest stores

✔ Time Design (800-637-9942) — mail order only

✔ Day Runner (800-635-5544) — available in most stationery stores

✔ Filofax (800-345-6798) — available in most stationery stores

✔ Day Timer (800-225-5005) — mail order and some stores

In addition to providing a system, some of these companies offer time management trainings — live and on tape. Call to inquire.

 Because so many good ideas are available for gaining control of your time, we strongly recommend that you buy a book, like *Time Management For Dummies* (IDG Books Worldwide, Inc.), or an audio tape that teaches the principles of time management. In addition, several companies offer seminars on time management where a system is provided as part of the course.

Improve your physical work environment

Your surroundings at work can be a contributing factor in your stress level. If you have worked in the same environment for a long time, you're likely to no longer notice the things around you that may be tying knots in your stomach. The three biggest environmental stressors are:

✔ noise

✔ clutter

✔ space

Noise

The next time you are at the airport notice how the airline personnel on the tarmac wear those little colored earplugs. This apparel is not a fashion statement, but rather a way of minimizing the noise level that is all around them. Noise pollution is one of the leading causes of stress in the workplace. If you regularly find yourself saying:

> *I can't hear myself think with all this noise.*

then you may want to talk with your supervisor about taking some actions to reduce the noise level.

Clutter

We learned the value of being clutter free in a time management course we took a few years ago. In short, mess is inefficient. It makes it harder to find the things you need when you need them. If you are one of those people who, peeking over a mile-high stack of papers, says:

> *I have a system — I know where everything is.*

you, too, can reduce unnecessary stress by spending a little time sorting and organizing. We recommend setting aside some time to do the following:

✓ **Clean out your desk.**

   Many people use their desk drawers as a storage area for all the items that they don't know what to do with but can't bear to throw out. If you are one of those people, you may find bottles of dried-out correction fluid, refills to pens that you no longer own, and old keys. We recommend you go through your desk drawers and ruthlessly discard anything you haven't used in the last year.

✓ **Sort your paperwork.**

   Sort your paperwork into three piles. The first pile is priority one and includes items that are important and must be handled right away. The priority two pile contains items that are important but can wait. Priority three items should probably just be thrown away.

✓ **Organize your files.**

   The point of having a filing system is to be able to find things quickly and easily. Papers that are misfiled or files that are out of order can be frustrating and time consuming when you are looking for something you need.

The pack rat's credo is:

> *If I throw it away today, I will need it tomorrow.*

This credo is a great excuse never to get rid of anything — which means you end up with everything cluttering up your work space. While there may be those rare occasions when you do throw away something you need later, most of the time what you need you already use.

Space

If you can't swing a cat in your work area, it's either because pets aren't allowed or you are crowded in by furniture, machinery, storage boxes, and so on.

You can do two things to help keep your work space from cramping your style:

✔ **Get out more.**

Make sure that on your breaks, no matter how short, you go outside or to someplace where you can get a feeling of spaciousness. Doing so periodically during the day helps refresh and renew you.

✔ **Reorganize.**

Examine how efficiently you are using the physical space you are in. More often than not, no real planning was involved in the arrangement of things in your work area. With a little thought, time, and reorganization, the same stuff can be rearranged to make a more comfortable and spacious work environment.

How to Reduce Stress for a Lifetime

In addition to the ideas we outlined for how to reduce stress at work, learning how to prevent and reduce stress for a lifetime is equally important. Following are three ways to incorporate stress reduction into your lifestyle. While your doctor (or more likely your mother) may have been suggesting these for years, recent research confirms that they are still the most effective ways to control stress and stay healthy.

Eat right

Your eating habits have an impact on your stress level. For example, certain foods can dramatically effect your mood:

✔ Caffeine (coffee, tea, and cola) stimulates the nervous system and imitates the process of stress arousal. In some people, too much caffeine can result in headaches, irritability, and nervousness.

✔ Sugar (cookies, doughnuts, and candy) is a favorite for many people at work because it gives you a quick energy boost. After a short while, though, the *sugar blues* set in and increased tiredness and irritability can result.

✔ Salt (chips and fast food) is bad for your blood pressure and stimulates stress arousal.

Learning to minimize your intake of the above foods and eating a balanced diet that includes lots of fresh fruit and vegetables, salads, and grains can make an immediate difference to the way you feel throughout your workday. If your eating habits could use a makeover, we recommend that you see your doctor or a nutritionist for guidance.

Most of the foods and drinks above are the kinds of snacks you find in the typical employee lounge vending machine. Do your staff and yourself a favor and start offering some healthy, lower-calorie alternatives.

Exercise regularly

In most cases, some exercise is better than no exercise at all. If you have a job where you spend most of your time sitting on your behind, try incorporating some easy physical activity into your day. You can reduce your stress by walking up stairs instead of using an elevator; going for a fifteen minute walk at lunch time; or parking your car at the far end of the parking lot and walking that extra twenty yards. If you want a more rigorous exercise program to do at home, you need to follow several important guidelines:

Make it something you enjoy

Boredom is the enemy of any exercise program. If you are just starting out, you may want to try a few different types of exercise and see which one you like the best.

Many people we know tell us that they incorporate reading a book, listening to an audio tape, or watching TV while on stationary bikes, stair steppers, and treadmills in order to keep the yawns from setting in.

Make it convenient

One well-intentioned friend of ours joined a state-of-the-art gym, but she hardly ever goes there because it's twenty minutes away from her home. When she joined, she didn't think the distance would be a problem, but now just the thought of making this drive stops her on most days. Any exercise expert will tell you that the more convenient it is for you to exercise, the more likely you are to do it.

Schedule it

This is one place where your can use your handy time management system to support you in your personal life. Many people find that if they make an appointment with themselves to exercise and schedule it in their book, they are more likely to carry through with it.

Make an appointment ♪ yourself ♪

See your doctor before you start

Be careful not to overdo it because doing so increases your risk of injury and only prevents you from continuing. Before you begin any exercise program, see your doctor. Taking your exercise routine at a pace that you are comfortable with is essential for long-term success.

If you own a company, consider setting up free or discount health club memberships for your staff at a location near your office. They will be healthier and happier employees as a result. The benefit to you is increased productivity and reduced absenteeism.

Practice relaxation techniques

Basic relaxation techniques (including meditation) have been practiced for thousands of years as a way to reduce tension, fatigue, and stress in the body and mind. The results of using these techniques can include:

- ✔ lowering of heart rate, blood pressure, and respiration rate
- ✔ increase of alpha waves, the brain waves associated with deep relaxation
- ✔ rapid decline of blood chemicals associated with anxiety

Following are two techniques that you can use at home or during your lunch break at work to reduce stress.

Tense and release

Sit in a comfortable chair and take a few deep breaths. With your arms bent at the elbow, tightly squeeze your hands into fists and then curl them up toward your shoulders so that your hand, arm, and shoulder muscles are tensed. Remember to keep breathing and hold this position for 5 seconds. Slowly release the tension and notice how it feels.

Next straighten out your legs and point your toes straight out in front of you so that your calf and thigh muscles are tensed. Hold this for 5 seconds and slowly release. Notice how your legs feel as the tension is released.

Continue the exercise by tensing the muscles in your neck, chest, shoulders, and back. When you finish, your body should feel more relaxed and at ease.

Gold liquid

Sit in a comfortable position with your eyes closed. Imagine that your body is a glass container full of gold liquid and that all the gold liquid is slowly draining out from your fingertips and toes. As the liquid drains out and the level goes down, imagine that it takes with it all the tensions, worries, and negative thoughts of the moment. Once you are drained out, go back over your glass vessel and see if you find any remaining traces of gold liquid. If you do, go back to that part of your body and clean the liquid out.

As a final step, take a few minutes to become aware of your breathing. Focus your attention on your breath as it goes in and out. Breathe deeply and naturally. As thoughts come to mind, just notice them and then go back to your breathing. Do this exercise for a few minutes until you feel relaxed (or have fallen asleep). When you are ready to finish, briefly imagine your immediate surroundings and then slowly open your eyes, feeling refreshed and relaxed. For a quick pick-me-up, do this exercise at work during a ten minute break. For a deeper relaxation at home, do the same exercise for 20 to 30 minutes.

Because both of these techniques can be done while you are sitting down, they work very well for reducing fatigue and stress on long airplane flights.

Chapter 17

It Takes Two to Tango: Getting in Step with Your Customer

*Y*our customers fall into two general categories: ones who think and behave similarly to you, and ones who don't. With the first group, it often seems that you know what they are going to say (even before they say it), how they will respond, and what it will take to have them be satisfied. The second group of customers are harder to relate to. You are often surprised by what they say, puzzled by how they react, and uncertain about how to satisfy them.

The most successful service providers have learned how to work with both groups of customers, especially the ones who think and act differently than they do. We call these differences *working styles,* and they reflect the various ways that people behave at work. Understanding your working style and the style of those around you dramatically improves your communication with customers, co-workers, and even your boss. Think of this as the customer service equivalent of learning a new language. When you are able to speak another person's language, it becomes easier to understand — and be understood — by them. The place to start is by identifying your own individual working style.

What's My Style?

Consider each of the following questions separately and circle the *one* letter (a, b, c, or d) that corresponds to the description that most fits you. If you have trouble selecting only one answer, ask yourself which response, at work, would be the most natural or likely for you to take.

Self-evaluation questionnaire

There are no *right answers* to these questions so base your response on how you are today, not how you think you should be or would like to be in the future.

1. When talking to a customer or co-worker . . .

a. I maintain eye contact the whole time.

b. I alternate between looking at the person and looking down.

c. I look around the room a good deal of the time.

d. I try to maintain eye contact but look away from time to time.

2. If I have an important decision to make . . .

a. I think it through completely before deciding.

b. I go with my gut instincts.

c. I consider the impact it will have on other people before deciding.

d. I run it by someone whose opinion I respect before deciding.

3. My office or work area mostly has . . .

a. Family photos and sentimental items displayed.

b. Inspirational posters, awards, and art displayed.

c. Graphs and charts displayed.

d. Calendars and project outlines displayed.

4. If I am having a conflict with a co-worker or customer . . .

a. I try to help the situation along by focusing on the positive.

b. I stay calm and try to understand the cause of the conflict.

c. I try to avoid discussing the issue causing the conflict.

d. I confront it right away so that it can get resolved as soon as possible.

5. When I talk on the phone at work . . .

    a. I keep the conversation focused on the purpose of the call.

    b. I will spend a few minutes chatting before getting down to business.

    c. I am in no hurry to get off the phone and don't mind chatting about personal things, the weather, and so on.

    d. I try to keep the conversation as brief as possible.

6. If a co-worker is upset . . .

    a. I ask if I can do anything to help.

    b. I leave him alone because I don't want to intrude on his privacy.

    c. I try to cheer him up and help him to see the bright side.

    d. I feel uncomfortable and hope he gets over it soon.

7. When I attend meetings at work . . .

    a. I sit back and think about what is being said before offering my opinion.

    b. I put all my cards on the table so my opinion is well known.

    c. I express my opinion enthusiastically, but listen to other's ideas as well.

    d. I try to support the ideas of the other people in the meeting.

8. When I make a presentation in front of a group . . .

    a. I am entertaining and often humorous.

    b. I am clear and concise.

    c. I speak relatively quietly.

    d. I am direct, specific, and sometimes loud.

9. When a customer is explaining a problem to me . . .

    a. I try to understand and empathize with how she is feeling.

    b. I look for the specific facts pertaining to the situation.

    c. I listen carefully for the main issue so that I can find a solution.

    d. I use my body language and tone of voice to show her that I understand.

10. When I attend training programs or presentations . . .

    a. I get bored if the person moves too slowly.

    b. I try to be supportive of the speaker, knowing how hard the job is.

    c. I want it to be entertaining as well as informative.

    d. I look for the logic behind what the speaker is saying.

11. **When I want to get my point across to customers or co-workers . . .**

    a. I listen to their point of view first and then express my ideas gently.

    b. I strongly state my opinion so that they know where I stand.

    c. I try to persuade them without being too forceful.

    d. I explain the thinking and logic behind what I am saying.

12. **When I am late for a meeting or appointment . . .**

    a. I don't panic but call ahead to say that I will be a few minutes late.

    b. I feel bad about keeping the other person waiting.

    c. I get very upset and rush to get there as soon as possible.

    d. I apologize profusely once I arrive.

13. **I set goals and objectives at work that . . .**

    a. I think I can realistically attain.

    b. I feel are challenging and would be exciting to achieve.

    c. I need to achieve as part of a bigger objective.

    d. Will make me feel good when I achieve them.

14. **When explaining a problem to a co-worker whom I need help from . . .**

    a. I explain the problem in as much detail as possible.

    b. I sometimes exaggerate to make my point.

    c. I try to explain how the problem makes me feel.

    d. I explain how I would like the problem to be solved.

15. **If customers or co-workers are late for a meeting with me in my office . . .**

    a. I keep myself busy by making phone calls or working until they arrive.

    b. I assume they were delayed a bit and don't get upset.

    c. I call to make sure that I have the correct information (date, time, and so on).

    d. I get upset that the person is wasting my time.

16. **When I am behind on a project and feel pressure to get it done . . .**

    a. I make a list of everything I need to do, in what order, by when.

    b. I block out everything else and focus 100 percent on the work I need to do.

    c. I become anxious and have a hard time focusing on my work.

    d. I set a date to get the project done by and go for it.

17. **When I feel verbally attacked by a customer or a co-worker . . .**

   a. I tell her to stop it.

   b. I feel hurt but usually don't say anything about it to her.

   c. I ignore her anger and try to focus on the facts of the situation.

   d. I let her know in strong terms that I don't like her behavior.

18. **When I see a co-worker or customer whom I like and haven't seen recently . . .**

   a. I give him a friendly hug.

   b. I greet him but don't shake his hand.

   c. I give him a firm but quick handshake.

   d. I give him an enthusiastic handshake that lasts a few moments.

Scoring the questionnaire

Once you have finished the questionnaire, review the following scoring sheet (shown in Figure 17-1). You will be scoring yourself on four specific working styles. They are:

✔ Driver (DR)

✔ Expressive (EX)

✔ Amiable (AM)

✔ Analytical (AY)

Later in this chapter, we explain each style in detail, but first transfer your answers from the questionnaire to the scoring sheet and then count up the number of times you circled each style. Enter these scores at the bottom of the scoring sheet. The style where you scored the most points is your primary working style.

FYI

The four terms (Driver, Expressive, Amiable, and Analytical) were originally coined by Dr. David Merrill, founder of Tracom Consulting Group. If you are interested in reading more about the research done by Dr. Merrill and his associates, read *Personal Styles and Effective Performance: Make Your Style Work for You* by David Merrill and Roger Reid (Radnor, Pa.: Chilton, 1981).

Scoring Form

1	7	13
a Driver	**a** Analytical	**a** Analytical
b Amiable	**b** Driver	**b** Expressive
c Analytical	**c** Expressive	**c** Driver
d Expressive	**d** Amiable	**d** Amiable
2	**8**	**14**
a Analytical	**a** Expressive	**a** Analytical
b Driver	**b** Analytical	**b** Expressive
c Amiable	**c** Amiable	**c** Amiable
d Expressive	**d** Driver	**d** Driver
3	**9**	**15**
a Amiable	**a** Amiable	**a** Expressive
b Expressive	**b** Analytical	**b** Amiable
c Analytical	**c** Driver	**c** Analytical
d Driver	**d** Expressive	**d** Driver
4	**10**	**16**
a Expressive	**a** Driver	**a** Analytical
b Amiable	**b** Amiable	**b** Driver
c Analytical	**c** Expressive	**c** Amiable
d Driver	**d** Analytical	**d** Expressive
5	**11**	**17**
a Driver	**a** Amiable	**a** Driver
b Expressive	**b** Driver	**b** Amiable
c Amiable	**c** Expressive	**c** Analytical
d Analytical	**d** Analytical	**d** Expressive
6	**12**	**18**
a Amiable	**a** Analytical	**a** Amiable
b Analytical	**b** Amiable	**b** Analytical
c Expressive	**c** Driver	**c** Driver
d Driver	**d** Expressive	**d** Expressive

Total Driver Score _____
Total Analytical Score _____
Total Amiable Score _____
Total Expressive Score _____

Figure 17-1:
The working
styles
scoring
form.

Understanding Your Working Style

Your working style describes how you primarily approach and deal with people and situations at work (although many of our clients tell us that they see similarities that carry over into their personal lives as well).

If you have two scores the same and are a little uncertain about which is your style, you should be able to pinpoint where you fit in by reading through the descriptions of each style presented later in this chapter. If this doesn't work, ask a co-worker, spouse, or close friend which working style they think you have — they usually know.

What does working style measure?

Research on the general concept of individual styles goes back to the work of the famous psychologist Carl Jung. Since then, many researchers, psychologists, and consultants have studied and further developed the concept of styles. One thing all the researchers agree on is that these styles measure two important aspects of a person's behavior:

- how emotionally expressive they are
- the degree to which they assert themselves

Emotional expression

The degree to which you show or hold back your emotions helps determine your style. In particular, emotions are expressed in four ways:

Verbal expression

What type of language do you use? Are your discussions filled with colorful metaphors and larger-than-life phrases, or do you tend to say things in an understated way? The types of words that you use and the way in which you use them is a direct reflection of your working style.

Vocal expression

Are you a fast talker or do you go at a slow and easy pace? Is there a lot of intensity and excitement in your voice, or do you usually sound calm and relaxed? The tone you use communicates as much about your working style as the words themselves.

Body language

Do you talk with your hands or hold them by your side when speaking? Do you walk at a brisk pace or do you prefer a leisurely stroll? Your body movement tells a story about which working style is the most natural to you.

Environment

Do you have a neat and tidy office with charts and graphs or do you prefer posters and motivational sayings plastered on your walls? Your office environment is a clue to the type of working style you have.

Assertiveness

Assertiveness relates to how much or how little you try to influence and control the actions and opinions of those around you. If your working style reflects a high degree of assertiveness, you are probably seen by others as forceful and direct. A lower degree usually signifies being more reserved and easygoing.

Don't make the mistake of thinking that one style is better or more desirable than another. Everyone expresses himself or herself differently, and each style adds to the richness of your working environment. Wanting to trade your style for the one that you've always yearned for is as fruitless as wanting another personality. Appreciate the way you are and read on to discover ways that you can adapt your style in order to better communicate with the people around you.

The working styles grid

Plot your scores on the working styles grid (shown in Figure 17-2) and read the description of your style written below each section. We recommend that you read through all four of the working style descriptions because understanding the other three styles will help you become more sensitive and flexible with customers and co-workers who have a style different than your own.

The analytical working style

The analytical working style, found in the top-left corner of the grid, has a low degree of assertiveness and a low degree of emotional expression. People with this style focus on facts more than feelings. They evaluate situations objectively and gather lots of data before making a decision. They prefer an organized work environment where they know exactly what is expected of them. Words that describe this style include the following:

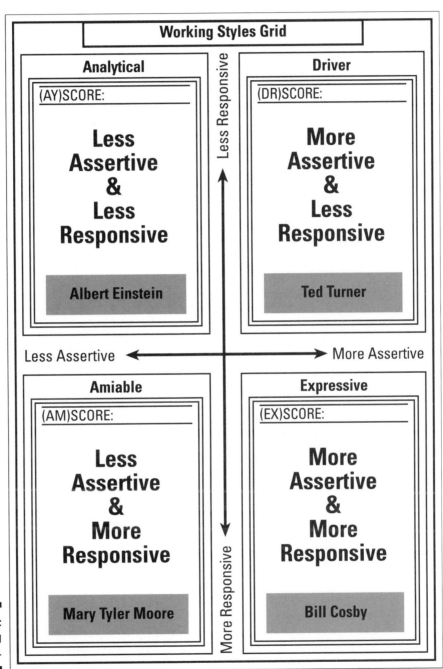

Figure 17-2:
The working
styles grid.

- ✔ serious
- ✔ well-organized
- ✔ systematic
- ✔ logical
- ✔ factual
- ✔ reserved

Strengths of the analytical style

Their natural inclination toward fact finding makes *analyticals* good problem solvers who have the patience to examine the details and come up with a logical solution. They can work independently, and as such they are well-suited to the finance, science, and computer fields. Albert Einstein was the perfect example of this working style.

Weaknesses of the analytical style

Analyticals place facts and accuracy ahead of feelings, and they are sometimes seen by others as emotionally distant. Under stress, they have a tendency to over analyze in order to avoid making a decision. Because analyticals are uncomfortable with feelings — their own and other's — they may avoid expressing feelings even when this would be the best thing to do.

Key analytical behaviors

People with the analytical working style tend to:

- ✔ show little facial expression
- ✔ have controlled body movement with slow gestures
- ✔ have little inflection in their voice and may tend toward monotone
- ✔ use language that is precise and focuses on specific details
- ✔ have charts, graphs, and statistics displayed in their office

The driver working style

The driver working style, found in the top-right corner of the grid, has a high degree of assertiveness and a low degree of emotional expression. People with this style know where they want to go and how they are going to get there. They are good at managing tasks and are results oriented. *Drivers* like competition (especially when they win). Words that describe this style include:

- ✔ decisive
- ✔ independent
- ✔ efficient
- ✔ intense
- ✔ deliberate
- ✔ achieving

Strengths of the driver style

The ability to take charge of situations and make quick decisions are what often make drivers high achievers. They put a single-minded focus on the goals they want and are not afraid to take risks in order to accomplish them. They do well in positions of authority, can work independently, and are well-suited to being lawyers, surgeons, and CEOs. Ted Turner is a good example of the driver working style.

Weaknesses of the driver style

When feeling stressed, drivers can be so focused on getting things done quickly that they can overlook details and make mistakes. They may push aside their own and other's feelings in order to get the job done, which can create tense situations with co-workers. Because of their hard driving, competitive nature, drivers can sometimes become workaholics.

Key driver behaviors

People with the driver working style tend to:

- ✔ make direct eye contact
- ✔ move quickly and briskly with purpose
- ✔ speak forcefully and fast-paced
- ✔ use direct, bottom-line language
- ✔ have planning calendars and project outlines displayed in their office

The amiable working style

The amiable working style, found in the bottom-left corner of the grid, has a low degree of assertiveness and a high degree of emotional expression. People with this style are responsive and friendly — but not necessarily forceful or direct. Words that describe this working style include:

- ✔ cooperative
- ✔ friendly
- ✔ supportive
- ✔ patient
- ✔ relaxed

Strengths of the amiable style

Amiables are generally good listeners to whom others come for support. Their sensitivity to the feelings of others makes them good collaborators who thrive in a team environment. They are well-suited to the helping professions, such as nurses, therapists, teachers, and so on. A good example of the amiable working style is Mary Tyler Moore.

Weaknesses of the amiable style

Amiables often have trouble asserting themselves and making decisions quickly. Generally, they do not like confronting disagreement with co-workers, and their reluctance to deal with conflict means that they don't always get what they really want. Their frustration about not resolving such issues can turn into resentment that is directed toward the same co-worker in later interactions.

Key amiable behaviors

People with the amiable working style tend to:

- ✔ have a friendly facial expression
- ✔ make frequent eye contact
- ✔ use non-aggressive, non-dramatic gestures
- ✔ speak slowly and in soft tones with moderate inflection
- ✔ use language that is supportive and encouraging
- ✔ display lots of family pictures in their office

The expressive working style

The expressive working style, found in the bottom-right corner of the grid, has a high degree of assertiveness and a high degree of emotional expression. People with this style are outgoing and persuasive. They are enthusiastic, friendly, and prefer to work with other people. Expressives thrive in the spotlight. Words that describe this working style include:

✔ outgoing

✔ enthusiastic

✔ persuasive

✔ humorous

✔ gregarious

✔ lively

Strengths of the expressive style

Expressives have a lively nature, and because of this, they are able to motivate and generate excitement in others. They work at a fast pace, and are good at building alliances and relationships to accomplish their goals. They are well-suited to high profile positions that require them to make public presentations, such as trainers, actors, salespeople, and so on. Bill Cosby is a famous example of the expressive working style.

Weaknesses of the expressive style

When expressives are upset, they can often communicate their feelings with a lot of intensity and, if criticized, may lash out with a verbal attack. They can seem overwhelming to less assertive styles because when they are enthusiastic about an idea, they press for a decision and may overlook important details.

Key expressive behaviors

People with the expressive working style tend to:

✔ use rapid hand and arm gestures

✔ speak quickly with lots of animation and inflection

✔ have a wide range of facial expressions

✔ use language that is persuasive

✔ have a workspace cluttered with inspirational items

Getting in Step with Different Styles

Customers and co-workers with different styles require different types of approaches. By understanding and adapting to the style of the person you are dealing with, you'll create stronger rapport and deliver better service. This technique of *style stepping* is especially important in difficult situations where there's a high probability for misunderstanding or confusion.

Your backup style

While there is usually one primary working style, many people have a backup style. This is the style that you fall back on when you are under pressure. Your second highest questionnaire score usually indicates your backup style. For example, your primary style may be expressive, but under pressure you take on some driver style behaviors. When under stress, all four styles go one of two ways: they get more active or more passive. Drivers and expressives (the more assertive of the four styles) become more active and aggressive under pressure. Amiables and analyticals (the less assertive of the four) become less active and less responsible under pressure. These are the general behaviors associated with each style when under pressure:

- Drivers will become more autocratic and demanding.

- Expressives will show their emotions by verbally attacking.

- Amiables will give in and put their own feelings aside.

- Analyticals will handle conflict by avoiding the situation.

None of these responses usually works to resolve conflict (see Chapter 18 for more in-depth information about resolving conflict). Therefore, being able to predict how you and others are likely to react under pressure and modifying those reactions can reduce conflict between you and your co-workers.

Everybody uses aspects from all four working styles to some degree. While the behaviors that you use the most reflect your working style, there are others — less frequently used — that are a smaller part of how you express yourself. Practicing style stepping gives you a chance to emphasize these little used aspects of yourself.

Meanwhile, back at the bookstore...

The following four scenarios, which take place between a bookstore sales clerk and a customer, show how people with different styles might typically interact with one another. The first sketch in each scenario takes place before *style stepping,* and although the sales clerk is polite and efficient, he or she misses the mark with the customer because the conversation is on the service person's terms rather than on the customer's terms.

The second sketch in each scenario shows how — by using *style stepping* — the clerk creates more rapport and understanding by adapting to the customers working style.

First, look for the scenario that features your own working style. Getting familiar with it will help you be more sensitive to how others view your style. Second, find the scenario that contains the style of a customer or co-worker. Notice what you would have to change in order to *get in step* with their style.

Part of becoming a good style stepper is quickly assessing what style your customer or co-worker has. Figuring out the styles of those you work with is easy because you are around them all the time. Customers can be trickier because you don't have a great deal of time to make an assessment of their style. The more you use style stepping, the better you will become at recognizing each working style. To begin with, when trying to evaluate a customer's style, we recommend that you keep it simple by asking yourself these two questions:

- ✔ Is this person asserting his or her needs, wants, and opinions a lot or a little?
- ✔ Is this person expressing his or her feelings and emotions a lot or a little?

The answers to these two questions should point you in the right direction.

Amiable and driver

In this scenario, the clerk has the amiable working style, and the customer has the driver working style.

Clerk	—	*(with a pleasant tone)* Good afternoon, how are you today?
Customer	—	Fine. I'm looking for a book called *How To Get 25 Hours Out Of Your Day.* Do you have it?
Clerk	—	I'm not sure, I'll have to look it up. Sounds like an interesting book, where did you hear about it?
Customer	—	*(impatiently looking at his watch)* A friend. The author is Stan Workmore. Do you have it?
Clerk	—	*(looking at computer screen)* Let me see. Mr. Workmore has written several books, have you read anything else by him?
Customer	—	I'm really in a hurry; do you have it?
Clerk	—	Yes, here it is! We have one copy left; it's in the back stock room. Why don't you relax and look around while I go find it for you?
Customer	—	I don't have the time. Could you get it for me now?
Clerk	—	Sure, I'll be back in just a minute.

Getting in step with drivers

From this scenario, it is obvious that drivers are not big on small talk, and they like to get speedy results. Style stepping behaviors for working with drivers include:

✔ making direct eye contact

✔ speaking at a fast pace

✔ getting down to business quickly

✔ arriving on time and not lingering

✔ being clear, specific, and brief in your conversation

✔ not over explaining or rambling

✔ being organized and well prepared

✔ focusing on the results to be produced

Using style stepping

In this scenario, the clerk's natural style is amiable, but he style steps to bridge the gap between himself and his driver customer.

Clerk	—	(*with a pleasant voice*) Good afternoon. How are you today?
Customer	—	Fine. I'm looking for a book called *How To Get 25 Hours Out Of Your Day.* Do you have it?
Clerk	—	I can find out. What's the author's name?
Customer	—	Stan Workmore.
Clerk	—	We have one copy left. My co-worker, Nancy, can ring it up for you while I get the book from the stock room.
Customer	—	Thanks for taking care of this so quickly.
Clerk	—	No problem.

Analytical and amiable

In this scenario, the clerk has an analytical working style, and the customer has the amiable working style.

Clerk	—	Can I help you with anything?
Customer	—	(*pleasantly*) I'm looking for a book called *How To Get 25 Hours Out Of Your Day.* Do you have it?
Clerk	—	(*matter-of-factly*) I've never heard of it, and I wouldn't want to guess. I can look it up in the books in print if you would like.
Customer	—	I would really appreciate it if you could.

Clerk	—	What is the exact spelling of the author's name, the publisher, and the year the book was published?
Customer	—	The author's name is Stan Workmore. I'm really sorry, but I don't know who the publisher is. Can you still help me?
Clerk	—	I will do my best, but Mr. Workmore has written several books, and without more specific information, it will take me that much longer to locate it.
Customer	—	That's okay. I'll be more than happy to wait while you look it up.
Clerk	—	Okay, here it is. I've managed to find it. The publisher is Toilaway & Company. It was published in June of 1993. I have one copy left, and that should be located in our back stock room. I will go and get it. Will you wait here?
Customer	—	I think I'll go have a cup of coffee in your cafe while I'm waiting.
Clerk	—	Where will you be sitting exactly so that I can find you?

Getting in step with amiables

This scenario shows how the amiable customer couldn't care less about any of the details that are so important to the analytical sales clerk. Style stepping behaviors for working with amiables include:

- ✔ making eye contact but looking away once in a while
- ✔ speaking at a moderate pace and with a softer voice
- ✔ not using a harsh tone of voice or language
- ✔ asking them for their opinions and ideas
- ✔ not trying to counter their ideas with logic
- ✔ encouraging them to express any doubts or concerns they may have
- ✔ avoiding putting excessive pressure on them to make a decision
- ✔ mutually agreeing on all goals, action plans, and completion dates

Using style stepping

In this scenario, the clerk's natural working style is analytical, but she will style step to bridge the gap between herself and the amiable customer.

Clerk	—	Can I help you with anything?
Customer	—	I'm looking for a book called *How To Get 25 Hours Out Of Your Day*. Do you have it?

Clerk	—	(*with empathy*) I'm sorry, but I haven't heard of it. Would you like me to look it up for you?
Customer	—	I would really appreciate it if you could.
Clerk	—	Can you tell me the author's name and perhaps the publisher?
Customer	—	The author's name is Stan Workmore. I'm really sorry, but I don't know who the publisher is. Can you still help me?
Clerk	—	Of course; this will take me a few minutes to look up. Here it is. We have one copy left in the stock room. Would you mind waiting here while I get it?
Customer	—	No problem. Thanks for helping me out.
Clerk	—	My pleasure.

Expressive and analytical

In this scenario, the clerk has the expressive working style, and the customer has the analytical working style.

Clerk	—	Good morning. How can I help you?
Customer	—	I'm looking for *How To Get 25 Hours Out Of Your Day*; it's by Stan Workmore and published by Toilaway & Company. Can you tell me where I can find it in the store?
Clerk	—	(*enthusiastically*) Now that sounds like something we could all use. What did you say that author's name was again?
Customer	—	Stan Workmore, W-O-R-K-M-O-R-E. Do you want to write it down?
Clerk	—	No, I've got it. What a perfect name for the author of that book. Okay, here it is. You'll be pleased to know we've one copy left in the back. If you hold on just a second, I'll run and get it for you.
Customer	—	How long exactly will this take? I have an 11 o'clock meeting.
Clerk	—	Just a second or two.

Getting in step with analyticals

Remember that analyticals focus on facts, details, and logic. They are uncomfortable with expressing feelings and are not very outgoing. When dealing with them, you should emphasize the rational, objective aspects of what you are discussing. Style stepping behaviors for working with analyticals include:

✔ not speaking with a loud or fast-paced voice

✔ being more formal in your speech and manners

✔ presenting the pros and cons of an idea, as well as options

✔ not overstating the benefits of something

✔ following up in writing

✔ being on time and keeping it brief

✔ showing how your approach has little risk

Using style stepping

In this scenario, the clerk's natural working style is expressive, but he will style step to bridge the gap between himself and his analytical customer.

Clerk	—	Good morning. What a great day. How can I help you?
Customer	—	I'm looking for *How To Get 25 Hours Out Of Your Day*; it's by Stan Workmore and published by Toilaway & Company. Can you tell me where I can find it in the store?
Clerk	—	(*seriously*) I can locate that for you. Can you spell the author's last name for me please?
Customer	—	Stan Workmore, W-O-R-K-M-O-R-E. Do you want to write it down?
Clerk	—	Yes. I'll make a note of it. I have it. There's one copy left. It's in the stock room; if you will please wait, I will go get it for you.
Customer	—	How long exactly will this take? I have an 11 o'clock meeting.
Clerk	—	No longer than five minutes.

Driver and expressive

In this scenario, the clerk has the driver working style, and the customer has the expressive working style.

Clerk	—	Can I help you?
Customer	—	(*enthusiastically*) Hi, how are you? I'm looking for *How To Get 25 Hours Out Of Your Day*. Isn't that a great title? All my friends have read it, and they just love it!

Clerk	—	(*looking at his watch*) Who's the author?
Customer	—	Oh, he's a wonderful man. I've met him. You won't believe his name: it's Stan Workmore. Isn't that the perfect name?
Clerk	—	We have it. I need to go in the back to get it. Why don't you pay Nancy here while I go get the book?
Customer	—	Sounds like a wonderful idea. I think I'll grab a cup of coffee in the cafe while you get the book.
Clerk	—	No, don't do that—you won't have time. I will be back in just a minute. Wait here. I will be right back with your book.
Customer	—	Sure, I'll just talk with Nancy while I wait. Hello Nancy . . . .

Getting in step with expressives

Expressives are the most outgoing and gregarious of all the styles, and they are best approached by focusing on generalities rather than on details. Expressives usually respond well to playful people who focus on the big picture. Style stepping behaviors for working with expressives include:

- ✔ making direct eye contact
- ✔ having energetic and fast-paced speech
- ✔ allowing time in the meeting for socializing
- ✔ talking about experiences, people, and opinions, as well as the facts
- ✔ asking about their intuitive sense of things
- ✔ supporting your ideas with testimonials from people whom they know and like
- ✔ paraphrasing any agreements made
- ✔ maintaining a balance between fun and reaching objectives

Using style stepping

In this scenario, the clerk's natural working style is driver, but she will style step to bridge the gap between herself and her expressive customer.

Clerk	—	Can I help you?
Customer	—	(*enthusiastically*) Hi, how are you? I'm looking for *How To Get 25 Hours Out Of Your Day*. Isn't that a great title? All my friends have read it, and they just love it!
Clerk	—	It sounds interesting. Can you tell me the author's name?

Customer	—	Oh, he's a wonderful man; I've met him. You won't believe his name: it's Stan Workmore. Isn't that the perfect name?
Clerk	—	It certainly is. Okay, you will be happy to know that I have found your book; it's in the back. Do you want to wait here while I go get it?
Customer	—	I think I'll go grab a cup of coffee in your cafe.
Clerk	—	Okay, I'll be back in just a minute. In the meantime, my co-worker Nancy can ring up the book for you if you would like.
Customer	—	Thanks. I'll see you in a few minutes.

The rule of thumb when it comes to stepping into another style is this: *a little goes a long way.* In all of the previous revised scenarios, the clerk did not go over the top when style stepping but showed just enough flexibility to make the customer feel comfortable and taken care of.

Many people get concerned that style stepping means being artificial with people. If you are thinking, "Won't I seem phony if I am always being flexible to the other person's style," take heart in knowing that style stepping doesn't replace your personality, but it does *enhance* your ability to get your ideas across to others.

Style Stepping Opportunities

Many situations at work provide good opportunities for using style stepping, including:

✔ **making a sales presentation**

We hear many success stories from our clients who tell how redesigning their sales pitch to fit their customer's *language* has closed a sale that had been previously elusive.

✔ **conflicts between you and a customer**

By stopping and listening to your customer's style, you can quickly redirect how you are approaching him or her and have a better chance of resolving disagreements.

✔ **presenting your ideas to your manager**

Style stepping with your manager can make the difference between your ideas being acted upon or ignored. In our workshops, we often see good ideas lost because the staff person was not able to present them in a way that made sense to the manager's way of thinking.

✔ **developing teamwork**

Style stepping, in many ways, is the essence of good teamwork. Knowing and appreciating the different styles of the people on your team makes understanding their point-of-view and coming to a consensus decision easier.

Create a Customer Profile

There are some situations where sitting down and pre-planning an upcoming conversation can be useful in getting to a win-win resolution. The customer profile form (shown in Figure 17-3) is best used when you have a challenging situation on hand and a specific objective that you want to achieve. There are four steps to creating a customer profile:

✔ Determine the customer's primary working style.

✔ Set your objective.

✔ Look at the big picture.

✔ Plan a rapport strategy.

You can also use the customer profile form to plan out conversations with co-workers and bosses, as well as customers.

Determine the customer's primary working style

Based on your observations, what is this customer's primary style? If you are not sure, read the description of each style found earlier in this chapter and choose the one that fits the best.

Set your objective

One of the keys to successful customer profiling is setting clear and achievable outcomes. Objectives that are too vague, such as, "I want to improve my relationship with, Liza, my co-worker, " make it difficult to assess what exactly needs to happen to achieve the goal. It will work better if you define your outcome more specifically, such as, "I want Liza and myself to agree on how we are going to solve the overtime problem."

Customer Profile Form

Primary working style:

My objective is:

The big picture:

My strategy for building rapport is:

Figure 17-3:
The
customer
profile form.

Look at the big picture

Step back for a moment and consider your working style and the working style of the customer. What are the potential trouble spots that you may encounter and where are you most likely to have agreement and common ideas? By thinking about these trouble spots ahead of time, you can plan for a more successful interaction.

Plan a rapport strategy

Once your analysis is complete, plan out what actions you will take in order to create a rapport with your customer (or co-worker) and achieve the result you want. At this point, you may want to review the previous section, "Getting in Step with Different Styles," and use the information provided as a basis for your strategy.

Be as specific as possible when you write down your strategy actions. For example:

- Be on time to my meeting with Bob.
- Prepare a chart with all the information on it.
- Ask Bob what his ideas are for solving the problem.
- Explain to Bob how I arrived at the solution, step-by-step.
- Give Bob a one-page overview of the proposed solution.

Chapter 18

Managing Conflict with Co-Workers

• •

In This Chapter
▶ How internal conflict effects the customer
▶ The four conflict traps and how to avoid them
▶ How to be more assertive
▶ Five basic truths about people

• •

*O*ne significant difference between managing conflict with your co-workers and managing conflict with your customers is that customers come and go, but your co-workers are here to stay. Managing conflict with workmates can also be harder because you have more contact with them, more often. All of the skills you use to deal with difficult customers (described in Chapters 15 and 17) work just as well with difficult co-workers; however, you need a few additional skills when you are having a hard time communicating with co-workers. Establishing good rapport and learning to resolve conflicts with co-workers results in less stress for you and better service to your customers.

The Weak Link in the Chain

When conflict between co-workers is badly managed or unresolved, it has a lasting impact on both staff and customers. The employee suffers because unresolved conflicts are a constant source of tension, and the customer suffers because the service they receive is only as good as the weakest link in the employee chain that delivers that service. The following scenario shows how a poorly managed conflict between two employees can seriously undermine the quality of service that the customer receives.

Yesterday's conflict

For the last few years, Geraldine and Becky have worked together at Desktop Office Supply. Geraldine is a customer service representative and Becky works in sales. Several weeks ago, they had a disagreement regarding an incorrect customer delivery date. Geraldine, who ended up taking the heat from the customer, was angry with Becky for giving her the wrong information and ended up losing her temper during the ensuing conversation. Becky, feeling attacked by Geraldine, became defensive, and the conflict was never resolved.

Today's problem

Two months later. A new customer calls the company to inquire about pricing and, unwittingly, is about to become a victim of Geraldine and Becky's disagreement.

Customer — I need a price on item #345 in a custom color. Can you tell me what the cost would be?

Geraldine — Sure. May I put you on hold a moment while I get that information for you?

Customer — Certainly.

Geraldine — Thank you.

Geraldine puts the customer on hold and calls the sales department to get the pricing information she needs. The problem begins when Becky unexpectedly picks up the phone.

Becky — This is Becky, how may I help you?

Geraldine — *(coldly)* This is Geraldine. I need a price on item #345 in a custom color.

Becky — *(off-handedly)* I don't have time to look that up right up now. Call me back later.

Geraldine — *(angrily)* I need it now; the customer is waiting on the line.

Becky — You will have to get back to him later — I have a deadline, and I can't look up the information right now.

Becky hangs up the phone and Geraldine, fuming, gets back on the line with the customer.

Geraldine — I can't get you that price right now.

Customer — But I have a meeting with the designer in an hour.

Geraldine	—	There's nothing that I can do. The sales department has the information I need, and they can't help me right now. I'll be happy to call you later when they give me the price.
Customer	—	I can't wait — and if you can't be more helpful, I'll take my business elsewhere.

Tomorrow's outcome

Desktop Office Supply just lost a customer because of an unresolved conflict between two of its employees. The cost of their continuing disagreement doesn't end there. After the call, they are both more edgy with the other customers they have to deal with, as well as the people they work around. Because Geraldine and Becky never effectively dealt with their original conflict, its shockwaves are felt every time they see or talk to one another.

The Four Conflict Traps

Geraldine and Becky fell into the trap of letting their initial conflict spiral way out of control. If they had been able to recognize when things started going wrong and taken steps to prevent the conflict, they would still be friends today. While avoiding occasional, job-related conflicts is impossible, they do not have to become so upsetting that they drive a wedge between you and the people you work with. Learning the four traps that keep you stuck in conflict — and how to get out of them — gives you a constructive way of resolving disagreements with co-workers. The four conflict traps are:

- ✔ fighting for the last word
- ✔ saying everything is okay when it isn't
- ✔ not wanting to talk about it — ever
- ✔ serving up put-downs

Trap 1: Fighting for the last word

This conflict trap is the vocal equivalent of dueling banjos. This trap usually begins when your co-worker makes a remark that you don't like and you up the ante by coming back with a snappy, even more disrespectful reply. The other person takes offense and does the same back to you — only one better — and you're off! Before you know it, voices are raised, tempers are hot, and the conversation is spiraling out of control. Following is a conversation between Lauren and Jon, two systems programmers who share the same work area in a large insurance company.

Lauren	—	I can't believe you forgot to turn on the copier — again.
Jon	—	Oh, yeah, like you never forget to turn it on.
Lauren	—	Actually, turning on the copier is the first thing I do when I come in the morning.
Jon	—	Well, you're just so together, aren't you?
Lauren	—	Why are you always in such a bad mood?
Jon	—	If you don't like the way I am, then don't talk to me.
Lauren	—	No wonder nobody in the office likes you.
Jon	—	Listen, Lauren, I haven't seen you winning any popularity contests lately.

Three ways to keep from spiraling out of control

If you find yourself in a conversation (such as the preceding one) where things seem to be spiraling out of control, you can pull yourself out by learning to back off. Follow these steps when you notice that you and your co-worker are stuck in fighting for the last word:

✔ Let your co-worker have the last word.

✔ Count to five before you respond.

✔ Use empathic phrases.

Let your co-worker have the last word

End the contest by letting your co-worker have the last word. If you can drop your defensive posture, you will be able to listen to his or her point of view, discuss it, and then present your ideas or opinions.

Count to five before you respond

Rather than allowing the conversation to bounce back and forth with the speed of a ping-pong ball, stay quiet for five seconds before you respond to what your co-worker has said. A moment of silence usually gives you the time you need to stop from zinging back with an automatic, negative response.

Use empathic phrases

Once you have broken the going-one-better chain, use an empathic comment to let the other person know that you are listening and appreciate his or her perspective — even though you may disagree.

Using these techniques, the previous conversation between Lauren and Jon might go something like this:

Lauren — I can't believe you forgot to turn on the copier — again.

Jon — Oh, yeah, like you never forget to turn it on.

Lauren — Actually, turning on the copier is the first thing I do when I come in the morning.

Jon — Well, you're just so together, aren't you?

Realizing that the conversation is spiraling out of control, Lauren decides to give Jon the last word. She counts to five before responding and then continues with an empathic comment.

Lauren — *(calmer)* I know how easy it is to forget to turn it on sometimes.

Jon — It is. I was just so busy this morning….

Lauren — I understand. I'm sorry I snapped at you.

Jon — That's okay. I'll try and remember to switch the copier on in the future.

I was once stopped by a California Highway Patrol officer because I was exceeding the speed limit (a rare occurrence). He walked up to the car window, looked me straight in the eye, and, with a slightly concerned look, asked me if I knew why he had stopped me. He waited while I performed a few verbal somersaults, and then, with a calm voice, he told me the specific details of my offense. He stuck to the facts and never once made any assumptions about why I had done what I did. He was so good at giving me the bad news that when he finished writing the ticket and said, "Have a nice day," I responded back with a genuinely enthusiastic, "You, too, Officer." I later found out that the California Highway Patrol Academy put officers through a 27-week training course that emphasizes dealing with confrontation and conflict with their *customers* — It works!

How to assert yourself

If you don't know how to strike that delicate balance between straight-forwardness and tact, you can unintentionally create conflict. By flying off the handle and becoming aggressive, you force your co-workers into a defensive posture that makes hearing what you have to say difficult for them. The opposite stance is also ineffective; being too tentative when presenting your point may result in a co-worker not taking you seriously.

Knowing how to assert yourself will help you to voice your thoughts, feelings, and opinions in a nonthreatening and balanced way. Following are six important tips on asserting yourself:

✓ **Be specific.**

Make sure that you describe the situation in specific terms so that the other person knows exactly what you are talking about. For example, saying, "You don't communicate" is not as effective as saying, "You didn't call me when you said you would."

✓ **Stick to the facts.**

Don't become a mind reader and assign reasons, attitudes, or motives for why your co-worker behaved as he or she did. Your co-worker will become defensive if you make incorrect assumptions about his or her feelings. Remember to only describe what is observable. For example, saying, "You felt so guilty, you couldn't even look at me" is not as effective as saying, "After I spoke with you, you turned your back to me."

✓ **Never say never.**

When you talk about the other person's behavior, stay away from absolute words such as *never* and *always* because those words are usually exaggerations of the facts. For example, saying, "You always ignore me" is not as effective as saying, "You didn't do what I asked you to do."

✓ **Let your face reflect your feelings.**

Your face should reflect the message that you want to convey. For example, if you are angry, resist the urge to smile and make light of the situation. In this case, a look of concern is most appropriate.

✓ **Make eye contact.**

Let your co-worker know that you mean what you are saying by making direct eye contact with him. However, be careful not to stare him down, as this could be interpreted as overbearing and aggressive behavior.

✓ **Don't fidget.**

Avoid nervous habits such as pacing, tugging at your hair, rattling change in your pocket, or tinkering with a pen. They are all distracting and weaken the impact of what you are saying.

Trap 2: Saying everything is okay when it isn't

By burying your head in the sand and smoothing everything over, you fall into the trap of convincing yourself that nothing is wrong and that no conflict exists. On the surface, you seem to be avoiding confrontation with this strategy, but in reality, the situation is a conflict waiting to erupt. Eventually, the conflict will bubble to the surface when you least expect it. Here is a conversation between

Cliff and Alex. Cliff is Alex's supervisor in the receiving department of a large consumer electronics company. Alex has fallen behind schedule but doesn't want Cliff to know.

Cliff — Did you inspect those amplifiers that came in yesterday?

Alex — Yes. They look fine.

Cliff — But some of the boxes haven't been opened.

Alex — Well, I've looked at most of them, and they were okay.

Cliff — How many did you look at?

Alex — Most of them.

Cliff — When will you inspect the rest?

Alex — Sometime today.

Cliff — We're expecting another shipment in this afternoon, so all of them need to be checked before the next lot comes in. This job is really important Alex, and I'm going to be very upset if it doesn't get done.

Alex — Don't worry, no problem.

Alex is avoiding telling his supervisor the truth because he wants the problem to go away without facing it head on. The trap is that Alex believes that the situation will somehow miraculously fix itself when, in reality, it won't. Avoiding the conflict now will only make matters that much worse later when Cliff realizes that the next shipment has arrived and the amplifier inspection is still not complete.

How to keep from smoothing things over

Both people were partly responsible for not dealing well with the conflict at the warehouse. As soon as he knew that there was a possibility that his work would not get done, Alex should have notified Cliff. By doing so, the potential conflict could have been prevented and then a solution could have been reached for completing the inspection on time. Alex has another problem as a result of avoiding the conflict: His stress level will steadily climb as the new shipment arrival gets closer. Focusing on his task will be more difficult, and unnecessary mistakes may easily be made.

Cliff, the supervisor, was too easily diverted from getting to the facts by Alex's vague answers. Be sure to ask specific questions to get to the truth of the matter when dealing with a co-worker whom you suspect is saying things are okay when they're not. Both parties need to take action to keep from falling into this conflict trap.

If you are the smoother:

If you find yourself in a situation where you are tempted to pretend everything is all right when it isn't, take the following steps:

✔ **Don't assume it will get better.**

   Although hope springs eternal, the chances of an uncomfortable situation just blowing over is very unlikely, so the sooner you come to terms with the situation, the sooner you resolve the problem.

✔ **Tell someone.**

   Find someone who can help you resolve the issue and tell that person exactly what is happening. He or she may get upset or react in a way that makes you feel uncomfortable at first, but a few minutes of direct heat is always better than several hours of slow simmering.

✔ **Pat yourself on the back.**

   Once the situation is out in the open and resolved, notice how much lighter you feel. Recognizing and reinforcing that you had the courage to face the circumstances and deal with them is important. Give yourself a pat on the back for taking the burden off of your shoulders.

If you are the smoothee:

When you are in a situation where you suspect *another* person is smoothing over a problem to avoid a conflict with you, take the following steps:

✔ **Ask general questions.**

   Start by asking general questions that probe a little deeper into what the facts of the situation might be. If you suspect that some important information is being left out, move on to the next step.

✔ **Ask specific questions.**

   Ask for details and don't settle for answers that seem too vague or general. Remember that if a person is holding something back, she is probably doing so because she wants to avoid conflict, not because she is dishonest. By keeping your tone soft and avoiding language that makes it sound as if you are accusing the other person, you make it easier for her to face the situation and tell you what you need to know.

✔ **Don't overreact.**

   Assuming that the other person hasn't done something really bad, like blown up the mainframe computer, most conflicts can be resolved by simple communication. If you react by jumping up and down with steam coming out of your ears, you make 'fessing up unsafe for the other person the next time something difficult has to be dealt with.

▹ **Work together on a new plan of action.**

Once the situation has been put on the table and discussed, look for mutual ways of resolving the problem.

Using the preceding suggestions for both the smoother and smoothee, a revised conversation between Cliff and Alex might go something like this:

Cliff	—	Did you inspect those amplifiers that came in yesterday?
Alex	—	Yes. They look fine.
Cliff	—	But some of the boxes haven't been opened.
Alex	—	Well, I've looked at most of them, and they were okay.
Cliff	—	How many did you look at?
Alex	—	Most of them.

Cliff must now ask more specific questions so that he can find out what is really going on. Alex uses these specific questions as his cue to face the conflict and talk to Cliff about the problem he has.

Cliff	—	How many exactly?
Alex	—	Sixty-three.
Cliff	—	That's only two-thirds of them.
Alex	—	I know. I'm really behind on my schedule. I don't think I will able to finish everything on time.
Cliff	—	(*annoyed but calm*) You assured me they would get done. This creates a problem.
Alex	—	I know, I'm sorry. I thought I could catch up, but I was wrong.
Cliff	—	Okay, well, let's figure out what we can do to get out of this jam.

Trap 3: Not wanting to talk about it — ever

This trap is that of trying to shut out conflict by staying silent and avoiding the problem at hand. This kind of withdrawal is a strategy used to keep conflict at arm's length so that it never has to be dealt with directly. The following conversation between Amber and Manuel, co-workers in the credit department of an auto parts company, shows what happens when one person withdraws from the conversation and just doesn't want to talk about the problem.

Amber — Manuel, I really need your monthly statistics for my report.

Manuel — (*busy working at his computer*) Later, okay?

Amber — I need them today. This report is due soon.

Manuel — I can't do it now, I'm busy.

Amber — I want them by lunch time.

Manuel — (*getting up from his desk*) I'll see what I can do.

Amber — (*frustrated*) This is the third time I've asked you for them.

Manuel — (*leaving the office*) I have to go over to shipping, talk to me when I get back.

Amber — (*loudly*) You're leaving? I can't believe it! You never want to deal with this problem or anything else!

Manuel — (*looking back as he leaves*) There's no point in yelling. I'll be back in an hour.

If you have ever been in a situation like this one, you know how frustrating it can be. In this example, Manuel, for whatever reason, does not want to give Amber the time of day — or the statistics she desperately needs. Rather than directly confronting the situation, he withdraws from it by only half listening to what Amber is saying. Eventually, as she becomes more persistent, he physically leaves the room to avoid the conflict.

Four ways of dealing with a withdrawing co-worker

This conflict trap is difficult to manage because, if someone is really intent on withdrawing from the situation, you can't do a whole lot about it. However, there are ways of talking to a withdrawing co-worker that help you deal more directly with the situation at hand. We recommend the following steps:

- ✔ Resist the urge to push.
- ✔ Use an empathic tone of voice.
- ✔ Seek out your co-worker's advice.
- ✔ Set a specific time.

Resist the urge to push

If a co-worker is starting to withdraw, resist the natural urge to chase after the response you want. The more you push your co-worker for an answer, the more he or she will pull back.

Use an empathic tone of voice

As you notice your co-worker beginning to withdraw, change your tone from one of frustration to one of understanding. Your co-worker always has a reason for not dealing with the issue at hand. Using an empathic tone is often all you need to get a dialogue going.

Seek out your co-worker's advice

Once your co-worker lets down his guard a little, ask him what he would do — if he were you — to resolve the situation. By doing so, you gently nudge him out of withdrawal by helping him to be more sensitive to your predicament.

Set a specific time

If the conflict cannot be resolved right away, set a specific, mutually agreeable date and time when you can sit down and resolve the problem.

Following these steps, the conversation between Amber and Manuel would go something like this:

Amber — Manuel, I really need your monthly statistics for my report.

Manuel — (*Busy working at his computer*) Later, okay?

Amber — I need them today. This report is due soon.

Manuel — I can't do it now, I'm busy.

Amber now realizes that pushing Manuel any harder will only make him withdraw even more. She continues speaking with a softer, more empathic tone that lets Manuel know she is sensitive to his circumstances.

Amber — (*softly*) I know how busy you are, and I'm sorry to be bothering you with this, but I don't know what else to do.

Manuel — Can't it wait until later?

Amber — (*gently*) The problem is that I'm running out of time. You know what that's like.

Manuel — I'm just so busy . . . .

The empathic tone diverts Manuel off of the withdrawal track, and he is now listening more attentively. Amber asks for Manuel's advice regarding what she should do to solve the problem.

Amber — I understand how busy you are. What do you suggest I do?

Manuel — (*with more interest*) Maybe we can talk about it later.

Amber — I would really appreciate that.

Lastly, Amber takes Manuel's general agreement to talk about it later and turns it into a specific time to which they both agree.

Amber — Let's set up a specific time so that we can do it and get it over with.

Manuel — Okay, how about two o'clock?

Trap 4: Serving up put-downs

Verbal assaults used to invalidate the other person lead to this conflict trap. Put-downs can be a co-worker's way of letting you know that she disagrees with something you have done or said. Because she wants to avoid direct conflict, she does not talk to you about the problem. Slowly, her unspoken feelings turn to resentment and eventually become outright attacks on your feelings, thoughts, and general character. The following conversation takes place between Mel and Betty, sales clerks at a retail furniture store:

Betty — Did you notice that I sold the walnut bedroom set?

Mel — All I noticed was the mess you made in the delivery book.

Betty — (*feeling put down*) I'm sorry. The customers were newlyweds, and they asked me so many questions I got confused.

Mel — It's a wonder you didn't scare them away. You always seem so put out when customers ask you a lot of questions.

Betty — (*hurt*) What do you mean? I'm never rude to my customers.

Mel — You probably don't realize it when you are.

Betty — Mel, you're the one who's being rude.

Mel — No. I'm just telling it like I see it.

Betty — You're so judgmental.

Mel — See, there you go, you just can't take any criticism.

In this situation, Mel has an attitude about Betty before the conversation begins. No matter what Betty says, Mel will use it to find fault with her and invalidate her character as well as her achievements. The next time they speak, Betty will hide what she is really feeling and the relationship between the two of them will rapidly deteriorate. By not dealing with the original conflict (whatever it was and whenever it happened), Mel internalized his disagreement and now it seeps out whenever an opportunity presents itself.

Three ways of avoiding the put-down trap

If you find yourself with a negative evaluation of a co-worker, remember that your attitude is *your* responsibility — not your co-worker's. Blaming the other person for a situation that *you* have been unwilling to confront never resolves anything. If, on the other hand, you are on the receiving end of a co-worker's negative evaluation, as Betty was, don't follow her example. Resist the urge to respond with more negativity, and try to get to the real issues that are causing the conflict. If you are in a situation where your co-worker is putting you down, do the following three things:

- ✔ Don't get defensive.
- ✔ Be interested.
- ✔ Get to the root cause.

Don't get defensive

Defending yourself against a co-worker's slurs never resolves the situation because it fails to get to the real issues that are fueling the insinuations. You just end up feeling like a hamster on a wheel, spending lots of effort going round and round and getting nowhere.

Be interested

Even though your co-worker is being indirect and may not be expressing himself very well, he does have something to convey. Try to listen to the message underneath his negative evaluation and address that.

Get to the root cause

Ask the other person if something you did in the past has upset him.

Using these steps, the revised conversation between Betty and Mel would go something like this:

Betty	—	Did you notice that I sold the walnut bedroom set?
Mel	—	All I noticed was the mess you made in the delivery book.
Betty	—	(*feeling put down*) I'm sorry. The customers were newlyweds, and they asked me so many questions I got confused.
Mel	—	It's a wonder you didn't scare them away. You always seem so put out when customers ask you a lot of questions.

Betty now realizes that Mel has a negative evaluation about her and getting defensive will serve no purpose. Instead, she becomes interested in what Mel is saying.

Betty	—	What do you mean?
Mel	—	I've noticed that you can be snappy with customers sometimes.
Betty	—	Can you give me an example?
Mel	—	You were snappy with me last week.
Betty	—	I'm sorry. Have there been any other times when I have treated you rudely?
Mel	—	Yes, three months ago when I asked you if you could work a Saturday for me, you jumped all over me.

Five Basic Truths

Leading seminars for so many years has given us the opportunity to meet all kinds of different people, and we've learned (sometimes the hard way) five basics truths that will help you prevent unnecessary conflict:

✔ When people's moods change, so does their receptivity.

✔ Different people have different working styles.

✔ People are more sensitive than they seem to be.

✔ We prefer some people over others.

✔ You can't tell a book by its cover.

When people's moods change, so does their receptivity

Your mood affects how receptive you are to input. For example, when you are angry, your attention is narrowly focused on the person or thing that is upsetting you. You probably have little room, if any, for input from another source. So when someone speaks to you when you are angry, you are more than likely unable to really listen to or accept what he or she has to say.

The opposite is also true. When you are in a good mood, you are much more open to receiving input. The point is, don't approach your co-worker with a heavy duty topic when she is in a bad mood because you won't get the attention or receptivity you deserve.

Different people have different working styles

Some people are very precise and organized, others are vague and untidy. We all have different working styles (see Chapter 17) and remembering this fact gives you more patience and understanding with co-workers who think and act differently than you do. Understanding and respecting these differences can help you to prevent conflicts caused by misunderstanding.

People are more sensitive than they seem to be

People get their feelings hurt more often and more deeply than they usually admit. Often, something said quite innocently can be taken as an offense by a co-worker. By being more sensitive to the feelings of others, you cut down the number of times you might inadvertently offend someone.

We prefer some people over others

Don't expect to like all your co-workers equally. Some people you just click with and some people you don't. Chalk it up to chemistry. Conflict can usually be resolved by focusing on having respect for your co-worker's point of view rather than how much you like him or her.

You can't tell a book by its cover

Sometimes we form a negative opinion about a co-worker because of our judgments about the way they look, how they talk, or where they are from. If you get to know the person on a deeper level, you usually find that he or she is nothing like your mental picture. When dealing with other staff members whom you don't know well, be careful not to let the way they present themselves on the outside keep you from getting to know them on the inside.

Part V
The Part of Tens

In this part...

We have created a bunch of *cheat sheets* for managers, sales people, and front-line staff. This Part of Tens is a quick and easy way for you to brush up on the main points listed in this book — as well as a way to pick up some new tips and techniques.

Chapter 19

Ten Good Customer Service Habits to Develop

• •

Most habits are actions you have taken for so long that they now come naturally and you no longer need to think about them. For example, when you first learned to drive a car you probably felt as if you would never be able to turn the wheel, press the accelerator, *and* signal all at the same time — now you can do it with your eyes closed (figuratively speaking). Following are some basic habits that we think every service person should develop to maintain a consistently high level of customer service.

Be on Time

Being on time for appointments with your customers (and co-workers) is a statement of respect. Conversely, making others sit around and wait until you show up creates a negative impression and is disrespectful of your customers' time. Now and again you'll encounter situations that force you to be late — traffic jams, bad directions, a total eclipse of the sun — the cardinal rule then is to call as soon as you know you are going to be late. The sooner you let your customers know you are delayed, the less irritated they will be. Don't wait until the last minute and hope that it all works out.

Follow Up on Your Promises

We hear one major pet peeve from many customers: service providers who promise something and then don't follow through. For example, a customer is told that she will be notified as soon as her order comes in and then — as if the promise were all a dream — no one from the company ever calls to notify her! Customers are so unaccustomed to good follow through that making it a habit scores you big points.

Always call a customer back by the time you promised — even if it's to say that you don't yet have the information they want and you'll get back to him or her later. Your credibility as a service provider hinges on how well you keep your promises.

Under Promise and Over Deliver

Sometimes, in your enthusiasm to give the customers what they want, you may find yourself promising them something that is difficult to deliver. By making a promise, you create an expectation in the customer's mind that can be difficult to fulfill. When you find yourself in this situation, your best approach is to only promise the customer what you can be sure of —not what you hope will happen.

For example, your customer wants his new couch delivered by 3 pm. You know that this delivery time is possible, but not guaranteed. By promising delivery by 4 pm, you avoid disappointing your customer and delight him if the couch arrives earlier.

Go the Extra Mile

Make going out of your way for your customers a habit. By doing small, extra things for them, your service is remembered and your company differentiates itself from its competitors. On those occasions when you cannot go as far out of your way as your customers would like — when you can't say *yes* and you have to say *no* — be sure that you get into the following habit . . .

Offer Your Customer Options

Two customer service situations lend themselves to offering options: when you have to say *no* to a customer, or when you have an option to offer that will make the customer's life easier or smoother. When you cannot provide your customers with what they want, giving them an alternative helps to soften their natural disappointment.

Too many options can overwhelm your customer, so keep them down to one or two.

Express Empathy

No matter how good your customer service skills, you will, at times, have an unhappy camper for a customer. At such times, developing the habit of expressing *empathy* is important. Empathy means understanding your customer's point of view, regardless of whether or not you agree. Some empathic phrases to practice and remember are:

- ✔ I understand why you feel that way.
- ✔ I see your point of view.
- ✔ I hear what you are saying.
- ✔ I'm sorry that happened.

Treat Your Customer as the Most Important Part of Your Job

When all the functions of your job — meetings, paperwork, telephone calls, and so on — start to get you down, develop the habit of changing your attitude. Viewing your customers as interruptions to the work that you have to get done is all too easy. By focusing on your customers as *the* reason why you do your job, you will make them feel important. After all, ultimately they are the ones who write your paycheck.

Treat Your Co-Workers as Customers

The quality of service you provide to your customers is only as good as the quality of relationships that you have with the co-workers around you. Treating your workmates as customers raises the overall quality of communication within your company. For example, if a customer calls asking for information that you do not have, you may need to contact another department. If the co-worker in that department is friendly and responsive to your needs, then you, in turn, can get back to the customer faster and provide him or her with better service.

Give the Customer Your Name and Telephone Number

Make finding you easy for your customers by giving them your name and telephone number. With telephone systems getting more sophisticated, customers can easily *get lost in the system* and waste a great deal of time trying to reach you, the person with whom they were dealing — the one who knows the ins and outs of the particular problem.

Smile and Use Inflection on the Telephone

Smiling on the phone changes the sound of your voice because it alters the shape of your mouth, making the sound waves more fluid (ask any singing teacher). Customers assess your service attitude (on the phone) almost entirely from your tone of voice. We know customers who will hang up and call back if a service provider says "Hello" in an unfriendly way.

How to remove a bad habit

The habits we outline in this chapter are all the good habits, but what if you have some bad customer service habits that you want to eliminate? Following are three simple ideas:

🖛 After you realize you have fallen back on the bad habit, think about what you could have done differently.

🖛 If you catch yourself in the middle of acting out the bad habit, stop and try something else.

🖛 Just before you are about to fall prey to the bad habit, stop yourself and pick a better action.

If you practice any of these actions often enough, you will replace the bad habits with good ones.

Chapter 20

Ten Ways to Be a Good Customer Service Role Model for Your Staff

• •

*F*rom years of talking to thousands of staff members all over the world, we've come to the conclusion that most managers don't realize just how closely their staffs watch them for direction and guidance. If you talk about good customer service but don't demonstrate it, then you've lost before you've even started. As a manager, the first step in motivating your staff to provide excellent service is to consistently demonstrate the attitudes and behaviors you want your staff to use with their customers. Following are ten actions that your staff use to gauge just how serious *your* commitment to good customer service is.

Start the Day off Right

Everyone has days when he gets up on the wrong side of the bed and rolls into work with a less than stellar attitude. As a manager, you need to remember that your mood affects the mood of your staff, which, in turn, affects their treatment of the customer. Believe it or not, the way you first greet your staff in the morning can set the tone for the rest of the day. Remember to greet your staff with a friendly smile when you first see them. After all, you would do the same for any customer.

Discuss Your Feelings, Don't Vent Them

Working life has its ups and downs, and nobody expects you to be calm and collected all the time just because you are a manager. However, if you find yourself getting angry with one of your staff, you don't have the luxury of venting your feelings to him or her in a negative way. Letting off steam with a dramatic outburst erodes your relationship with your staff and only encourages them to reciprocate by venting at their customers in a similar fashion. Instead, if you get angry with one of your staff, do the following:

- ✔ Remain calm.

- ✔ Discuss the matter in *private,* never in front of other people.

- ✔ Explain in *detail* why you are upset, not in general terms that force the staff member to guess why you're angry.

- ✔ Give the person a chance to respond and say how he or she feels, thus avoiding a one-way conversation.

- ✔ Come to a *mutual* solution to the problem.

Do the Right Thing

When you find yourself face-to-face with a difficult customer, your staff will carefully watch and listen to your every move to see how well you deal with the situation (and if you practice what you preach). If you handle it like a pro and practice the kinds of recommendations we make in this book (for more information on dealing with difficult people, see Part IV), you teach your staff, by example, how they should act in similar situations.

Support Your Staff's Decisions

When customers are upset and they can't get what they want, they often ask to speak to you — the manager or supervisor. If your staff have made a decision that enforces company policy and you reverse it, you have just taken the first step toward disempowering them. Why should they bother to stand up for the company if the company won't stand up for them? We recommend talking to the customer and then discussing the issue briefly with the staff member. If you *and* the staff member decide to reverse the decision, have the staff member be the one to tell the customer so that the staff member can be the hero in the customer's eyes. By taking the extra few minutes to collaborate with your staff, you empower and encourage them to be more flexible and resourceful.

Be Willing Not to Know the Answer

Some supervisors think that being a manager means having to know all the answers to every question that's fired at them. There will always be times when you won't be able to answer a question, so don't try and bluff it. Admitting that you don't know can be a sign of strength that garners trust from those around you. By being open to discovering answers, you encourage your staff to do the same.

Learn to Listen

Service providers spend a good deal of their day listening to what their customers need. Your staff are continually told that they should not interrupt their customers or jump to conclusions about what the customers are saying. The best way for you to reinforce this message is to learn to listen to your staff when they speak to you. If you cut your staff short or ignore what they are saying, you can guess how well your next *listen to your customer* pep talk will go over.

Take Time to Socialize

Know your staff and what they are up to in their lives. By all means have your privacy, and respect theirs, but don't be so distant that you are out of touch with major events such as birthdays, anniversaries, weddings, and so on. Celebrate noteworthy occasions and develop a relationship with your staff that is based upon respect for them as complete individuals rather than just the results they produce.

Use Good Telephone Etiquette

You should be your staff's best example of excellent telephone manners. Whenever you pick up the phone, follow the telephone etiquette guidelines we outline in Chapter 6. If you do so consistently, your staff will naturally follow your example. *Anytime* you pick up the phone is an opportunity for you to demonstrate good telephone etiquette.

Thank Your Staff Often

Be generous with compliments to your staff and acknowledge their service skills when they've done a good job. Don't assume that they know you appreciate the good job they do — nothing has the same impact as hearing it straight from you. By fostering an environment of recognition and appreciation, you encourage your staff to maintain consistently high levels of service. The negative attitude that some managers have toward praise. . .

> *Why should I thank them for doing their job? That's what they get paid for.*

. . . guarantees staff resentment which, in one way or another, is reflected back to customers.

Say What You Mean and Mean What You Say

Your staff are appreciative when you are straightforward with them. If difficult situations need to be dealt with, your words should match what your body language and tone of voice are already communicating. By being honest and straightforward with your staff, you gain their trust. If they can count on you to *say it the way it is* when things aren't going well, they are that much more appreciative of your praise when things are going right.

Chapter 21

Ten Major Don'ts (and Do's) of Customer Service

• •

*E*very day you face situations when what you say to your customers makes or breaks the service interactions. Following, we list ten phrases to avoid — because they drive customers nuts — and our recommended alternatives for delivering the message in a more polite and helpful way.

"I Don't Know."

SAY: "I'll find out."

When you say "I don't know," your customers often hear it as, "I don't have the information you want, and I'm not going out of my way to get it." By offering to find the answer to your customers' questions, even if doing so means taking a little extra time researching or checking with another department, you score service points for going the extra mile.

"No."

SAY: "What I can do is . . ."

Inevitably, you sometimes have to say no to a customer's request. Rather than using what we call a hard no — where no options or alternative are provided — focus on what you *can* do for your customers. Starting your sentence with "What I can do is . . ." shows customers that you are taking a problem-solving approach to their situation.

"That's Not My Job."

SAY: "This is who can help you . . ."

When customers ask you to do something that you don't have the authority or knowledge to carry out, become a catalyst by leading the customer to the person or department who can help him solve his problem.

"You're Right — This Stinks."

SAY: "I understand your frustration."

If a customer expresses annoyance at something another person or department has done, don't make matters worse by commiserating with him. Instead of agreeing by saying something like, "You're right, this place stinks," express empathy for the customer's feelings by saying "I understand how frustrating this must be." Empathy is showing care and concern without agreeing or disagreeing with what the customer is saying.

"That's Not My Fault."

SAY: "Let's see what we can do about this."

If an angry customer seems to be accusing you of creating a problem for her, the natural reaction is to become defensive. However, if you allow this reaction to take over, your mind becomes closed to hearing what the customer has to say. So when you find the words "That's not my fault" on the tip of your tongue, stop, take a breath, and then, with all the empathy you can muster, say, "Let's see what we can do about this." By resisting the urge to defend yourself, you can resolve the problem faster and with less stress.

"You Need to Talk to My Manager."

SAY: "I can help you."

Customers sometimes ask you for things that are a little outside of company policy or procedure. At such times, quickly passing them off to your manager is tempting. Instead, focus on what you *can* do to help them. If your manager does need to be involved, take the initiative to go to him or her yourself and return to the customer with a solution in hand. Doing so makes you the service hero in the customers' eyes.

"You Want It by When?"

SAY: "I'll try my best."

When customers make demands by asking you for something that is unreasonable and difficult to provide, your first reaction may be annoyance. However, because you have little control over your customers' requests, the best approach is to hold off on your negative judgments and try your best to accommodate the requests. Don't promise something with the hope that you can deliver. Giving customers unrealistic expectations may get them off your back now but will blow up in your face later. Do make promises that you know you can accomplish and assure them, with confidence and enthusiasm, that you know how important their deadline is and that you will try your best to meet it.

"Calm Down."

SAY: "I'm sorry."

When customers are upset, angry, frustrated, or concerned, telling them to calm down is like saying that their feelings don't matter. If you want your customers to calm down, take the opposite approach and apologize. Apologizing does not mean you are agreeing with the customers' point of view, or that you are admitting guilt, it means that you are sorry for what has happened and the negative impact it has had on them.

"I'm Busy Right Now."

SAY: "I'll be with you in just a moment."

Stopping and assisting another customer who is asking for your help isn't always easy, especially when you are already in the middle of serving a customer. Some service providers handle this situation by tossing out a curt, "I'm too busy right now" at the customer, which is their way of saying, "Why are you bothering me, can't you see I'm busy?" Stellar service providers use a better approach by saying, "I'll be with you in just a moment." This little sentence, along with a pleasant tone of voice, lets your customer know that you are aware of his presence and you will help him as soon as you are able.

"Call Me Back."

SAY: "I will call you back."

Some customer requests take time for you to research and investigate and require a further conversation at a later date. Follow-up phone conversations should always be initiated by you — not by the customer. When you are so busy that you are tempted to ask him or her to call you back — stop, be proactive, and take the initiative to call the customer back when you have taken care of the problem.

Chapter 22

Ten Ways to Sell with Service

*W*hile sales and service are usually thought of as two separate activities they are really just different sides of the same coin. The skills you use to provide excellent service are not all that different from those that you use to sell to customers in a service-oriented way. These ten skills are the ones we consider fundamental to the selling process.

Get Your Customer's Attention

We can't stand it when an over-enthusiastic telemarketer calls us at dinner time and starts rattling on about his product or service. He thinks that by forcing himself on us we will listen more attentively — and, of course, it doesn't work that way. These types of foot-in-the-door, attention-grabbing methods aren't *customer focused,* and they make customers angry. One of the first steps in selling with service is getting the customers' attention in a positive manner and on their terms. We suggest these three ways to do so:

✔ **Send literature first and then follow up.**

By sending prospective customers a letter with written material about your company and the product you are selling, you are introducing your services and paving the way for a follow-up call. When you subsequently speak to them, they will have a better idea of who you are and what you are selling. By creating this comfort zone for the customer, you have a better chance of getting their undivided attention.

✔ **State what you want and ask if they have time to talk.**

Always start a conversation with customers by asking, "Is this a good time to talk?" or "Do you have a moment to speak with me?" Don't start off by blurting out your sales pitch, especially on a cold call. If you do, the customer will get annoyed, impatient, and block out most of what you are saying.

✔ **Use a third-party reference.**

If a prospective customer was referred to you by someone he or she knows, make this clear right away. Customers are usually more willing to listen to someone when they have been referred by a third party the customer knows and trusts.

Customers won't always say *yes* when you ask them if they have the time to speak with you. When it isn't convenient, ask if there is a better time to contact them. If they still say *no,* hit the road and move on because when someone is not interested in what you are selling, pushing her will only make her angry.

Ask Lots of Questions

Many salespeople are so intent on getting through their sales pitch that they forget to ask customers what is important to them. The heart of service-oriented selling is focusing on the customers' needs, rather than on your own, and you do this by asking lots of questions. There are two flavors to choose from:

Open questions — Use open-ended questions to gather general information about what customers want and their receptivity to what you are selling. Open ended questions don't elicit or require a *yes* or *no* answer. They usually begin with:

- How
- Why
- What
- Who
- When
- Which
- Where

For example:

> *What do you need?*

> *How do you think this would fit your needs?*

> *Which feature appeals to you the most?*

Closed questions — Use close-ended questions when you are looking for a basic *yes* or *no* answer. These questions are useful when you want the customer to make a decision about something. They usually begin with:

- ✔ Is
- ✔ Are
- ✔ Do
- ✔ Does
- ✔ Have
- ✔ Has
- ✔ Can
- ✔ Will
- ✔ Would

For example:

Is this a convenient time for you to talk?

Have I answered all of your questions?

Will Thursday be a good day for delivery?

State the Benefits of What You Are Selling

Clearly present the value of what you are selling by explaining to your prospective customer the benefits of using your product or service. Be careful not to get too bogged down in explaining the features or facts about your product because, although they may be interesting to you, the customer is more concerned with the impact your product/service will have on his or her business. For example, if you are trying to sell your travel agency services to a potential corporate client, one feature might be

We have locations throughout the country.

The benefit of this feature, and what you should present to your customer, would be

Because we have locations throughout the country, there's always a local branch available to ensure fast and easy service to your staff.

Mirror Back What the Customer Tells You

This is sometimes called *paraphrasing* or *active listening*. By reflecting back to a customer your understanding of what he or she has said, the customer knows that you are listening. For example, say that you are selling encyclopedias over the phone and your customer says:

> *I need to speak to my wife before going any further. We always like to talk these things over together.*

A customer-focused response would be:

> *I understand, you would feel more comfortable discussing this with your wife and making a joint decision. Is that correct?*

Next, make an appointment to call the customer back after he has had a chance to talk to his spouse.

Get in Step with Your Customer's Style

In Chapter 17, we cover how to analyze the four different working styles of your customer. These styles also apply to potential buyers. Being flexible to your buyers' working style means presenting your product or service in a way that has the most meaning to them — and not necessarily in the way that feels the most normal to you. Below is a list of how each working style is best approached in the selling process:

The Analytical Buyer — This style is focused on facts, not feelings, and views purchase decisions from a logical perspective. Some of the important things to do when selling to someone with this style are

- Put the information in writing with lots of detail.
- Show the buyer hard proof of the claims you are making about your product.
- Be professional in your presentation style.
- Show how the product has little or no risk.

The Driver Buyer — This style focuses on producing bottom-line results quickly. The driver style makes decisions fast and independently. Once they make a decision about something, changing their minds is difficult. Some of the important things to do when selling to customers with this style are

✔ Let them feel that they have control over the selling/buying process.

✔ Make it easy and convenient for them to purchase from you.

✔ Assure them that you will follow through and deal with any loose ends once the sale is over.

✔ Show them how your product will help them reach their objectives.

The Expressive Buyer — The expressive style is the most enthusiastic of all the styles. Expressives make their buying decisions based on how excited they feel about your product or service. Here are some of the important things to do when selling to customers with this style:

✔ Make your presentation fun and interesting.

✔ Assure them that you will take care of the details.

✔ Follow up with them on agreements made.

✔ Let them know how the product/service will make them more successful.

The Amiable Buyer — Amiable buyers are the most feeling oriented of the four styles. They often take a little longer to decide and base their decisions on how comfortable they feel with the salesperson and the product. Some of the important things to do when selling to someone with this style are

✔ Don't try to rush their decisions; let them decide in their own time.

✔ Work with them as a partner.

✔ Explain to them, with confidence, how the product/service will work.

✔ Ask them questions during the sales presentation to find out how they feel about what's being discussed.

Learn Your Customers' Critical Sales Factors

What are the things that your prospective customers consider to be of prime importance in deciding to purchase your service or product? What specific criteria will influence their buying decision? Find out their top five buying criteria by asking questions and listening carefully. Build your sales presentation around those five things. For example, if you are selling a refrigerator to a new home buyer, you might discover in your initial conversations with her that what will most affect her decision to purchase is:

✔ price

✔ guarantee against defects

✔ color

✔ size of freezer

✔ free delivery service

Knowing this, you can address those factors and not waste time addressing other issues that are of little relevance to your customer.

Turn Incoming Service Calls into Sales Opportunities

If customers call into your customer service department with an inquiry or a problem, be prepared to furnish them with information on other services or products your company offers. Many times sales are lost because service providers don't take a *proactive* role by asking the customers if they are interested in other options. Organize your business so that you can sell other services and products on the spot with the minimum of inconvenience to the customers.

Learn to Take "No" for an Answer

We believe that the old sales rule of *never take no for an answer and keep asking until you get a yes* is outdated and not customer focused. If you have discussed your product/service with your customers and they give you a firm *no*, they are not interested at this time, so listen to them. By graciously accepting their *no,* you may not make a sale today — but you may get future business or referrals from them.

Present New Options

We know one salesperson who works in the men's suits department of a local department store. When a customer goes in to buy a suit, our friend ends up selling him a tie, shirt, and shoes to go with it. All he does is ask simple questions that broaden the focus of the customer's original purpose for visiting the store. By saying something like, "I have a tie that I think will look great with this suit; would you like me to show it to you?", the salesman presents his customers with a new option that they can either accept or refuse. Most of his customers accept — and appreciate the extra care and concern he has shown!

Embrace the Customers' Concerns

When prospective customers begin to tell you what they are concerned about and why they are not sure about buying your product or service, don't hide your head in the sand like an ostrich and ignore what they are saying. Most people won't say *yes* and purchase from you until they have talked about and resolved their worries, concerns, and considerations. The best strategy is to address each of a customer's concerns, one at a time, with empathy and honesty. You will find that a customer's confidence level in you and your product will be elevated when you take the time to do this.

The 5th Wave

By Rich Tennant

"JERRY! OVER THERE, NEAR THE ESCALATOR. I THINK IT'S A SALES CLERK. QUICK! LIGHT ANOTHER TIE ON FIRE!"

Chapter 23

Ten Questions to Ask before Hiring a Customer Service Consultant

. . . .

*A*t some time, you may consider hiring a consulting company to help you implement the ideas we have discussed in this book. Some of the activities outside consultants can help you with include:

- ✔ conducting customer surveys
- ✔ conducting staff surveys
- ✔ helping executive teams to develop an overall strategy for service improvement
- ✔ conducting customer service trainings
- ✔ conducting service management trainings
- ✔ setting up quality groups
- ✔ facilitating off-site management retreats

Consulting companies vary greatly in the services they offer and their ability to deliver these services. These ten questions will help you pick a firm whose style, methods, and approach will fit with your objectives and the culture of your company.

Do You Have Any References I Can Call?

Ask the consulting company for a selection of references from a variety of their clients with a specific contact person in each company. It's also a good idea to ask the consultant to contact the persons they are referring to let them know you will be calling.

What Makes You Experts in the Area of Quality Service?

Because the topic of quality service has become so popular in the last few years, many consulting companies have added a customer service training module to their existing programs. This addition does not make them experts and doesn't mean they can help you implement an entire service improvement program from soup to nuts.

Make sure that the consultants you hire are experts in customer service improvement. For example:

✔ Do they conduct customer/staff surveys?

✔ Can they help set up a quality group program?

✔ Do they coach senior executives?

Our experience (which is admittedly biased) shows the best customer service consulting companies are those that offer a comprehensive program in customer service improvement and not just a one- or two-day training program.

What Is the Background of Your Company?

Gather as much general information about the consulting company as possible. Some questions to ask include:

✔ How long have you been in business?

✔ What industries have you worked with?

✔ Who are your clients?

✔ What is your company philosophy?

✔ How many people work for you?

Don't base your decision to hire a consulting company solely on the convenience of their geographic location. While we realize that this is a consideration, don't sell yourself short and hire the wrong company for the job just because they operate in the same city as you do.

Do You Customize the Training Programs and Materials to Our Business?

For a training program to be really effective with your staff, it has to have examples, demonstrations, and content that they can relate to. Generic training programs usually miss the mark because they rely on universal examples that don't hit home.

Ask what *specific steps* the consultants will take to customize their programs and materials to your company.

Who Delivers the Training?

Larger consulting companies usually have one group of people selling the product and a different group delivering the training and consulting. Some businesses have complained to us about hiring a consulting company (because they were impressed with the salesperson) but then being disappointed with the consultant or trainer who subsequently worked with them. While there is nothing wrong with having one person sell and another deliver the programs, make sure that you get to talk to the actual person(s) who will be working with you.

Can You Put Together a Proposal for Me?

Many ideas get tossed around during initial meetings with a consulting firm. At the conclusion of your first meeting, ask for a written proposal that outlines the major points of your discussion and provides specifics such as:

- how long it will take to implement
- how soon it will start
- fees
- travel and material costs
- maximum number of attendees allowed in each workshop

The quality of the proposal can say a lot about the consulting company. Is it neat, correctly spelled, and well laid out? Or does it look haphazardly slapped together? Does it reflect the conversation you had — or some other meeting that you don't remember attending?

How Will We Keep This Going in the Future?

You don't want to spend the rest of your life depending on an outside consultant to keep service alive and well in your company, so ask how the consulting firm plans to empower you to maintain the changes once they have left the scene.

Continuing the process of service improvement is mostly your responsibility, not the consultants'. Once they have finished their part and left you with the knowledge, tools, and training you need, it's up to you to keep it going.

How Do You Deal with Managers Who Aren't Behind This?

A reality of implementing a company-wide service improvement program is that some managers will be more gung ho about it than others. Because managers are so important to this process, it is good to find out what approach the consulting company takes to help get resistant managers to support the program.

How Will We Get New Hires Up to Speed?

If you are a small business, you may want to hire the consulting company to come back once or twice a year and deliver their program for your new hires. If you are a larger company, conducting the customer service training in-house may be more cost effective. Find out if the consulting company has a train-the-trainer program or video-based training for getting new hires up to speed.

What Do You Think the Most Difficult Part of This Project Will Be?

At the end of the interview, ask the consultants to give you their impression (based on what's been discussed so far) as to what they anticipate will be the most difficult part of the project. What will their strategy be to overcome this difficulty? Asking these questions should give you an insight into how well the consultants understand your company's issues.

Chapter 24

Ten Ways to Maintain Service in a Growing Company

• •

*A*s your company grows, your business will pass a plateau where the actions that worked below the plateau — in terms of your company's culture, structure, strategy, and management style — no longer work above the plateau. This chapter outlines ten ways that you can help your company establish a solid foundation upon which you can continue to grow with service excellence.

Write a Mission Statement

Often, with a small company, spelling out the importance of quality and service in a mission statement isn't necessary. However, as you grow, so does the need to specifically highlight your commitment to customer service. A mission statement helps by providing guidance and focus. For more information on mission statements and how to write them, see Chapter 10.

Develop a Long-Term Strategy

As your business grows, you may notice that you get so wrapped up in day-to-day concerns that you stop planning for the future. If you keep reacting to what's in front of you, customer service gets degraded by having to continually patch up the symptoms of service problems rather than fixing the real causes of the problem. To get yourself out of this trap, create and implement a one-year strategy that covers six key areas:

- ✔ marketing and sales
- ✔ technology
- ✔ company culture

- ✔ quality service
- ✔ finance
- ✔ human resources

Hold an Off-site Retreat at Least Once a Year

It will become necessary, as you grow, to form a *core management team*. This team is made up of the owner of the company and his or her top managers. We recommend taking your core management team on a one- to three-day off-site retreat for big picture strategic planning.

Hire a Human Resources Director

Human resources need to grow along with your company. Staying up to date on employment laws, hiring and training new staff, dealing with compensation and performance reviews, and so on, require more time the bigger your company gets. Business life is a lot easier if you hire an expert human resources person to watch over this part of your company.

Write and Implement a Marketing Plan

A continual challenge for many companies is striking a balance between delivering quality service to current customers while, at the same time, marketing to find new ones. Writing and implementing a formal marketing plan can help you to organize your activities by planning:

- ✔ how you will allocate your sales and marketing resources
- ✔ how to further develop the markets you already have
- ✔ which new markets are worth going after

Update Your Technology

Technology, being a capital investment (and usually an expensive one at that), is often the last area a growing company invests in. However, in order to maintain excellent service as you grow, telephone systems, hardware, software, and other related technology must be able to adequately handle the increased workload.

Invest in Developing Your Staff

Don't take the sink-or-swim approach by hiring staff, throwing them into the job without any training, and hoping that, by some process of osmosis, they will learn what they need to. This approach always results in poor quality, bad service, and frustrated staff. As you grow, continue to develop your staff by training them in the specifics of their jobs so that they are empowered to help customers to the best of their ability.

Invest in Developing Your Managers

Being a manager requires a different set of skills than those of being a staff member. Growing companies often promote from within, which is a good thing as long as managers are provided with appropriate training. By coaching them in the skills of being successful supervisors and motivators, you help them to have better relationships with their staff — who consequently provide better service to your customers.

Create an Orientation Program

Communicating your company's service philosophy to new hires right from the start is essential. Once upon a time, when your company was a smaller *family*, service values were probably easier to communicate. As you grow, these guiding principles of service can get lost in the daily work load, and an employee orientation helps introduce and formalize the priority your company places on customer service. Orientation programs also familiarize your staff with the rest of the company, what different departments do, how they interrelate, and the chain of events that deliver service to the customer.

Conduct a Customer Survey

Small business owners sometimes say to us, "We don't need to survey our customers, we know who they are and what they want." While this may be true when you are small, it's easy to get out of touch with your customers as you grow bigger. Get into the habit of conducting a formal survey at least once a year so that you have a dependable and up-to-date method of collecting information necessary for future developments within your business.

Index

The Internet For Macs® For Dummies,® 2nd Edition	by Charles Seiter	ISBN: 1-56884-371-2	$19.99 USA/$26.99 Canada
The Internet For Macs® For Dummies® Starter Kit	by Charles Seiter	ISBN: 1-56884-244-9	$29.99 USA/$39.99 Canada
The Internet For Macs® For Dummies® Starter Kit Bestseller Edition	by Charles Seiter	ISBN: 1-56884-245-7	$39.99 USA/$54.99 Canada
The Internet For Windows® For Dummies® Starter Kit	by John R. Levine & Margaret Levine Young	ISBN: 1-56884-237-6	$34.99 USA/$44.99 Canada
The Internet For Windows® For Dummies® Starter Kit, Bestseller Edition	by John R. Levine & Margaret Levine Young	ISBN: 1-56884-246-5	$39.99 USA/$54.99 Canada

MACINTOSH

Mac® Programming For Dummies®	by Dan Parks Sydow	ISBN: 1-56884-173-6	$19.95 USA/$26.95 Canada
Macintosh® System 7.5 For Dummies®	by Bob LeVitus	ISBN: 1-56884-197-3	$19.95 USA/$26.95 Canada
MORE Macs® For Dummies®	by David Pogue	ISBN: 1-56884-087-X	$19.95 USA/$26.95 Canada
PageMaker 5 For Macs® For Dummies®	by Galen Gruman & Deke McClelland	ISBN: 1-56884-178-7	$19.95 USA/$26.95 Canada
QuarkXPress 3.3 For Dummies®	by Galen Gruman & Barbara Assadi	ISBN: 1-56884-217-1	$19.99 USA/$26.99 Canada
Upgrading and Fixing Macs® For Dummies®	by Kearney Rietmann & Frank Higgins	ISBN: 1-56884-189-2	$19.95 USA/$26.95 Canada

MULTIMEDIA

| Multimedia & CD-ROMs For Dummies,® 2nd Edition | by Andy Rathbone | ISBN: 1-56884-907-9 | $19.99 USA/$26.99 Canada |
| Multimedia & CD-ROMs For Dummies,® Interactive Multimedia Value Pack, 2nd Edition | by Andy Rathbone | ISBN: 1-56884-909-5 | $29.99 USA/$39.99 Canada |

OPERATING SYSTEMS:

DOS

| MORE DOS For Dummies® | by Dan Gookin | ISBN: 1-56884-046-2 | $19.95 USA/$26.95 Canada |
| OS/2® Warp For Dummies,® 2nd Edition | by Andy Rathbone | ISBN: 1-56884-205-8 | $19.99 USA/$26.99 Canada |

UNIX

| MORE UNIX® For Dummies® | by John R. Levine & Margaret Levine Young | ISBN: 1-56884-361-5 | $19.99 USA/$26.99 Canada |
| UNIX® For Dummies® | by John R. Levine & Margaret Levine Young | ISBN: 1-878058-58-4 | $19.95 USA/$26.95 Canada |

WINDOWS

| MORE Windows® For Dummies,® 2nd Edition | by Andy Rathbone | ISBN: 1-56884-048-9 | $19.95 USA/$26.95 Canada |
| Windows® 95 For Dummies® | by Andy Rathbone | ISBN: 1-56884-240-6 | $19.99 USA/$26.99 Canada |

PCS/HARDWARE

| Illustrated Computer Dictionary For Dummies,® 2nd Edition | by Dan Gookin & Wallace Wang | ISBN: 1-56884-218-X | $12.95 USA/$16.95 Canada |
| Upgrading and Fixing PCs For Dummies,® 2nd Edition | by Andy Rathbone | ISBN: 1-56884-903-6 | $19.95 USA/$26.95 Canada |

PRESENTATION/AUTOCAD

| AutoCAD For Dummies® | by Bud Smith | ISBN: 1-56884-191-4 | $19.95 USA/$26.95 Canada |
| PowerPoint 4 For Windows® For Dummies® | by Doug Lowe | ISBN: 1-56884-161-2 | $16.99 USA/$22.99 Canada |

PROGRAMMING

Borland C++ For Dummies®	by Michael Hyman	ISBN: 1-56884-162-0	$19.95 USA/$26.95 Canada
C For Dummies,® Volume 1	by Dan Gookin	ISBN: 1-878058-78-9	$19.95 USA/$26.95 Canada
C++ For Dummies®	by Stephen R. Davis	ISBN: 1-56884-163-9	$19.95 USA/$26.95 Canada
Delphi Programming For Dummies®	by Neil Rubenking	ISBN: 1-56884-200-7	$19.99 USA/$26.99 Canada
Mac® Programming For Dummies®	by Dan Parks Sydow	ISBN: 1-56884-173-6	$19.95 USA/$26.95 Canada
PowerBuilder 4 Programming For Dummies®	by Ted Coombs & Jason Coombs	ISBN: 1-56884-325-9	$19.99 USA/$26.99 Canada
QBasic Programming For Dummies®	by Douglas Hergert	ISBN: 1-56884-093-4	$19.95 USA/$26.95 Canada
Visual Basic 3 For Dummies®	by Wallace Wang	ISBN: 1-56884-076-4	$19.95 USA/$26.95 Canada
Visual Basic "X" For Dummies®	by Wallace Wang	ISBN: 1-56884-230-9	$19.99 USA/$26.99 Canada
Visual C++ 2 For Dummies®	by Michael Hyman & Bob Arnson	ISBN: 1-56884-328-3	$19.99 USA/$26.99 Canada
Windows® 95 Programming For Dummies®	by S. Randy Davis	ISBN: 1-56884-327-5	$19.99 USA/$26.99 Canada

SPREADSHEET

1-2-3 For Dummies®	by Greg Harvey	ISBN: 1-878058-60-6	$16.95 USA/$22.95 Canada
1-2-3 For Windows® 5 For Dummies,® 2nd Edition	by John Walkenbach	ISBN: 1-56884-216-3	$16.95 USA/$22.95 Canada
Excel 5 For Macs® For Dummies®	by Greg Harvey	ISBN: 1-56884-186-8	$19.95 USA/$26.95 Canada
Excel For Dummies,® 2nd Edition	by Greg Harvey	ISBN: 1-56884-050-0	$16.95 USA/$22.95 Canada
MORE 1-2-3 For DOS For Dummies®	by John Weingarten	ISBN: 1-56884-224-4	$19.99 USA/$26.99 Canada
MORE Excel 5 For Windows® For Dummies®	by Greg Harvey	ISBN: 1-56884-207-4	$19.95 USA/$26.95 Canada
Quattro Pro 6 For Windows® For Dummies®	by John Walkenbach	ISBN: 1-56884-174-4	$19.95 USA/$26.95 Canada
Quattro Pro For DOS For Dummies®	by John Walkenbach	ISBN: 1-56884-023-3	$16.95 USA/$22.95 Canada

UTILITIES

| Norton Utilities 8 For Dummies® | by Beth Slick | ISBN: 1-56884-166-3 | $19.95 USA/$26.95 Canada |

VCRS/CAMCORDERS

| VCRs & Camcorders For Dummies™ | by Gordon McComb & Andy Rathbone | ISBN: 1-56884-229-5 | $14.99 USA/$20.99 Canada |

WORD PROCESSING

Ami Pro For Dummies®	by Jim Meade	ISBN: 1-56884-049-7	$19.95 USA/$26.95 Canada
MORE Word For Windows® 6 For Dummies®	by Doug Lowe	ISBN: 1-56884-165-5	$19.95 USA/$26.95 Canada
MORE WordPerfect® 6 For Windows® For Dummies®	by Margaret Levine Young & David C. Kay	ISBN: 1-56884-206-6	$19.95 USA/$26.95 Canada
MORE WordPerfect® 6 For DOS For Dummies®	by Wallace Wang, edited by Dan Gookin	ISBN: 1-56884-047-0	$19.95 USA/$26.95 Canada
Word 6 For Macs® For Dummies®	by Dan Gookin	ISBN: 1-56884-190-6	$19.95 USA/$26.95 Canada
Word For Windows® 6 For Dummies®	by Dan Gookin	ISBN: 1-56884-075-6	$16.95 USA/$22.95 Canada
Word For Windows® For Dummies®	by Dan Gookin & Ray Werner	ISBN: 1-878058-86-X	$16.95 USA/$22.95 Canada
WordPerfect® 6 For DOS For Dummies®	by Dan Gookin	ISBN: 1-878058-77-0	$16.95 USA/$22.95 Canada
WordPerfect® 6.1 For Windows® For Dummies,® 2nd Edition	by Margaret Levine Young & David Kay	ISBN: 1-56884-243-0	$16.95 USA/$22.95 Canada
WordPerfect® For Dummies®	by Dan Gookin	ISBN: 1-878058-52-5	$16.95 USA/$22.95 Canada

For scholastic requests & educational orders please call Educational Sales at 1. 800. 434. 2086

FOR MORE INFO OR TO ORDER, PLEASE CALL ▶ 800. 762. 2974

For volume discounts & special orders please call Corporate Sales, at 415. 655. 3000

PC PRESS

IDG BOOKS WORLDWIDE

7/29/96

"A lot easier to use than the book Excel gives you!"

Lisa Schmeckpeper, New Berlin, WI, on PC World Excel 5 For Windows Handbook

Official Hayes Modem Communications Companion
by Caroline M. Halliday

ISBN: 1-56884-072-1
$29.95 USA/$39.95 Canada
Includes software.

1,001 Komputer Answers from Kim Komando
by Kim Komando

ISBN: 1-56884-460-3
$29.99 USA/$39.99 Canada
Includes software.

PC World DOS 6 Handbook, 2nd Edition
by John Socha, Clint Hicks, & Devra Hall

ISBN: 1-878058-79-7
$34.95 USA/$44.95 Canada
Includes software.

PC World Word For Windows® 6 Handbook
by Brent Heslop & David Angell

ISBN: 1-56884-054-3
$34.95 USA/$44.95 Canada
Includes software.

PC World Microsoft® Access 2 Bible, 2nd Edition
by Cary N. Prague & Michael R. Irwin

ISBN: 1-56884-086-1
$39.95 USA/$52.95 Canada
Includes software.

PC World Excel 5 For Windows® Handbook, 2nd Edition
by John Walkenbach & Dave Maguiness

ISBN: 1-56884-056-X
$34.95 USA/$44.95 Canada
Includes software.

PC World WordPerfect® 6 Handbook
by Greg Harvey

ISBN: 1-878058-80-0
$34.95 USA/$44.95 Canada
Includes software.

QuarkXPress For Windows® Designer Handbook
by Barbara Assadi & Galen Gruman

ISBN: 1-878058-45-2
$29.95 USA/$39.95 Canada

Official XTree Companion, 3rd Edition
by Beth Slick

ISBN: 1-878058-57-6
$19.95 USA/$26.95 Canada

PC World DOS 6 Command Reference and Problem Solver
by John Socha & Devra Hall

ISBN: 1-56884-055-1
$24.95 USA/$32.95 Canada

Client/Server Strategies™: A Survival Guide for Corporate Reengineers
by David Vaskevitch

ISBN: 1-56884-064-0
$29.95 USA/$39.95 Canada

"PC World Word For Windows 6 Handbook is very easy to follow with lots of 'hands on' examples. The 'Task at a Glance' is very helpful!"

Jacqueline Martens, Tacoma, WA

"Thanks for publishing this book! It's the best money I've spent this year!"

Robert D. Templeton, Ft. Worth, TX, on MORE Windows 3.1 SECRETS

For scholastic requests & educational orders please call Educational Sales at 1. 800. 434. 2086

FOR MORE INFO OR TO ORDER, PLEASE CALL ▶ 800. 762. 2974

For volume discounts & special orders please call Corporate Sales, at 415. 655. 3000

IDG BOOKS WORLDWIDE ™

Order Center: **(800) 762-2974** *(8 a.m.–6 p.m., EST, weekdays)*

Quantity	ISBN	Title	Price	Total

Shipping & Handling Charges

	Description	First book	Each additional book	Total
Domestic	Normal	$4.50	$1.50	$
	Two Day Air	$8.50	$2.50	$
	Overnight	$18.00	$3.00	$
International	Surface	$8.00	$8.00	$
	Airmail	$16.00	$16.00	$
	DHL Air	$17.00	$17.00	$

*For large quantities call for shipping & handling charges.
**Prices are subject to change without notice.

Ship to:

Name _____

Company _____

Address _____

City/State/Zip _____

Daytime Phone _____

Payment: ☐ Check to IDG Books Worldwide (US Funds Only)

☐ VISA   ☐ MasterCard   ☐ American Express

Card # _____ Expires _____

Signature _____

Subtotal _____

CA residents add
applicable sales tax _____

IN, MA, and MD
residents add
5% sales tax _____

IL residents add
6.25% sales tax _____

RI residents add
7% sales tax _____

TX residents add
8.25% sales tax _____

Shipping _____

Total _____

Please send this order form to:

**IDG Books Worldwide, Inc.
Attn: Order Entry Dept.
7260 Shadeland Station, Suite 100
Indianapolis, IN 46256**

*Allow up to 3 weeks for delivery.
Thank you!*

IDG BOOKS WORLDWIDE REGISTRATION CARD

Visit our
Web site at
http://www.idgbooks.com

Title of this book: Customer Service For Dummies

My overall rating of this book: ❑ Very good [1] ❑ Good [2] ❑ Satisfactory [3] ❑ Fair [4] ❑ Poor [5]

How I first heard about this book:

❑ Found in bookstore; name: [6]

❑ Advertisement: [8]

❑ Word of mouth; heard about book from friend, co-worker, etc.: [10]

❑ Book review: [7]

❑ Catalog: [9]

❑ Other: [11]

What I liked most about this book:

What I would change, add, delete, etc., in future editions of this book:

Other comments:

Number of computer books I purchase in a year: ❑ 1 [12] ❑ 2-5 [13] ❑ 6-10 [14] ❑ More than 10 [15]

I would characterize my computer skills as: ❑ Beginner [16] ❑ Intermediate [17] ❑ Advanced [18] ❑ Professional [19]

I use ❑ DOS [20] ❑ Windows [21] ❑ OS/2 [22] ❑ Unix [23] ❑ Macintosh [24] ❑ Other: [25]_____

(please specify)

I would be interested in new books on the following subjects:
(please check all that apply, and use the spaces provided to identify specific software)

❑ Word processing: [26]

❑ Data bases: [28]

❑ File Utilities: [30]

❑ Networking: [32]

❑ Other: [34]

❑ Spreadsheets: [27]

❑ Desktop publishing: [29]

❑ Money management: [31]

❑ Programming languages: [33]

I use a PC at (please check all that apply): ❑ home [35] ❑ work [36] ❑ school [37] ❑ other: [38] _____

The disks I prefer to use are ❑ 5.25 [39] ❑ 3.5 [40] ❑ other: [41]_____

I have a CD ROM: ❑ yes [42] ❑ no [43]

I plan to buy or upgrade computer hardware this year: ❑ yes [44] ❑ no [45]

I plan to buy or upgrade computer software this year: ❑ yes [46] ❑ no [47]

Business title: [48] _____ Type of Business: [49] _____

)

Name: _____

Address (❑ home [50] ❑ work [51]/Company name: _____

Street/Suite# _____ Country [55] _____

City [52]/State [53]/Zipcode [54]: _____

❑ **I liked this book!** You may quote me by name in future
IDG Books Worldwide promotional materials.

My daytime phone number is _____

IDG
BOOKS
WORLDWIDE

THE WORLD OF
COMPUTER
KNOWLEDGE®

 **YES!**

Please keep me informed about IDG Books Worldwide's World of Computer Knowledge. Send me your latest catalog.